PERCY H. FITZGERALD

GW00771023

THE HISTORY

OF

PICKWICK

AN ACCOUNT OF ITS

CHARACTERS, LOCALITIES, ALLUSIONS

AND ILLUSTRATIONS

WITH A BIBLIOGRAPHY

Elibron Classics
www.elibron.com

Elibron Classics series.

© 2005 Adamant Media Corporation.

ISBN 1-4021-0319-0 (paperback)
ISBN 1-4021-0309-3 (hardcover)

This Elibron Classics Replica Edition is an unabridged facsimile
of the edition published in 1891 by Chapman and Hall, Ltd.,
London.

THE

HISTORY

OF

PICKWICK

AN ACCOUNT OF ITS

CHARACTERS, LOCALITIES, ALLUSIONS,

AND ILLUSTRATIONS

WITH A BIBLIOGRAPHY

BY

PERCY FITZGERALD, M.A., F.S.A.

LONDON—CHAPMAN AND HALL, LIMITED

1891

LONDON :
PRINTED BY GILBERT AND RIVINGTON, LD.,
ST. JOHN'S HOUSE, CLERKENWELL ROAD, E.C.

Inscribed

TO

HENRY FIELDING DICKENS,

THE SON

OF

THE AUTHOR OF "PICKWICK."

INTRODUCTION.

THERE are many who look back with delight to the days of their childhood, when "Pickwick," in its green wrappers, was coming out month by month, and furnished nearly two years · of sustained enjoyment to people of all ages and conditions. The cherished numbers, bound into a volume, now lie before me, and bring back the recollection of the almost feverish expectancy with which its mirth-moving incidents were awaited or listened to, as the head of the family read them aloud, to increase, it might be, his own sense of the relish. Not the least merit in this book is that it should have been thus appreciated by children; but the aged found no less enjoyment in its humours; so those of the old and new fashion were alike recreated. This was in itself a phenomenon. If it be not read by the children of our generation, it is owing to the change in habits and manners; it is too much to expect such an exertion from the juvenile mind, as to assume the existence of duelling, stage coaches, elopements, old inns, and other obsolete things.

The book is so rich in suggestion, so stored with humorous touches and allusions, that each reading—as Professor Ward has pointed out—brings out something that has escaped notice: while the general hilarity is so overpowering that many delicate touches escape notice, and require pause and deliberation to discover.

It may be that objection will be taken to the somewhat minute character of the following speculations, and it may be thought that the praises are exaggerated; but the position held for over half a century by "Pickwick" is really a unique one. Edition after edition comes out, and the stock of allusions and metaphors drawn from it increase every day. The book is regularly studied, and the ardent Pickwickian will find in these pages much that will assist him in his labours. As the form of humour now in fashion is of a somewhat trivial kind, founded on verbal quips and fancies, it were to be heartily desired that something of the old Pickwickian, laughter-moving humour, illustrating comic adventure, could be revived. We cannot, of course, revive a young and buoyant Dickens; but where genuine humour exists, it can be turned into new and varied channels, and by careful study, something of the original pattern may be caught: like Boswell's German, who, when surprised jumping over chairs, explained, "*J'apprends d'être vif.*"

I have shown in the text how much this work has engrossed the labours of bibliographers, topographers, critics, students of manners and customs, even of professors of " Folk lore." The illustrations, with their " stages," the artists themselves, and their history, have excited the curiosity and research of the inquirer. All these topics have been dealt with, not too copiously, I hope; they offer an interest even for the general reader. The imitations, translations, dramas, &c., still further show the singular vitality and fascination of the subject. We may look around in vain for any work of modern times which has excited such interest or prompted so much commentary, except it be the " Life of Johnson." But Boswell's hero *lived*. Mr. Pickwick, however, is quite as familiar to us as Boswell's idol, and almost as living.

In conclusion, I have to acknowledge the assistance I have received from all quarters, assistance given cordially and heartily, as though it were felt that the service was rendered to their old esteemed friend Mr. Pickwick, for whom too much could not be done. I have been particularly aided by the Rev. Alfred Buss, son of one of the early illustrators of " Pickwick," and by Mr. W. Wright of Paris, who opened to me his extraordinary " Dickens Collections." I am also indebted to Dr. Brougham, the Dean of

Lismore; to Mr. Sketchley, Librarian of the Forster and Dyce Collections; to Mr. Grego; to the Vicar of Cobham ; and to several other persons who have aided in various ways.

I may add that a small portion of this book has already made .its appearance in the *Cornhill Magazine*, where it excited some interest and discussion. I have also included some papers on the same subject, from the *St. James's Gazette*.

ATHENÆUM CLUB,
          January, 1891.

THE

HISTORY OF PICKWICK.

I.

Tʜɪs cheerful and inspiring work, which of all modern inventions has most increased the gaiety of nations and the public stock of harmless pleasure, appeared over fifty years ago, and its Jubilee has recently been celebrated by a sumptuous edition, the "Victoria," enriched with "extra" illustrations, and notes explaining its origin. Such is a tribute almost of affection; while any new information about its characters seems to be always welcomed, much as are fresh biographical details concerning some popular favourite. During the last half-century all that relates to the composition of the immortal book, the allusions, the personal history of the author and of all concerned, has been greedily sought for, and gathered up; the work itself has come to be treated as a classic, and laborious persons are already exhausting themselves in commentaries, collections and discussions on its text and illustrations. None are so interested as our American cousins, and, it may be added, the booksellers; while a standing entry in every catalogue is half a column or so of " Pickwicks."

In this marvellous " Pickwick" panorama the work of a young man of two-and-twenty, there are some seventy or eighty characters, round, clearly drawn, original, and distinct. Of these about twenty are leading or working performers, as they may be called, who carry the piece regularly through, and appear in all the acts. These are Mr. Pickwick, and his three friends, Tupman, Winkle, and Snodgrass; Wardle, his daughter Emily, and the " Fat Boy;" Jingle and Job Trotter; Ben Allen and Arabella; Bob Sawyer, Perker, with Lowten his clerk; the two Wellers, and Mary the pretty housemaid; Stiggins and Mrs. Weller. In addition there are fifty and more minor figures, who appear little more than once, and then go their way. This amusing miscellany is all marshalled without confusion or crowding, and furnishes entertainment to the close. We have only to call up the list to marvel at the author's power of gay invention. We have Dr. Slammer, Dr. Payne, and the widow; the dockyard magnates; Mr. and Mrs. Pott, Slurk, the Leo Hunters, and Count Smorltork; the spinster aunt and her mother, the "long game-keeper," Magnus, Miss Withersfield, and Dowler. Then come the characters of the Fleet: Roker, Mivins, Smangle, the Cobbler, the Butcher, Parson, &c.; the M.C. at Bath, with Lord Mutinhed; the card-playing ladies, and the immortal "Bath footmen;" Nupkins the Mayor, and his servant Muzzle; the constable, Grummer, Dodson and Fogg and their clerks; the attorney Pell, Justice Stareleigh, Serjeants Buzfuz and Snubbin, with the other barristers; the chemist-juryman; Mrs. Cluppins and Mrs. Rogers, and old Winkle; to say nothing of a crowd of inferior characters who appear but for a few moments, but who serve their purpose, helping on the story and amusing the reader. The remarkable thing is, that not only are there characters of one class, but there are classes of the same character—all distinct.

The figures of Mr. Pickwick and his party are known wherever an English story is read. A more artistic and suitable character for suggesting or provoking situations could not have been devised. He is universally popular, and his popularity is declared in all sorts of ways. At the interesting Dickens sale, a set of small apostle spoons ornamented with Pickwick figures were fiercely contended for, and we recall the triumph with which the late Andrew Halliday, one of the

master's own "merry men," displayed to us a
single spoon which he had secured for the enormous
price of sixty-nine odd pounds ! The Christmas-
trees in Germany and elsewhere are often hung
with Wellers, Winkles, &c., in their habits as they
were etched. The fund of happy and ready quota-
tions has been amply enriched by points and
allusions from the same story, the most useful and
humorous being that of "the Pickwickian sense,"
which removes offence from an offensive speech.
The sale of this extraordinary work has never
flagged during fifty years, and we are told that,
since the death of the author, over a million
copies have been disposed of by its publishers.
One of the most touching, practical tributes
to the popularity of the story—one which would
have given the author gratification—is that
at the Bodleian Library, "they show a stained
and battered volume in the Russian language,
which the besiegers of Sebastopol found among
the dreadful ruins of the Redan," a tattered
copy of "Pickwick." Topographers, Bibliographers, critics, booksellers, annotators, artists,
have all been attracted and kept at work by this
extraordinary book. It may be said indeed, without exaggeration, that there is a regular "Pickwick" literature. So real are the characters and
scenes, that in reading it over and over again,
we find no more sense of familiarity or same-

ness than we do in meeting friends or acquaintances. In these fictitious beings, as in real
life, we seem to discover on further intimacy
fresh points of interest which have escaped us
before.

The oft-told but always interesting story of the
origin of " Pickwick " has been clearly and satisfactorily related by Mr. Forster, in his admirable
biography of the author. In its way it is as interesting, and even romantic, as anything known
in the history of authorship. There was living in
Furnival's Inn, a bright, vivacious, energetic young
fellow, then a reporter on the press, and who
was indeed scarcely more than a magazine writer.
Young as he was—not more than three and twenty
—his childhood and youth had been the severest
discipline conceivable. He had passed through
much privation, had been familiar with the inside
of debtors' prisons, had been glad to snatch a
morsel at a tavern, like the " Fox under the Hill," a
sort of shanty on the river, which disappeared only
yesterday—thus picking up a sort of " extensive
and peculiar " knowledge of London life and
manners. These experiences he had already set
out in some vivid and amusing local sketches,
which had attracted attention.

But in 1835 came a chance which he hailed
with delight, and which promised an opening. It
really amounted to no more than a clever piece

of " drudgery " which was to consist in
illustrating certain illustrations that were to be
executed by an artist of much popularity. This
was a combination then in favour. The public
was partial to a coarse sort of coloured
caricature, and illustrated adventure. The publishers of the present volume, Messrs. Chapman and Hall, were then at No. 186, Strand, and
it was Mr. Edward Chapman who was chiefly
concerned in arranging the plan. In a letter
dated July 7, 1849, he furnished his recollections
to the author himself—which corresponded in
every particular with the latter's own. Dickens's
account is given in the preface to the edition of
1847, and is an interesting piece of personal
history.

The way in which the happy chance offered
was this :—

" In November," says Mr. Chapman, " we
published a little book called the ' Squib
Annual,' with plates by Seymour, and it was
during my visit to him, to see after them,
that he said he should like to do a series of
cockney sporting plates of a superior sort to
those he had already published. I said I thought
it might do if accompanied by letterpress and
published in monthly parts ; and this being agreed
to, we wrote to an author of " Three Courses and
a Dessert " (a Mr. Clarke). I proposed it ; but

receiving no answer, the scheme dropped for some months, till Seymour said he wished us to decide, as another job had offered which would fully occupy his time. And it was on this we decided to ask you to do it." As they had already formed a connection with him, this was natural. " But I am quite sure," he goes on, " that from the beginning to the end nobody but yourself had anything whatsoever to do with it."

It was evident that the intended new work was little more than " a job," or piece of hack-work as it might be called, in which the writer was to be useful to Mr. Seymour. Mr. Buss states in his memoir that others besides Dickens and Mr. Clarke were thought of as literary " illustrators " of the Illustrations. Leigh Hunt was at one time proposed, and Mr. Mackenzie Bell tells us that Charles Whitehead, a friend of Dickens, and some years older, " used constantly to affirm that he had been asked to write to Seymour's sketches; but that feeling uncertain as to his being able to supply the copy with regularity, he had recommended Dickens."

Mr. Edward Chapman further relates the nature of the contract between the firm and the young author. " There was no agreement about 'Pickwick' except a verbal one. Each number was to consist of a sheet and a half, for which we were to pay fifteen guineas, and we paid him for the first two numbers at once, as he required the money to go and get married with. We were also to pay more according to the sale, and I think " Pickwick" altogether cost us three thousand pounds." Mr. Forster thinks that the share of profit thus calculated would have come to four times as much, and his impression is that the sum received was not so large. When arrangements were made for a new venture it was agreed that, after five years, the author should have a share in the copyright of " Pickwick." But all through the firm behaved to him with fairness and liberality.

"I was a young man of three-and-twenty, when the publishers, attracted by some pieces I was at that time writing in the *Morning Chronicle* newspaper (of which one series had lately been collected and published in two volumes, illustrated by my esteemed friend, Mr. George Cruikshank), waited upon me to propose a something that should be published in shilling numbers —then only known to me, or, I believe, to anybody else, by a dim recollection of certain interminable novels in that form, which used to be carried about the country by pedlars.

" When I opened my door in Furnival's Inn to the managing partner who represented the firm, I recognized in him the person from whose hands I had bought, two or three years previously, and whom I had never seen before or since, my first copy of the Magazine in which my first effusion —dropped stealthily one evening at twilight, with fear, and trembling, into a dark letter-box, in a dark office, up a dark court in Fleet Street—appeared in all the glory of print; on which memorable occasion (how well I recollect it) I walked down to Westminster Hall, and turned into it for half-an-hour, because my eyes were so dimned with joy and pride, that they could not bear the street, and were not fit to be seen there. I told my visitor of the coincidence, which we both hailed as a good omen; and so fell to business.

"The idea propounded to me, was, that the monthly something should be a vehicle for certain plates to be executed by Mr. Seymour; and there was a notion, either on the part of that admirable humorous artist, or of my visitor, that a 'Nimrod Club' would be the best means of introducing these. I objected, on consideration, that although born and partly bred in the country, I was no great sportsman."

Within the memory of the present generation there used to be in the Haymarket a well-known print shop, whose windows displayed coloured caricatures, chiefly representing sporting cockneys in old-fashioned costume—strange beings, whose guns were always going off by accident, whose fishing-hooks caught in ladies' bonnets.

These were coarsely drawn and highly coloured, and underneath was usually some punning title, such as "A Good Bite," &c. The favourite purveyor for these things appears to have been this Mr. Seymour, an artist of skill, but who seems to have brought his humour down to the level of the street public. Mr. Buss gives a very plausible account of how the idea of a club came to suggest itself to the artist. He lived at Islington, which was then a great resort of cockney sportsmen, who were ever firing at the cats and sparrows, or fishing in the New River, and their oddities impressed him forcibly. He himself was fond of angling and of sport of all kinds.

He had the most marvellous fertility and facility in his work; his sketches amount to thousands, and display a great deal of clever invention. Underneath each plate is put some rather vulgar or "slangey" jest: these, however, were condescensions to the public taste, for he was capable of better things, had exhibited at the Academy, and could etch with freedom and refinement. It was the fashion then in the trade that for such works the plate should be the leading feature; the artist in fact told the story as he pleased, and the author was expected to "write up" to him. It was in this way that Dr. Syntax had made such a success, the "hack" Combe, from his prison furnishing copy to any amount and for any subject. It seems to have been expected that the young Dickens was to follow the usual course.

Seymour had been engaged on a paper called the *Figaro*, edited by a clever member of a witty, clever family, and showed extraordinary versatility and energy in his work. At one time he took up " High Art," and retired with a fellow-student to practise his art, to that interesting old monument near Islington, Canonbury Tower, which has furnished shelter to Goldsmith and other remarkable persons. The result of these ardent studies was an enormous and ambitious picture, representing scenes of German *Diablerie*, " The Giant of the Brocken," " The Skeleton Hunt," the " Casting of the Bullets " from " Der Freischütz," and other goblin incidents. The picture was exhibited without success, and the artist soon abandoned this line.

Dickens, heartily accepting his *rôle*, tells us that he put in Winkle "expressly for the use of Mr. Seymour," who introduced one of his most favourite types to represent him, and which figures in many of the cockney sporting caricatures, with check neckcloth, turned-up nose, and long gaiters. On the green cover of " Pickwick " he is seen firing at a sparrow. A design of this kind is also to be found in one of the caricatures.

More interesting and a greater matter of

discussion has been the question of the origin of
the central figure of the story, "the immortal
Pickwick." The first type for this personage
was, according to Mr. Chapman's statement,[1]
" a long thin man. The present one he made
from my description of a friend of mine at
Richmond, a fat old beau, who would wear, in
spite of ladies' protests, drab tights and gaiters.
His name was John Foster." [2] Seymour would
also appear to have designed Tupman and Snodgrass, but they are rather indistinct and colourless.
His family, however, claimed that the gaiters, and
Pickwick himself, was his conception also, and an
attempt was made to support this by reference to
one of his old caricatures of a portly old gentleman
fishing. But there is little resemblance.

The very name of "Pickwick," so natural and
yet of quaint sound, unfamiliar, and yet recognizable, was one of the happiest selections ever
made. It is interesting to consider how it came
to be suggested to him. It was said that when it
occurred to him, he rushed off in triumph to the
publishers, calling out, " I have got it,—' Pickwick ' ! "

The coaches running between Bath and London
belonged to a well-known proprietor named Pickwick, of a family established in Bath. There can be

---

[1] Forster's Life of Dickens i. 91.
[2] Mr. Forster pleasantly calls attention to this odd coincidence.

little doubt that Dickens had abundant experiences of coaching, when on his reporting expeditions, which brought this exceptional and quaint name to his mind when he was looking out for one for his hero. It had been better, according to strict artistic propriety, that the master and servant had not the same name, Samuel. But in this case, "Sam" might be considered a different name from "Samuel," for no one would think of calling Mr. Pickwick "Sam," or his servant "Samuel."

It will be recollected how bewildered Sam was at discovering the name of his master upon the coach that was to take them to Bath :—

"Here's rayther a rum go, sir," replied Sam.

"What?" inquired Mr. Pickwick.

"This here, sir," rejoined Sam. "I'm wery much afeerd, sir, that the properiator o' this here coach is a playin' some imperence vith us."

"How is that, Sam?" said Mr. Pickwick; "aren't the names down on the way-bill?"

"The names is not only down on the vay-bill, sir," replied Sam, "but they've painted vun on 'em up, on the door o' the coach."

"Dear me," exclaimed Mr. Pickwick, quite staggered by the coincidence; "what a very extraordinary thing!"

"Yes, but that ain't all," said Sam, again directing his master's attention to the coach door; "not content vith writin' up Pickwick,

they puts 'Moses' afore it, vich I call addin'
insult to injury," as he paused.

I have always fancied that Dickens could not
fairly have avoided noting the coincidence of
Mr. Pickwick's travelling in Pickwick's coach.
Having adopted the proprietor's name, he
probably wished to pass it off, in a good-natured
way, making a sort of *amende* by the bold
advertisement; or felt that unless he took
some notice of the fact, there would be good-
natured persons to note it.

Mr. R. Peach, of Bath, who has written several
agreeable works on his native city, full of
interesting details, has furnished some facts
concerning the Pickwick family. "At the
close of the last century," he writes to
me, "Eleazer Pickwick (from these names,
Eleazer and Moses, it must have been a Jewish
family), who had been for some years a postboy at
the Old Bear Inn, succeeded a Mr. Brockman
at the White Hart; he made the hostelry very
popular and famous. He had two sons who
succeeded him, the elder of whom was the father
of Charles Pickwick and of Major Pickwick, who
was the father of Moses Pickwick. The old Pickwick, who kept the hotel and who was living at
the time of Dickens' visit, died soon after, and was
succeeded by Mr. Cooper, but the posting and
coaching business was carried on by Moses, whom

I knew very well. Charles died before I came to Bath, he left one son and two daughters. The son entered the army, and for some reason changed his name to Sainsbury." The reason probably was the awkwardness of bearing a too familiar name associated with grotesque adventures.

Thus far Mr. Peach's narrative. But it would seem as if everything connected with the family should have a quaint flavour. Witness these entries in a newspaper :—

" In his 19th year, 1795, after a long, often flattering, but at last fatal illness, Mr. William Pickwick, son of Mr. P. of the White Hart Inn, Bath. He had been but a short period entered at Oxford, when the rupture of a blood-vessel impaired a constitution not naturally good, and terminated in depriving society of a valuable young man, his distressed parents of an only child, as amiable in manner as his genius was promising." And again :—

" This evening (October, 1807), George Hawkins, driver of Mr. Pickwick's coach from Southampton to Bath, was taken suddenly and very alarmingly ill on Slanderwick Common. When all apprehensions of immediate danger were over, he was unwilling to be carried to one of the neighbouring cottages, and was at his own request removed to the inside (of the coach), where he expired before the coach reached Bath."

This might have been one of Sam's own very appropriate anecdotes related on the top of the coach. Mr. Charles Pickwick died in 1835. A contributor to *Notes and Queries*, a paper from which I have taken much that is interesting about the story, writing in 1887, says that there was then living in Penarth, close to Cardiff, an efficient police officer, Sergeant Eleazer Pickwick. And a friend informs me that there is, or was until lately, engaged on the coach running between Ross and Pontypool, a well-known and exceedingly popular guard of the name of Pickwick.

In the first two numbers the author seems to have accepted as a type for his hero a rather disagreeable, sour and " cantankerous " cast of person. He had not, however, as yet developed the milder and more placid elements in Mr. Pickwick's character. He was much pleased with the pains the artist took to realize his ideas. Witness the modest letter, to be quoted later, which he addressed to him in reference to one of the illustrations.

Two or three years ago a curious and amusing coincidence brought the author's son, a barrister in good practice, into connection with his father's famous book. It occurred at a trial on the circuit.

Mr. Dickens, who was counsel for the defence, announced that he meant to call Mr. Pickwick.

The judge entered into the humour of the thing. "Pickwick," he said, "is a very appropriate character to be called by Dickens". (*laughter*). With much pleasantness the advocate replied: "I fully believe that the sole reason why I was instructed in this case *was* that I might call Mr. Pickwick" (*laughter*), "and it may interest your lordship to learn that the witness is a descendant,— a grandnephew, I believe, of Mr. Moses Pickwick who kept a coach at Bath, and that I have every reason to believe that it was from this Moses Pickwick that the name of the immortal Pick-wick was taken. I daresay your lordship will remember that that very eccentric and faithful follower of Mr. Pickwick—Sam Weller—seeing his name outside of the coach, was indignant because he thought it was a personal reflection upon his employer." This little bit of comedy harmonizes well with our old Pickwickian associations.

Meanwhile the young author had lost not a moment in setting to work; and, full of spirit and overflowing with humorous ideas, got ready his opening chapters.

On March 26th, 1836, the following advertisement appeared in *The Times* :—

" THE PICKWICK PAPERS.

" On the thirty-first of March will be published,

to be continued monthly, price 1s., the first number of *The Posthumous Papers of the Pickwick Club*, containing a faithful record of the perambulations, perils, travels, adventures, and sporting transactions of the corresponding members. Edited by 'Boz.' Each monthly part embellished with four illustrations by Seymour. Chapman and Hall, 186, Strand, and all Booksellers." [3]

We may assume that it was thought that " Boz " would be a more attractive name than the then obscure one of " Charles Dickens." The first number was arranged in the well-known "green leaves" which for over fifty years were to be the familiar joy of every lover of harmless pleasure. Their success at first was not remarkable—indeed the venture would seem to have " hung fire " a little.

Seymour prepared some seven illustrations in all, of which four were to appear in the first number. Some of these are excellent in the drawing and composition—done with a firm touch and much dramatic spirit, and in a wholly different style from that of his caricatures; and there is no scene we recall better than that of Jingle's

[3] On the same day was announced the first part of the "Library of Fiction," containing "The Tuggs's at Ramsgate," by Boz, and also some recognizable Pickwickian figures by Seymour, such as Jingle and Doctor Slammer.

altercation on the stairs with Dr. Slammer.
Jingle's attitude is excellent. So with the drawing of the "tall quadruped." The horse, in his
struggle, is admirably sketched, and capitally
modelled. It is superior in these points to one
substituted for it later. Mr. C. Thomson, in his
handsome volume · on Hablot Browne, gives a
facsimile of one of the original drawings for the
Stroller's Tale, which is really graceful and spirited.
It is after Rowlandson's fashion, outlined with
a pen, and lightly washed or tinted with water-
colour. His etchings indeed promised well, and
would no doubt have improved as he felt his way.
It is, however, worth noting that the face and
character of Mr. Pickwick had not then been
settled, and in the altercation with the cabman
and the club scene it appears very hostile and
uninviting.

The news of the important contract the author
communicated to his betrothed, Miss Kate
Hogarth, on one evening in 1835, when the
responsibility of his venture obliged him to deny
himself the pleasure of a visit to her. "My
dearest Kate, the house is up, but I am very sorry
to say I must stay at home. I have had a visit
from the publishers this morning, and the story
cannot be any longer delayed ; it must be done to-
morrow. As there are more important considerations than the mere payment for the story involved

too, I must exercise a little self-denial and set to work. They (Chapman and Hall) have made me an offer of fourteen pounds a month, to write and edit a new publication they contemplate, entirely by myself, to be published monthly, and each number to contain four woodcuts. I am to make my estimate and calculations, and to give them a decisive answer on Friday morning. The work will be no joke, but the emolument is too tempting to resist." This characteristic letter is the most interesting piece associated with Pickwick, or, indeed, with the course of the author. He was but just twenty-three, and it shows the reserve and self-denial of one far older—the thoughtful restraint which takes time to consider before deciding. *"But the emolument is too tempting to resist."* How natural and characteristic is this ! He seemed to be quite delighted with the modest honorarium. Shortly after the arrangement was concluded, Mr. James Grant, who had taken the editorship of the " Monthly Magazine," to which Dickens had furnished " Mrs. Joseph Porter " and other pieces, applied to him to continue his contributions. The young writer wrote that he had just concluded with Messrs. Chapman and Hall, and that he would be obliged to raise his terms to eight guineas a sheet, or ten shillings a page.

In an "illustrated" copy of the Forster Life, prepared by Mr. Harvey of St. James's Street, there was a letter of Dickens' to Harley, the actor, which shows how devotedly he applied to his task: 'I am so engaged with my respectable friend Pickwick, on whom I have only just commenced, that I cannot get out this week."

In the same ardent spirit he wrote to his betrothed after the work had commenced, excusing himself from a visit. "I have at this moment got Pickwick and his friends on the Rochester coach, and they are going on swimmingly in company with a very different character from any I have yet described, who I flatter myself will make a decided hit. I want to get them from the Ball to the Inn before I go to bed, and I think that will take me until one or two o'clock at the earliest. The publishers will be here in the morning, so you will readily suppose I have no alternative but to stick at my desk." This short scrap gives a fair notion of the spirit and high pressure, under which the work was carried out by all concerned.

The passage "I want to get them from the Ball to the Inn," seems to indicate that his first intention was to exhibit Mr. Pickwick and all his friends at the Rochester Ball; so that it would

almost appear that the capital device of the
borrowing of the coat, and Mr. Winkle's
adventure, had been an inspiration that came
to him as he wrote. We can fancy it would
have been amusing enough to have seen Mr.
Pickwick figuring away at the dance. On the
other hand " them " may have been intended only
for Jingle and Tupman.

It will be seen also from his little note that he
was accustomed to give his friends an anticipatory
enjoyment of his plans and characters, and to
consult with them on the treatment. This was
his fashion all through; and it bespeaks his open
and unaffected nature. Indeed, it is said that
at this time his Pickwick used to be read to a few
friends by Talfourd, and criticisms and suggestions were freely given and adopted.

We must always look with interest at Furnival's
Inn, No. 15—now marked with one of the Society
of Arts tablets—where he wrote the larger portion of the " Pickwick Papers,"—a year's work
from March to March. He married his wife two
days after the appearance of the first number
of the work, and in the March of the following
year removed to Doughty Street, No. 48, where
the last portion of Pickwick was written.

Some little versicles written to the printers or
engravers have been preserved, and were lately
" sold in America " for a large sum.

Private and Confidential.

TO MR. HICKS.

Oh, Mr. Hick
—s, I'm heartily sick
Of this sixteenth Pickwick,
Which is just in the nick
For the publishing trick,
And will read nice and slick
If you'll only be quick,
I don't write on tick,
That's my comfort, avick.

Mr. James Grant insists that the early numbers rather fell flat, or, as he puts it, were "a signal failure," and adds that "Charles Tilt, the bookseller, out of friendship for the firm, made great exertions to push the sale, taking 1500 copies of each number, which he sent into the country " on sale or return," as it is called. He even goes so far as to say it was proposed to stop the whole when Seymour died, but that on the appearance of Samuel Weller, the flagging interest revived. All which is most inaccurate, and inconsistent with well-established facts. It, may however, represent the story current in " the trade."

---

[4] He adds some further mythical details as to Dickens' remuneration; how the firm "gave Dickens a present of 500*l.* in November," and more by-and-by, amounting in all to 3500*l.*, while the publishers netted over 20,000*l.* This, however, is nothing to what appears in the preface to a French translation of the little story of " The Baron Grogswig," an elegant little

The general tumultuous success that attended
the work became pronounced after the appearance
of Sam Weller, when the whole kingdom was reading the numbers, in a state of eager expectancy
and delight. As Mr. Croker tells us, a notable
and exceptional point in this success was, that,
" with the exception of occasional extracts in
the newspapers, he received little or no assistance from the Press. Yet, in less than six months
from the appearance of the first number of the
Pickwick Papers, the whole reading world was
talking about them—the names of Winkle, Wardle,
Weller, Snodgrass, Dodson and Fogg,—had become familiar in our mouths as Household Words.
Nay, Pickwick chintzes figured in linen-drapers'
windows, and Weller corduroys in breeches-
makers' advertisements ; Boz cabs might be seen
rattling through the streets, and the portrait of the
author of Pelham or Crichton was scraped down
or pasted over to make room for that of the new
popular favourite in the omnibuses." [5]   There

book, prettily illustrated. M. de Bedolière there speaks of the
50,000 subscribers to Pickwick, and of two American editions,
each of 100,000 copies. The author, according to this authority,
received 50*l*. for the first number, 100*l*. for the third, and for
the whole, 16,000*l*!

[5] This was a characteristic element in the conduct of what is
called "the vehicular traffic" of the city. Now the omnibus
traveller is recreated with portraits of some popular performer,
or notability.

were to be seen " Pickwick canes," " Pickwick gaiters," " Pickwick Hats," with narrow curled brims ; and even tobacco-stoppers. Many years later a tobacco-merchant brought out a small, cheap and convenient cigar, " the penny Pickwick," which has ever since been patronized by 'Arry when out for his holiday.

A further testimonial to this popularity was the formation of " Pickwick clubs " all over the kingdom, in which the members supported the characters, or at least took the names of Winkle, Weller, &c. Even in our day the tradition is kept by one of the most flourishing of bicycle clubs, " the Pickwick," and many of these pages have been written, appropriately, with a " Pickwick " pen.[6] There are still sold Pickwick menus.

Mr. Carlyle's graphic testimony to its popularity is well known. " An Archdeacon," he wrote to Forster, " with his own venerable lips repeated to me the other night, a strange profane story of a solemn clergyman, who had been administering ghostly consolation to a sick person : having finished satisfactorily as he thought, and got out of the room, he heard the sick man ejaculate, ' Well, thank God, Pickwick will be out in ten days any way.' On the whole, I think nothing

Advertised for years in the familiar couplet:—
They come as a boon and a blessing to men,
The Waverley, Owl, and Pickwick pen.

more forcible or better than this has been said of
Pickwick." This passage is quite Pickwickian in
character, and the sketch of the patient turning
wearily from his proper clerical comforter, to the
ephemeral instalment of the story, has a grim air
of humour.

"How I envy," says Mr. Herman Merivale, "the
generation which read Pickwick as it came out in
numbers,—and my father has told me that it was
the phenomenon of the time. My grandfather's
whole family of sons and daughters (a very
large one), used to cluster round him to hear
number after number read out to them. He always
studied them himself for an hour or two, in order
to be able to read them aloud with decent gravity,
and his apoplectic struggles and occasional shouts
made them feel bad—longing for their turn."
Another thus forcibly recalls the same feverish
enjoyment with which each instalment was awaited.
" Few works of this or any other age have enjoyed
greater or more universal popularity. The unani-
mous (with one or two modified exceptions) approval
of the press ; the unprecedented sale of copies :
the feverish anxiety with which every one watched
the coming ' first ' as being to usher in a new
number of the engrossing series ; the voracious
eagerness with which each precious morsel was
literally devoured as soon as presented ; the feeling of half disappointment, half anticipation in

which we closed each number, with the knowledge that a long month must elapse before curiosity could be satisfied or anxiety relieved—these every reader will recollect as furnishing an index of public favour." But the most impressive testimony to this success is Miss Mitford's letter of rebuke to some incurious Dublin friends who knew nothing of *Pickwick :*—

"So you never heard of the *Pickwick Papers !* Well, they publish a number once a month, and print 25,000. It is fun—London life—but without anything unpleasant; a lady might read it aloud; and this so graphic, so individual, and so true, that you could courtesy to all the people as you see them in the streets. *I did think there had not been a place where English is spoken, to which Boz had not penetrated.* All the boys and girls talk his fun—the boys in the streets ; and yet those who are of the highest taste like it the most. Sir Benjamin Brodie takes it to read in his carriage between patient and patient ; and Lord Denman studies *Pickwick* on the Bench while the jury are deliberating. *Do take some means to borrow the 'Pickwick Papers.'* It seems like not having heard of Hogarth." This unaffected belief in the reality of the story, with a sort of compassion for the benighted creatures who " had never heard of Pickwick," is a truly genuine tribute.

II.

ONE reason for the exuberance and the life-like
originality which distinguished the characters of
the new story has, I think, not been suggested
before. In those happy, buoyant days, when
the author was busy with newspaper work, he
was encountering the varieties that are found
in courts and taverns, as well as all the curious
adventurers who "hung loose" upon this sort of
society. No one was more accessible, or met every
one so much "half-way," as it is called, a charm
which he retained to the end of his life. His
quick eye, therefore, caught up and appropriated
all odd types of character in abundance, wherever
he encountered them. At that time he appears to
have been a most brilliant, clever being, exuberant
in fancy and full of life.

But as he prospered, and rose out of this sphere,
the old opportunities became lost to him, and he
ceased to encounter these inspiring if grotesque
types. He had then to trust to his imagination
and invention. Hence those more fanciful figures
which crowd his later stories, and whose attrac-

tion rests upon curious turns and oddities of manner and speech, and which are admired for their ingenuity rather than for their nature.

His friend Forster had an important share in the revision and correction of proofs, and was entrusted, in the author's absence, with the nice duty of "cutting," when there was an excess of matter. We thus have not all that the author wrote in his pleasant exuberance and superabundance of ideas; and whereas, in later works, he was generally "short" of matter to fill a number, in Pickwick there was nearly always an overplus which had to be compressed or cut away.[1]

To Forster, when he reached No. 15, he wrote full of enthusiasm for his work—he was "getting on like a house o' fire," and thought the next Pickwick would "bang all the others." In this was the well-known account of the Fleet Prison and the debtors. "Every point was a telling one," says his friend, "and the truthfulness of the whole unerring. *The dreadful restlessness* of the place, undefined and yet unceasing, was pictured throughout with De Foe's minute reality." That dreadful restlessness actually expresses the *tone* of his description, which is apart from its details, and could only be imparted by one who was inspired by

[1] We find him writing to Forster, "I send you revise of the Pickwick by Fred,—you will see my alterations of it are very slight."

a vivid sense of what he was drawing. Mr. Forster
notes a fine point in his character in the indiffer-
ence he showed to any praise of his work " on the
literary side," compared with its higher recognition as bits of real life, set forth with the
purpose of doing good to his fellow-creatures.
Pickwick might seem to be an exception, from its
jovial, farcical character; but a "first Book" has
its immunities and privileges. He had to feel his
way and make sure of his ground. " It has been
often noted that the later portion seemed inconsistent with the first, not only in its more serious
tone—which this sense of responsibility made
him adopt—but in the actual characters;" and this
charge was ingeniously justified by the author for
this reason. He argued " that the mere oddities
of a friend were apt to strike us at first; but as
we grow acquainted with him the better and more
serious qualities reveal themselves."

This trusty friend of nearly forty years whom
he was then addressing as "My dear sir," was
editing the *Examiner*, and, as the work went on,
identified himself thoroughly and generously with
the interests of the author. When the work
reached the fifteenth number he wrote a review of
it which was cordial and enthusiastic. It will be
interesting to note how ardent were these praises.
" In this number the author has achieved his
masterpiece. Every point tells and the reality of

the whole is wonderful. We place the picture by the side of those of the greatest masters of this style of fiction in our language, and it rises in comparison."

He then speaks of "the exquisite sketches of Mr. Smangle and his friends. All is real life and human nature. It is not a collection of humorous or pathetic dialogues about people who have no tangible existence in the mind; but it is a succession of actual scenes, the actors of which take a place in the memory. We recognize in this fine writer a maturing excellence which promises at no distant day the very greatest accomplishment of that great style in which Fielding, honouring humanity while he exalts literature, achieved those books which are now appealed to as we appeal to truth or nature. We see in every succeeding work he takes in hand a superior insight into the general principles of character, joining itself to the old and exquisite representations of local peculiarities and humours; and we can rarely now find anything that approaches to caricature without finding also some very shrewd and sound truths concealed beneath it.

"The illustrations are as usual full of excellent character. The ease and skill with which they are drawn are among the least of his merits, they leave an artistic feeling and amazement most rare in things of the kind."

It is strange to think that the composition of this festive, jocund work, presumed to have been written in a whirl of good spirits, should have been marked by two events of a very tragic kind. The first, which occurred before the second number was reached, was the death of the illustrator, almost at starting. This alone might have proved a serious check to the success of the work, and, but for the good luck which attended the spirited author, might have shipwrecked it altogether. The other was the death of his wife's sister.

The young writer had only a short time before written to Seymour with a kindness and tact remarkable in one of his years :—

"Furnival's Inn, No. 8a.

"MY DEAR SIR,—I had intended to write to you, to say how much gratified I feel by the pains you have bestowed on our mutual friend Mr. Pickwick, and how much the result of your labours has surpassed my expectations. I am happy to be able to congratulate you, the publishers and myself, on the success of the undertaking, which appears to have been most complete. I have now another reason for troubling you. It is this. I am extremely anxious about the Stroller's Tale, the more especially as many literary friends on whose judgment I place great reliance, think it will create considerable sensation. I have seen your design for an etching to accompany it. I think

it extremely good, but still it is not quite my
idea; and as I feel so very solicitous to have it
as complete as possible I shall feel personally
obliged to you if you will make another drawing.
It will give me great pleasure to see you, as well
as the drawing, when it is complete, with this
view I have asked Chapman and Hall to take a
glass of grog with me on Sunday evening (the
only night on which I am disengaged), when
I hope you will be able to look in. The
alterations I want, I will endeavour to explain.
I think the woman should be younger, the dismal
man decidedly should, and he should be less
miserable in appearance. To communicate an
interest to the plate, his whole appearance should
express more sympathy and solicitude, and while
I represented the sick man as emaciated and
dying, I would not make him too repulsive. The
furniture of the room you have depicted *admirably*.
I have ventured to make these suggestions, feeling assured that you will consider them in the
spirit in which I submit them to your judgment.
I shall be happy to hear from you that I may
expect to see you on Sunday evening." [2]

---

[2] It may be mentioned here that the *Athenæum* did not favour
" Pickwick :"—

" A wit or humourist should remind you of human nature—
in its vivid and lustrous colours—and not hunt you back to a
foregone work. The writer of the periodical (for such it is)

D

But the catastrophe which was to be so perilous
for the interests of "Pickwick" was at hand.
Though a person of gay and pleasant disposition,
the artist had latterly been much depressed.
This state of mind seems to have had little or
no relation to a quarrel with the *Figaro*, with
which he had renewed his connection. The
truth was, he was overwhelmed with work, as,
indeed, the vast number of his sketches in every
direction and form, proves.   It was likely enough
that his sketches did not give complete satisfaction to the proprietors of " Pickwick," but no
doubt the strain of getting ready no less than four
illustrations for a number was excessive.   The
" copy," too, was delayed to the last moment, and
could have left him little time.   As, however, he
was so facile a workman—he had contributed no
less than 300 designs to the *Figaro*—and could
dash off his designs rapidly, one is not inclined to
lay much stress upon this.   On April 20th, on the
eve of the appearance of the second number, he was
found to have committed suicide.   This he carried
out in the most deliberate manner.   He retired to a

which is now before us has great cleverness, but he runs closely
upon some leading hounds in the humorous pack, and when he
gives tongue (perchance a vulgar tongue) he reminds you of the
bay of several *deep dogs* who have gone before.   The ' Pickwick
Papers' are in part made up of two pounds of Smollett, three
ounces of Sterne, a handful of Hook, a dash of a grammatical
Pierce Egan, incidents at pleasure served with an original sauce."

summer-house in the back garden of his house at Islington, and, attaching a string to the trigger of a fowling-piece, shot himself through the head. Much commiseration was shown for the fate of the unfortunate artist, and the following accounts appeared in the papers :—

"Mr. R. Seymour, the caricaturist, it appears, with all his relish for and quick perception of the humorous, was subject to dreadful fits of despondency and melancholy, in one of which he committed suicide. He was undoubtedly a man of considerable talent, at his outset there was too much of mannerism in his designs, and that mannerism was not original. But latterly, especially, in his illustrations of the 'Book of Christmas' and the 'Library of Fiction,' he gave good promise of being a distinguished artist. He supplied, we believe, from its commencement to his death, a period of nearly five years, the political sketches of the *Figaro*."

An address, dated April 27th, and written by Dickens, was issued with the next number. It spoke in sympathetic terms of the loss of the artist :—

"We do not allude to this distressing event in the vain hope of adding by an eulogium of ours to the respect in which Mr. Seymour's memory is held by all who ever knew him. Arrangements are in progress which will enable us to present the ensuing number of the 'Pickwick Papers' on an improved plan which we trust will give entire satisfaction to our readers."

After the artist's death, the connection was destined to be the source of annoyance to the author. Almost at once the family began to put forward a claim that their deceased relative was entitled to the credit of originating the idea of "Pickwick." A pamphlet or leaflet of a few leaves only—now extraordinarily scarce, and for a single copy of which ten pounds was asked some years ago [3]— was circulated, in which this claim was seriously maintained. Seymour, it urged, was an amateur gardener, and his experiences and failures in this direction suggested to him the subject of "Pickwick and his Club." He offered it to Mr. Spooner, the well-known print-seller, and etched some plates as a beginning. This was in 1835. In the following year Mr. Chapman called on him and mentioned "Pickwick" to him, with a proposal that it should be issued in half-guinea volumes, but the artist insisted on the "numbers" or "parts." "Boz" was, as we have seen, called in: they concocted the details together, and Seymour having one of his four plates before him, representing a poor author in a garret, suggested the

[3] This seems an enormous price, but last year a copy was sold at Mr. Mackenzie's sale for over seven times that amount.

subject of "The Stroller's Tale," which was adopted. Dickens, he said, was to receive 15*l.* a month; he himself, though reported to have 5*l.* for each drawing, really only had 1*l.* 15*s.* "Pickwick" was already exhibited in a series of plates called "The Heiress." One of his plates he had brought to Dickens on a particular Sunday, but returned home much discontented, and from that time—whatever time it was—did nothing more for "Pickwick," destroying all his corrections, &c.

Such was this very incoherent story, which is disposed of by Mr. Chapman's version already given, and by the admission that the artist was allowed the full credit of designing Mr. Winkle, and of suggesting the sporting character of the story. This idea, as Dickens said, was to have been enlarged "for the benefit of Mr. Seymour," so that his hitherto scattered caricatures of this kind might now have a sort of cohesion, owing to the advantage of narration. But nearly thirty years later the claim was once more put forward with more particularity : and, in an indignant strain, the author wrote to the *Athenæum*, on March 31st, 1866, to repudiate the whole story :—

"Mr. Seymour, the artist, never originated, suggested, or in any way had to do with, save as illustrator of what I devised, an incident, a character (except the sporting tastes of Mr. Winkle), a name, a phrase, or a word to be found in the ' Pickwick Papers.'

" I never saw Mr. Seymour's handwriting, I believe, in my life.

" I never even saw Mr. Seymour but once in my life, and that was within eight-and-forty hours of his untimely death. Two persons, both still living, were present on that short occasion. Mr. Seymour died when only twenty-four printed pages of the ' Pickwick Papers ' were published ; I think before the next twenty-four pages were completely written ; I am sure before one subsequent line of the book was inserted."

In a letter to his son, the author throws some more light on the subject :—

" 6, Southwick Place, Hyde Park,

" April 4th, 1866.

" MY DEAR CHARLEY,—There has been going on for years an attempt on the part of Seymour's widow, to extort money from me, by representing that he had some inexplicable and ill-used part in the invention of Pickwick ! ! ! I have disregarded it until now, except that I took the precaution some years ago, to leave among my few papers Edward Chapman's testimony to the gross falsehood and absurdity of the idea.

" But last week I wrote a letter to the *Athenæum* about it, in consequence of Seymour's son re-

viving the monstrosity. I stated in that letter
that I had never so much as seen Seymour but
once in my life, and that was some eight-and-
forty hours before his death. I stated also that
two persons still living were present at the short
interview. Those were your uncle Frederick and
your mother. I wish you would ask your mother
to write to you, for my preservation among the
aforesaid few papers, a note giving you her re-
membrance of that evening—of Frederick's afterwards knocking at our door before we were up, to
tell us that it was in the papers that Seymour had
shot himself, and of his perfect knowledge that the
poor little man and I looked upon each other for
the first and last time that night in Furnival's
Inn. It seems a superfluous precaution, but I take
it for the sake of our descendants long after.

"Yours ever affectionately,

"C. D."

In a new preface, added later, he also took
care to put on record his view of this transaction:—

"It is with great unwillingness that I notice
some intangible and incoherent assertions which
have been made, professedly on behalf of Mr. Seymour, to the effect that he had some share in the
invention of this book, or of anything in it, not
faithfully described in the foregoing paragraph.
With the moderation that is due equally to my
respect for the memory of a brother-artist and to

my self-respect, I confine myself to placing on
record here the facts :—

"That Mr. Seymour never originated or suggested an incident, a phrase, or a word, to be
found in this book. That Mr. Seymour died
when only twenty-four pages of this book were
published, and when assuredly not forty-eight
were written. That I believe I never saw Mr.
Seymour's handwriting in my life. That I never
saw Mr. Seymour but once in my life, and that
was on the night but one before his death, when
he certainly offered no suggestion whatsoever.
That I saw him then in the presence of two
persons both living, perfectly acquainted with all
these facts, and whose written testimony to them
I possess. Lastly, that Mr. Edward Chapman
(the survivor of the original firm of Chapman and
Hall) has set down in writing, for similar preservation, his personal knowledge of the origin and
progress of this book, of the monstrosity of the
baseless assertions in question, and (tested. by
details) even of the self-evident impossibility of
there being any truth in them. In the exercise
of the forbearance on which I have resolved, I do
not quote Mr. Edward Chapman's account of his
deceased partner's reception, on a certain occasion,
of the pretences in question."

Nothing but the brilliancy of the young author
and the spirit of the publishers could have saved

the venture after this serious check, at its very starting. Yet the loss of Seymour, tragic as were the circumstances, was certainly an unmixed benefit; for had he continued to be connected with it, the "sporting" character of the work must have developed; and scenes and situations would have had to be supplied, or " put in for the benefit of Mr. Seymour;" and the writer have been unable to take that free, unfettered course which has made the book what it is.[4]

[4] Seymour furnished some clever etchings to a little book, published by Messrs. Chapman and Hall in 1835, and called "The Squib Annual." One of the plates represents a sort of prison yard, and the warder is somewhat of an anticipation of Mr. Pickwick, having his short portly figure, low-crowned hat, shorts and boots.

III.

THE embarrassment caused to the new venture
by this casualty was excessive. An artist had to
be supplied at once, and it was difficult to know
to whom to apply. Who was now to work out the
"sporting-cockney" theme, for which Seymour
had such a gift? In the new number the indulgence of the public was humbly solicited:—

"Some apology is due to our readers with only
three plates. When we say they comprise Mr.
Seymour's last efforts, and that upon one of them
in particular (the Stroller's Tale) he was engaged
to a late hour of the night preceding his death,
we feel confident the excuse will be deemed a
sufficient one.

"Some time must elapse before the void the
deceased gentleman has left can be filled up.
The blank his death has occasioned in the society
which his amiable nature won and his talents
adorned, we can hardly hope to see supplied."

In the dearth of suitable talent for the purpose
—Cruikshank and Seymour were indeed the only

etchers of reputation—the publishers esteemed
themselves fortunate in having selected an
artist of note—viz. Mr. Buss. This gentleman was a painter of much merit, and had
exhibited at the Academy. He had a talent
for painting pictures suitable for engraving and
likely to hit the public taste. One of these, which
was highly popular, exhibited " Sir Walter Raleigh
smoking his first pipe," where the consternation of
the servant on entering is humorously conveyed.[1]
Mr. John Jackson, a well-known wood-engraver,
at the time working for the firm, had been applied
to, to help them out of their difficulty, and suggested this artist, who was unacquainted with the
mystery of etching. He had been a pupil of that
capital theatrical portrait-painter, Clint, and was
employed to illustrate Cumberland's " British
Theatre" with sketches of Harley and other
comedians. We may suppose, however, from his
acquaintance with Jackson, that he could design
on the wood. Sixteen years later we find him,
in announcing a course of lectures, thus describing
himself :—" Mr. R. W. Buss, painter, designer on

Another picture now in the possession of his son, the Rev.
Alfred Buss, was even more popular. It is entitled "Satisfaction," and represents with bitter irony the issue of a duel, in
which one of the combatants has been killed and the other
mortally wounded. The scene is dramatically expressed, and
the costumes—the long cloaks, caps, &c., are quite Pickwickian.

wood, and etcher, begs to inform the committee,"
&c.

One of the firm now waited on him and explained their difficult situation, promising, moreover, due consideration for his lack of practice.
His son, Mr. Alfred Buss, writes :—"After much
pressure, he consented to put aside the picture he
was preparing for exhibition, and to undertake
the work. He began at once to practise the
various operations of etching and biting in. The
subjects were then selected. When, however,
he began to etch them on the plate, he found the
wax break up under the etching point, as he had
little or no experience in laying it. Time was
precious, but as the pressure was very great, and
the time so short, he secured the services of a
professional etcher." The result was the unsatisfactory "Buss Plates" now found in a few copies
of the first edition, and which, by a curious com-
pensation, are sought for with as much avidity by
collectors as though they were rare gems of art.
One represented the " cricket match," with very
stout players, and an elderly gentleman " fielding,"
the other Tupman and the " spinster aunt" in
the arbour, not very successful either in design
or execution.[2]

___

[2] I have seen many of his little experiments in pen and
ink, which are spirited enough, and dashed off with much
freedom.

Among the artist's sketches and finished drawings are several designs for these two scenes. One of the cricketers is shown receiving a blow of the ball on his face, which no doubt was found too farcical. He confessed candidly enough that "there was a vague impression on my mind that these etchings were *abominably bad*, and utterly devoid of promise and hope;" so the result was not surprising.

By the time the next number was ready a great alteration had been made in the plan of the undertaking. Before the dismissal of Mr. Buss, a change was made in the length of each part and number of illustrations, the pages being increased to thirty-two, and the plates reduced to two. This was announced in the following address, dated May 30, 1836:—

"We announced in our last, that the ensuing numbers of the 'Pickwick Papers' would appear in an improved form; and we now beg to call the attention of our readers to the fulfilment of our promise.

"Acting upon a suggestion which has been made to them from various influential quarters, the Publishers have determined to increase the quantity of letterpress in every monthly part, and to diminish the number of plates. It will be seen that the present number contains eight additional pages of closely printed matter, and

two engravings by Mr. Buss, a gentleman
already well known to the public as a very
humorous and talented artist.

" The alterations in the plan of the work entail
upon the Publishers a considerable expense, which
nothing but a large circulation would justify
them in incurring. They are happy to have it
in their power to state that the rapid sale of the
two first numbers, and the daily increasing
demand for the periodical, enables them to
acknowledge the patronage of the public in the
way which they hope will be deemed most acceptable.

" May 30th, 1836."

The artist was now busy designing other plates
for the succeeding numbers—among which were
the " tipsy scene " in Wardle's kitchen ; " The
elopement," which is curiously like Browne's plate,
and Winkle's accidental shooting of Tupman, all
three a vast improvement on the first attempts—
when he received a communication that his
further services were to be dispensed with. This
dismissal was felt bitterly, and brought great
mortification. It must be said the fault was not
altogether his. In an elaborate statement which
he drew up for his children, he set out his case,
under a sense of having been dealt with unjustly.[3]

[3] With his son, the Rev. Alfred Buss, the Vicar of St. James's,
Curtain Road, Shoreditch, I lately spent an agreeable morning,

This feeling lay dormant for nearly forty years, until it was awakened by an allusion in Mr. Forster's " Life of Dickens." It must be said, however, that his style of humour was unsuited to that of " Pickwick," though it is quite clear that he had to bear the consequences of his unlucky ignorance of the art of etching. It is this part of the work that is inferior. He gives this account of the matter in his statement :—

"I was in an evil hour induced to place my designs in the hands of an engraver to be etched and bitten in. The work he did very well indeed, but, as might have been expected, had I time for thought, the free touch of the original work was entirely wanting. The etching itself failed, but the biting in was admirably done. Time was up. The plates must be placed at once in the printers' hands. Thus my name appeared to designs, not one touch of which was on the plates. I felt greatly annoyed at all this, and, had I been allowed time, would have cancelled these two plates." He had carefully prepared a third design, which he had submitted to the firm as a specimen, and this is executed with some delicacy and cleverness, and with humour too.

"I also got ready," he says, "a Pickwick

during the course of which he was kind enough to lay before me all his father's papers, sketches, proofs, &c. ; on a careful examination of which the account just given is based.

design to try my power. It is taken from the description of Mr. Pickwick at the review, when he was pushed forward by a crowd behind him, and jammed backward by a tall grenadier. As might be expected, it is thin and scratchy in execution."[4] Of this plate there are believed to be only one or two copies. The others have been reproduced.

The artist was later much employed as an illustrator of books, and had considerable success. Mr. Colburn engaged him to illustrate the diverting story of Mrs. Trollope, " The Widow Married," which " ran " in the *New Monthly*. We find his work also in the *Penny Magazine*. But his more remarkable efforts, which have merit for their drawing and etching, are his illustrations to Captain Marryatt's " Peter Simple," which show much spirit and correct colouring in their costumes and incidents. There we see in the limbs and attitudes his knowledge of drawing.[5]

The firm had fortunately secured another illustrator, a difficult task indeed, though they had offers enough. "I can remember," so Mr.

---

[4] Memoir.

[5] He also was engaged to illustrate Mrs. Trollope's "Michael Armstrong,' and Harrison Ainsworth's "Court of James II.," for the *New Monthly*, where he tried to imitate the grim, realistic style of Cruikshank.

Thackeray told the story at one of the Academy dinners, " when Mr. Dickens was a very young man, and had commenced delighting the world with some charming humorous works, in covers which were light green, and came out once a month; that this young man wanted an artist to illustrate his writings. I recollect walking up to his chambers in Furnival's Inn, with two or three drawings in my hand, which strange to say, he did not find suitable." Thackeray's sketches for his own works have a certain attraction of individuality and even humour, but they have what may be called an "amateurish" air.[6] They are moreover uncertain, as though the result did not answer the artist's intentions. He would have been unsuited to the task.[7]

By a fortunate chance, selection was made of Mr. Hablot K. Browne, a most competent person, whose work was exactly adapted to the story, and who through his long connection with Dickens showed an extraordinary flexibility and genius, that was really invaluable for a work that spread over so vast a field of adventure and character.

[6] Thackeray's style, Mr. Buss tells us, was founded on that of the caricaturist Bunbury, and was therefore old-fashioned and not original.

[7] Another candidate was Leech, one of whose delicately drawn sketches, for Tom Smart's story, is reproduced in the Victoria edition.

Much interesting detail, as to " Phiz's " connection with Dickens, will be found in the handsome quarto volume, on " Phiz," written by Mr.
Thomson.

It was indeed later stated, that "Phiz " also, like
Buss, was inexperienced in the technical parts of
etching, and, like him, had to call in assistance.[8]
Mr. Jackson, the engraver, however, states
that Phiz could etch perfectly, and mentions a
large plate of John Gilpin's ride, which was his
work. It would seem this very etching led to
his engagement. It was Mr. Jackson, it will be
recollected, who recommended Buss, and after
the latter was engaged, Mr. Chapman chanced to
call on Jackson, and was attracted by this picture.
" Mr. Chapman in common with every one who
had seen it, was delighted with it, and forthwith
applied to Browne." The truth, however, was
that Phiz was already a most competent artist,
having been long in Messrs. Finden's employment;
and only transferred the work to an assistant
when he was pressed for time.

---

[8] Mr. Buss, in his Memoir, speaks of some " proofs " of the
plates in "Nicholas Nickleby," which were "worked on only
by 'Phiz,' and which may be compared with their finished
state after they had been treated by Sands." The latter, who
was an old friend of Buss's, naturally claimed as much credit as
he could for his assistance, and appeals to one of the drawings on
which this direction by Browne was written : " The outlines of
the figure I have etched in with a broad point, intentionally ;
bite them slightly that they may not be too hard."

All the characters, indeed, who were attracted to the bright and buoyant Dickens seemed to have something of his spirit in their nature. The new illustrator found for "Pickwick" was a young fellow, just one-and-twenty, shrewdly observant, and pleasant, and known as Hablot Knight Browne. He was one of the youngest of fifteen children. The family had good connections, and two of his brothers distinguished themselves in the army and in the Church. He was called "Hablot" after a French officer who was engaged to one of the family, and who was killed at Waterloo.

In his line, Browne was as industrious and fertile and as much in demand as Dickens. Two of his early plates to "Pickwick" are marked with "Nemo" in faint characters in the corner, but he later adopted the well-known "Phiz," to be in harmony with his collaborator "Boz."[9] He became, indeed, the author's second self in the designing of these pictures, adapting himself with infinite resource to the hurried conditions of the venture. Dickens used to tell how often he had merely to explain to the artist in a few words, the character of the situation, which the latter caught

---

[9] "Phiz, whizz, or something of the kind," was T. Hook's joke. "I think," said the artist, "I signed myself as 'Nemo' to my first etchings, before adopting 'Phiz' as my *sobriquet,* to harmonize, I suppose, better with Dickens's 'Boz.'"

with admirable instinct and intelligence.   On other more fortunate occasions the proofs were read to him.   It need not be said that there is an art, not merely in giving a representation of the described scene, but in supplying what the public will accept as expressing what they have read.   Mr. Thomson has some shrewd observations on this point.

It was felt that a work containing specimens of three artists, two of whom were scarcely in "touch" with the narrative, could not be considered as well harmonized.   Buss's productions impaired the effect as the leaves were turned over, and it was determined that the industrious Browne should supply substitutes for these.   He accordingly re-drew Seymour's plates in the early parts, and substituted others for the two of Buss's. Indeed the demand for the work was so great, that three sets of the illustrations were etched. When the work had run half its course, on issuing the tenth number, for December, 1836, "Boz" added this address to the reader, written without any affectation :—

"Ten months have now elapsed since the appearance of the first number of the ' Pickwick Papers.' At the close of the year, and the conclusion of half his task, their author may perhaps without any unwarrantable intrusion on the notice of the public, venture to say a few words of himself.

" He has long been desirous to embrace the first

opportunity of announcing, that it is his intention
to adhere to his original pledge of confining this
work to twenty numbers. He has every temptation to exceed the limits he first assigned to
himself, the brilliant success, an enormous and
increasing sale, the kindest notice and the most
extensive popularity can hold out. They are one
and all sad temptations to an author; but he has
determined to resist them; firstly, because he
wishes to keep the strictest faith with his readers;
and secondly, because he is most anxious that
when the posthumous papers of the Pickwick
Club form a complete work, the book may not
have to contend against the heavy disadvantage
of being prolonged beyond his original plan.

" For ten months longer, then, if the author be
permitted to retain his health and spirits, the
' Pickwick Papers ' will be issued in their present
form, and will then be completed. By what
fresh adventures they may be succeeded is no
matter for present consideration. The author
merely hints that he has strong reason to believe
that a great variety of other documents still lie
hidden in the repository from which these were
taken, and that they may one day see the light.

" With this short speech Mr. Pickwick's stage
manager makes his most grateful bow, adding, on
behalf of himself and his publishers, what the late
eminent Mr. John Richardson, of Horsemonger

Lane, and the yellow caravan with the brass
knocker, always said on behalf of himself and
company, at the close of every performance,
"Ladies and gentlemen, for these marks of your
favour, we beg to return you our sincere thanks,
and allow us to inform you, that we shall keep
respectively going on, beginning again, and
regularly until the end of the fair."

The work, as we said, must have been prosper-
ing exceedingly to triumph over the periodical
shocks or blows that it received in its course. It
is rare that we find an undertaking planned to
exhibit the talents of a particular artist, all but
shipwrecked after starting, by the sudden death
of that person. But a greater danger even arises
from any interruption in supplying the public with
what it expects to receive, and has contracted for.
The general reader is touchy and capricious, and
resents such freedoms.

Dickens was tenderly attached to one of his
wife's sisters, Mary Hogarth, an interesting person.
It was in the month of May, 1837, when his
"Pickwick" was riding on the swelling tide of
popularity that this young lady died suddenly.
He felt the blow in an extraordinary way, and so
poignant was his grief that he found it impossible
to apply his thoughts to the humorous story he
was conducting. It was actually suspended—to
the consternation of the publishers—to wait his

return to composure. The first of the month went by without the flutter of the customary green leaves, and the fretted, eager public had to wait all the month of June without their supply. He found it necessary, with the July number, to issue an address explaining the delay, and this address, it may be said, showed that he was still nervous and overwrought.

"186, Strand, June 30, 1837.

"The author is desirous to take the opportunity afforded him by his resumption of this work to state once again, what he thought had been stated sufficiently emphatically before, namely, that its publication was interrupted by a severe domestic affliction of no ordinary kind, that this was the sole cause of the non-appearance of the present number in its usual course, and that henceforth it will continue to be published with its accustomed regularity. However superfluous this second notice may appear to many, it is rendered necessary by various idle speculations and absurdities which have been industriously propagated during the past month, which have reached the author's ears from many quarters, and have grieved him exceedingly. By one set of intimate acquaintances, especially well informed, he has been killed outright; by another driven mad; by a third imprisoned for debt; by a fourth left per steamer for the United States; by a fifth rendered incapable of mental exertion for evermore ; by all, in short, represented as doing anything but seeking a few weeks' retirement, the restoration of cheerfulness and peace, of which a sad bereavement has necessarily deprived him."

A curious form of " Address," with jocose comments by the editor, had been used by Hood and others in the *London Magazine*. They are too familiar, but are in the spirit of the time. Our author prints for his readers a ludicrous remonstrance addressed to him, on the score of the cabman's supposed cruel treatment of his horse :—

"If it is carelessness only, it may be corrected if it be bad taste ; but perhaps you could in another paper point out to the obtuse like myself, the wit or humour of depicting the noblest of animals faint, weary and over-driven, subjected to a brute, only to be tolerated because he at least is ignorant of the creature and his Creator."

" This is evidently," said the author, " a very pleasant person, a fellow of infinite fancy. We shall be happy to receive other communications from the same source, and on the same terms, that is to say, post paid." This is the style of the "Mudfog" papers.

In November, 1837, the last number of " Pickwick " was issued, and the happy conclusion was celebrated by a dinner, " with himself in the chair, and Talfourd in the vice-chair, everybody in hearty good-humour with every other body."

In Mr. Forster's library at South Kensington there is a handsome copy of " Pickwick," a pretty specimen of binding, delicately tooled. There were three copies sent to him by the publishers, "extra super bound," as he called them, in the month of December, 1837, the work being now complete. He presented one to his wife, another to Ainsworth, and the third to Forster.

When the last number had been issued, and the work was published in its final shape, the pseudonym of " Boz " was discarded, and the real name of the writer placed on the title-page.[1]

Another of the wonders connected with this wonderful book is that while he was furnishing his pleasant contingent of fun and humour, month by month, and before he was half way through it, he had begun, in January, 1837, another story, " Oliver Twist." Thus, for eleven months there were two streams of fun and humour gushing forth, without the slightest sign of confusion, or of flagging power and interest. He was also editing a magazine. Nor was this all. He had actually contracted with Macrone, the publisher, to furnish him with a third novel!

[1] This epigram was in one of the magazines:—
>   Who " the Dickens " " Boz " could be,
>   Puzzled many a learned elf,
>   But time unveiled the mystery,
>   And " Boz " appeared as Dickens' self.

"Monday, May 8, 1836.

"MY DEAR MACRONE,—I shall have great pleasure in accepting from you the sum of 200*l.* for the first edition of a work of fiction (in three volumes of the usual type) to be written by me, and to be entitled 'Gabriel Vardon, the Locksmith of London,' of which not more than 1000 copies are to be printed.

"I also understand that the before-mentioned 200*l.* are to be paid by you, on delivery of the entire manuscript—on or before the 30th day of November next, or as soon afterwards as I can possibly complete it."[2]

This impossible agreement was, however, cancelled, at a heavy sacrifice. During this busy year, the author also brought out two plays![3]

Talfourd, an accomplished, many-sided character, was a dramatic critic of delicacy, skill and power, as also a writer of much finish and art in works of "long breath," such as his life of Lamb. He moreover worked at his profession with great success, and on the circuit contended for the lead with such an opponent as Maule. This versatile

[2] Nearly two hundred letters of Dickens were in Mr. Ouvry's possession, and, at his death, were disposed of to an American newspaper. Some of these, including the one just quoted, were published in the *Times* of November 2, 1883.

[3] Nor, again, was this all. He wrote a pamphlet, "Sunday under Three Heads," now literally worth *more* than its weight in gold !

man had recently entered Parliament, and, after
some minor efforts, had taken up a subject which
was near to Dickens's heart, viz. the right of
authors to enjoy the fruits of their labours, with
protection from pillage. Talfourd, who sat for his
native town, Reading, introduced his Copyright
Bill early in the year 1837, in a speech of singular
elegance and finish. It is likely indeed, from some
of the pathetic turns, that his friend aided him in
the composition. He, with the " trusty " Forster,
were the friends whom Dickens regarded with
most affection. He had watched over and followed the career of Pickwick and his followers,
and at the happy close it was Talfourd who
presided at the dinner given in celebration of the
event. It was to Talfourd that he inscribed the
work, in a dedication breathing a warm affection
and gratitude.

" To Sergeant Talfourd, M.P., etc., etc.

" My dear Sir,—If I had not enjoyed the happiness of your private friendship, I should still have
dedicated this work to you as a slight and most
inadequate acknowledgment of the inestimable
services you are rendering to the literature of your
country, and of the lasting benefits you will confer
upon the authors of this and succeeding generations, by securing to them and their descendants a
permanent interest in the copyright of their works.

"Many a fevered head and palsied hand will gather new vigour in the hour of sickness and distress from your excellent exertions; many a widowed mother and orphan child, who would otherwise reap nothing from the fame of departed genius but the too frequent legacy of poverty and suffering, will bear, in her altered condition, higher testimony to the value of your labours than the most lavish encomiums from lip or pen could ever afford.

"Besides such tribute, any avowal of feeling from me on the question to which you have devoted the combined advantages of your eloquence, character and genius, would be powerless indeed. Nevertheless, in thus publicly expressing my deep and grateful sense of your efforts in behalf of English literature, and of those who devote themselves to the most precarious of all pursuits, I do but imperfect justice to your strong feelings on the subject, if I do no service to you.

"These few sentences would have comprised all I should have to say, if I had only known you in your public character. On the score of private feeling let me add a word more.

"Accept the dedication of this book, my dear sir, as a mark of my warmest regard and esteem, as a memorial of the most gratifying friendship I have ever contracted, and of some of the pleasantest hours I have ever spent, as a token of my fervent admiration of every fine quality of your head and heart, as an assurance of the truth and sincerity with which I shall ever be,

"My dear Sir,

"Most faithfully and sincerely yours,

"CHARLES DICKENS."

"48, Doughty Street,

"September 27th, 1837."

Talfourd, undistracted from the serious purpose of his life by his connection with the stage, or his intimacy with this choice spirit of literature, was eventually appointed a judge, and it was in the year 1854, when holding the assizes at Stafford, that he died suddenly under tragic circumstances. The calendar was a heavy one, and marked by an unusual amount of dreadful crime. This seems to have affected him, and in his address he spoke in a very feeling way of the lack of sympathy that existed between the upper and lower classes, urging the former to show a livelier interest in those who were below them. Suddenly he fell forward on his book, and, being "carried from the Court by six gentlemen," was found to have expired.

It is curious to find—and many have been perplexed at the omission—that, when a new edition of the story was issued in 1847, this affectionate dedication to Talfourd was withdrawn; and a simple "inscription as a memorial of friendship" substituted. Even this has disappeared from the later editions. Mr. Frederic Chapman has, however, informed me, that this omission was really owing to lack of room, when the cheaper editions came to be issued.

"The popularity of 'Pickwick,'" wrote Mr. Forster, " outstripped at a bound that of all the most famous books of the century. The charm of its gaiety and good-humour, its inexhaustible fun, its riotous overflow of animal spirits, its brightness and keenness of observation, and, above all, the incomparable ease of its many varieties of enjoyment, fascinated everybody. Judges on the bench, and boys in the street, gravity and folly, the young and the old alike found it to be irresistible."

This is sound and excellent criticism. Farther on, he adds, " We had all become conscious in the very thick of the extravagance of adventure and fun set before us, that here were real people."

IV.

BIBLIOGRAPHY has in our time become a regular science and supplies a minute and logical system of appraisement for settling the market value of books. The original edition of " Pickwick " takes a high place in the list of valuable books, but it engages all the skill of an expert to settle if a particular copy has all the requisite " points." This subject of what Mrs. Malaprop might have called the Biblio-idolatry of Dickens has of late years been carried to an extraordinary pitch. There can be no doubt there is a sort of fascination about it, which is founded to a great extent on the superior artistic merits of the books themselves, as specimens of typography, as also on their history and associations. Further, " Pickwick " is so sincere and genuine, so full of allusions and so characteristic of its era, that it bears study and investigation, and what might seem trivial helps to increase the interest. The special form of issue in numbers or parts, each number set off with illustrations of a high character, resulted in a volume of particular form and character, which was a whole, and yet at the same time had the air of a number of separate episodes. The shape became, therefore, rather peculiar and exceptional—a large octavo, in amount equal to two volumes bound together. The paper was superfine, and the printing executed with much care; and the illustrations, when fresh, and the plates unworn, have an attraction from their spirit and brilliancy. It must be remembered that the ordinary trade issues of our day are often *machined*, and the plates electrotyped; whereas the delicacy of the original illustrations, which are etchings, forms an adornment to a volume. They are different from the hasty, carelessly drawn engravings which set off the common works of commerce.

It is indeed astonishing to find to what extent the principles of Bibliography have been applied to these works. There are already some half-dozen books dealing in the most minute way with the different editions and their illustrations. Such are Mr. F. Kitton's "Dickensiana" Mr. Dexter's "Memorial of Dickens," Mr. J. Cook's "Bibliography," Mr. R. Herne Shepherd's, Mr. C. Thomson's, and Mr. Johnson's volumes, all full of research and comparison; with Mr. Anderson's, of the British Museum, "Bibliography," the fullest and most scientific of all.

Mr. Plumptre Johnson, in his pretty volume, speaks very seriously of the difficulties that beset the collector, who yearns, like the owner of the " blue" teapot, to live up to a proper copy of the first edition of Pickwick. It might seem an easy thing, on the first thought, to obtain such a *trouvaille*, scarce though it may be : an order to an experienced bookseller might readily secure it. But there is as much difficulty here, as in being certain as to the originality of a picture. The first object is to see that the work is in its original *numbers* or parts, with the old green covers on. This is at least *primâ facie* evidence of genuineness in the illustrations ; for later on the book was issued complete. Next must be pointed out the danger which besets the collector, owing to three "states" of each illustration being issued, after number 10 had appeared ; and these, being mixed together, are found indiscriminately in all the succeeding parts, the "first state" of one plate being in the same number with the "second state" of another. Mr. Johnson knew of a collector who possessed four copies in numbers, all in this unsatisfactory condition ; but, by a system of exchanges and purchases, he at last succeeded at infinite toil in forming a perfect set, homogeneous as it were, when all the plates were of the same state. We may smile at this, but as we said, the perfect article is a different thing

F

altogether from the ordinary edition of commerce. Everything, to be " desirable," should be complete, in its best and most natural shape, and in its proper order ; and degrees of merit are found in every work that comes from man's hand.

Another danger is from the spurious imitations and forgeries. To meet the demand, shall we say, of crazy amateurs, eager to have the two " suppressed Buss plates," these have been reproduced in different ways and offered as genuine. Evidences of later editions have been removed from the title-pages by the aid of chemicals ; portions have been reprinted, and sets " made up," as it is called, ingeniously " adulterated," as the old dry-asdusts used to say of the Shakespearian Folios.

" Pickwick " was published, as Mr. C. Plumptre Johnson tells us, " in twenty numbers, in green wrappers, one of which should be preserved." Of these seven plates were by Seymour, thirty-six by Phiz, and two by Buss. The last two are not essential as they were " suppressed," and two others " The influence of the salmon," and the " Arbour scene," by Phiz, substituted. The collector should see that all these plates are good impressions, and mark that they have no letterpress descriptions under them. He should also see that the plates by Buss are original impressions, as they have been republished in so-called *facsimile*.

The spurious plates were first issued on India paper only, in which form they could deceive nobody, but I have since seen copies on ordinary paper. It is also desirable to have the four notices issued with numbers 2, 3, 10 and 15 respectively.

Browne's first specimens were singularly successful, and are now pleasing to look at, from the softness of the treatment and delicacy of the tints. These were "the upset," and the scene in the White Hart Inn—so interesting as a record of the days when the inn yards, with picturesque galleries running round in tiers, were frequented. The faces are almost as delicate as those of Cruikshank's, whose work the plate suggests, and the details are sketched in a very artistic style. It is worth while putting one of the later copies—when the plate had been re-drawn, and re-issued again and again,—beside it. They are virtually different works. There is a good deal of persiflage, and perhaps contempt, displayed, at the expense of amateurs who collect mezzotints and engravings in different "states," who will give twenty pounds for a proof impression, and reject the ordinary engraving, though offered for five shillings: the truth being that, placed side by side, the inferior copy seems unendurable, half the shadows being worn away, the other half blackened and confused. The very dainty and interesting volume written by Mr. Dexter,

entitled a "Dickens Memento," deals minutely
with all the little notes and varieties by which
the genuine plates and true first edition are to be
known.   As he shows, Part I. contains four
etchings by Seymour; " at least it should do
so, " but ninety-nine copies out of every hundred
have only Phiz's copies of these etchings.
Part II. has only three etchings by the same
artist, but these are not difficult to obtain as
they were used in all the sets in parts and also in
the first cloth issue."

The publishers, pressed by the demand for
copies, for which an insatiate, delighted public
were clamouring eagerly, were at their wits'
end to supply them.   It has been often
repeated that they started with the modest
impression · of 500 copies, but at the close
were furnishing 30,000.   As in the case of
appreciating the value of money in old days, this
circulation, considering the restrained dimensions
of publishing, and the difficulties of dis-
seminating books, was certainly equivalent to
double that amount in our time.   These figures
may be gathered from what was called "The
Pickwick Advertiser," the leaves sewed up at
the end of each number, and which, in number
18, for Oct. 2, 1837, sets out that, "The impression of the advertising sheet is limited to 20,000,
but the circulation of the work being 29,000, that

number of bills is required." It will be seen that before the close the work must have risen by another 1000.

We have spoken of the curious variations that occur in the replicas of the plates : and it may be asked how these are to be accounted for. As mere slavish copying, whether in writing or drawing, is found infinitely more tedious than original work, our artist copied rather freely and with such improvements and variations as occurred to him. Hence is opened up a great field for collectors, who must look warily to see that their plates are in the first or second state, as it may be.[1]   The

---

[1] Dr. Brougham, the Dean of Lismore, an enthusiastic Pickwickian, has kindly collated for me the variations of the etchings in his three copies, with this result :—

"Frontispiece. A. and B. the same, and signed " Phiz fecit." In C. it is signed " Phiz del." In C. Pickwick's footstool is different, and his glass is empty, also the faces on the pillars differ from those in A. and B. Opposite picture in A. and B. "Phiz fecit." In C. "Phiz fect;" also the Marquis of Granby's pigtail is different, and *W*eller is spelt with *W.* instead of *V.* as in A. and B.

p. 69. Cricket match at Dingley Dell "drawn and etch'd by S. W. Buss," not in A. or C.

p. 74. Arbour scene in B. " Drawn and etch'd by S. W. Buss," a totally different version of same scene by "Phiz" in A. and C.

p. 313. Skating scene. Same in A. and B. In C. Winkle's skates and gloves are given, also a stake in the ice, at right front. Snodgrass's face, and Emily Wardle's bonnet strings are also different, and there is a little church steeple in background.

p. 343. The Valentine, same in A. and B   In C. Sam's face.

truth is, the whole impression was mixed, the
publishers issuing such plates as they had to hand,

and the buttons on old Weller's coat are different, and there is
a bow on the bell cord, which is not in A. and B.   "Grimes"
is misspelt in *all*, and the σ in Dublin is turned wrong.

p. 354. The Trial.   Missing from C.   A. differs from B. in
the figures of the lawyers in back benches, the face of Buzfuz
and the shape of his brief.   Mr. Perker's hat is beside him in
B. but *not in A.*, and they differ in several small details in
foreground.

p. 409. A. and C. the same.   B. is different in book-case in
background; man's face at window; position of Mr. Winkle's
cigar, and the spoon in his tumbler.   Bob Sawyer's face is also
different in B. from A. and C.

p. 434. A. and C. the same.   In B. the window is different,
also the hands of the clock, the back of Pickwick's chair, and
the pewter on floor in front.

p. 441. "The Zephyr."   Same in A. and C. ; in B. the
clothes on the line are different; also the bedclothes to right;
the Zephyr's cap and face of man singing.   In A. and C. there
are two balls in front ; in C. it looks like a glass.

p. 453. A. differs from B. and C., first in the potato falling from
Job Trotter's dish, the face of the girl watering the flowers, the
faces of the old man and child in front.   A. is signed "Phiz,"
but B. and C. "Phiz *del.*"

p. 495. Contents of basket in foreground, and Mrs. Cluppins'
profile, different in A. from B. and C.

p. 533. (Bob Sawyer on top of chaise.)   In B. the man cheering in background has a bundle hanging on his stick.   This is
not in A. and C.; also the following are same in A. and C.
and different from B. :—Sam Weller's cuffs, the face of the
coachman and man beside him.   Left leg of fallen child in foreground.

p. 553. "The rival Editors."   Missing from C.   In A.,
"Phiz del." (very small); in B., "Phiz del."   All the details
in these, contents of dresser, mantlepiece, differ.

whether of the first or second state. In many copies, which are apparently first editions, the plates of the last portion of the volume are the re-engraved ones, and this is known by their having a description under each plate, whereas the earliest set of plates had only a reference to the page.

Browne soon acquired freedom and boldness of touch, and his plates appear to have been re-engraved in a dashing, rapid style, and in rough, vigorous fashion; though the faint, delicate strokes, the velvety textures, have disappeared, every line is thick, strong, and black; witness the stretched reins of the horse in Winkle's scene with the "tall quadruped." Thus, a large circulation has its drawbacks.

Some of these variations which ingenious students have puzzled out, are certainly curious and interesting. Such, for instance, as the scene of Mr. Pickwick seated in his wheel-

p. 579. A. and B. the same. In C. Mary has no shoe-strings, and one of the hind legs of the fat boy's chair is seen, which is not in A. and B.

p. 590. In A. and B. there is a little bottle beside Mr. Pell's glass, not in C. The oyster shells on floor and table are the same in A. and B., but different in C.

It is curious how sometimes A. and B. differ from C., and sometimes A. and C. from B.; and also, how much oftener these differences occur in the beginning and end, than towards the middle of the work."

Thus far the Dean: but at the close of the work we shall return to the subject.

barrow in the pound, where there were originally *two* donkeys, but one was later "taken
out."

Some editions have at the bottom of the title-
page, "Phiz fect.," and the amateur must look to
it that it is thus abbreviated. In other editions
over the inn door there is read in legible
characters, "Tony Veller, licensed to sell beer,
spirits, tobacco." In the first edition we find
"PHIZ fecit" in large characters and in full;
while "Tony Veller" only, can be made out over
the door. The frontispiece has "Phiz Fect."
on the left hand at the bottom. On some
frontispieces "Phiz" is on one side of the
shield, and "fect." on the other. This information we owe to Mr. Morris of Eastbourne.
Unluckily, there is no certainty in the matter,
and the point of priority is hotly debated.

But even these varieties, carefully ascertained,
do not bring rest or security. Some urge that
the true first edition should have "*V*eller" on
the signboard; other copies have "*W*eller."
This was carrying idiomatic particularity too far,
as the sign-painter must have spelled the name
correctly : for we have Mr. Weller's own
authority, "put it down a *Wee*."

A true copy of "Pickwick," with all the conditions and in a fine state, was lately sold at Sotheby's
for over 20*l*. But here is a choice "well-found"

copy which Messrs. Robson and Kerslake were
" offering " some time ago :—

" Pickwick Papers, 1837. Bound in 2 vols.,
and containing 2 cancelled plates by Buss, in
addition to those substituted for them ; 1 unpublished plate by Buss (" The Review "), in two
states, plain and coloured; a set of 32 extra
coloured plates by Onwhyn ; 2 sets of Pailthorpe's
Illustrations, India proofs and coloured; a set of
extra coloured plates by Crowquill; a set of
' Original Illustrations to the Pickwick Papers,'
being 16 wood engravings ; a set of coloured
plates by Phiz, from the Household Edition ; 2
India-proof plates by F. Barnard; 2 engraved
vignettes ; 6 very pretty full-page wood engravings, by Phiz; frontispiece to the 'Charles Dickens'
edition, by Leslie ; and specially printed titles."

This shows what " capability," as Mr. Robins
used to say, there lies in our good and sound
Pickwick. It can be developed to any extent,
a " swellin' wisibly " by all sorts of adornments.
A list of the artists who have illustrated
" Pickwick " would be a long one. It would
include Seymour, Buss, " Phiz," Onwhyn,
Pailthorpe, Crowquill, Barnard, Leslie ; besides
many American and Australian artists.

There is a curious mystery, or it may be finality,
in this connection of *original* illustrations with
the text, from which, bad, indifferent or good, they

are not to be divorced. They have been engendered with it : they have come, in response
to the author's ideal; he at least has accepted
them. They have been produced under his
prompting and direction. Such are strong
recommendations; but a more important cause
for their acceptance is that the reader has
come to know the characters and scenes in this
shape. The newer designs have no authenticity,
and are distasteful because strange. Within the
last few years Mr. F. Barnard, a clever artist,
has issued some elaborately finished drawings of
some of Dickens' leading characters. They are
full of force, and, being on a large scale, the
expression of the features is brought out with many
minute and distinct touches. Yet somehow this
very precision seems to remove them from us to
a distance. They are not like our old favourites,
which were generalized by a few vigorous strokes.
This artist, has, for instance, given a capital
portrait of the housebreaking ruffian in "Oliver
Twist," but it is not *our* Sikes. So has Mr. Frith
done Dolly Varden and Kate Nickleby, very
charming and popular portraits; but we find
ourselves objecting that Dolly's mouth is "not
like," or not like what we expected.

In truth we must feel to these posthumous
illustrations much as we do in the case of some
celebrated person whom we are to meet, and

whom we have been hearing of all our lives, but whose face and figure do not correspond, because our imagination has formed for us another ideal. Nothing physical, indeed, could correspond to the fanciful sketch of our imagination. But when the idea and the expression have grown together, they harmonize. It is so with the illustrations which have been presented to us in company with the writer's fancies.

The later illustrator of "Pickwick" should hardly venture to touch scenes that have been already treated; they seem sacred. But it might be allowable to treat others that have not been attempted, provided they are treated in the same style. Thus Mr. Pailthorpe has done some etchings on this principle, which, when bound up, match very fairly with the original series. There is one plate happily selected, depicting a truly humorous incident, when Mr. Pickwick is refused hospitality at an inn, being suspected of having stolen the "tall quadruped," and which is worthy of all praise.

Many years ago "Phiz" was employed to illustrate a cheap edition of "Pickwick" which Messrs Chapman and Hall were about to issue. These drawings were on the wood, and offer a curious contrast to the original work of the artist. We look in vain for the familiar lineaments of the various "Pickwickians." There was little

attempt to carry out the accepted likeness of
Pickwick, Winkle, &c., and any faces or figures
that occurred to him seem to have been dashed
in or off, as hurriedly as possible. The only
solution is that the artist had lost his former
"cunning," and, what was more sad, only eager
to earn his crust, with as little exertion of his
talents as possible.

Dickens had marvellous tact in appreciating
the nice proprieties of illustration, and freely
made objection and suggestions when he was not
satisfied. These were often written on the drawing itself. As when the plate of Mrs. Leo Hunter
at her party was sent to him: "I think it would
be better," he wrote, "if Pickwick had hold of
the Bandit's arm. If Minerva *tried* to look a
little younger, more like Mrs. Pott, who is perfect,
I think it would be an additional improvement."
The hostess had been represented as tall and
rather stout. It is pleasant to have glimpses of
these councils.

One naturally believes that if a writer minutely
and carefully describe his scene in such a way
that it rises to the mind's eye, the artist can
have no difficulty. But the more minutely the
writer describes the scene, the harder will it be
for the artist to give effect to the description. If
the writer mark the principal characters well,
and leave the remainder of the incident in what

artists call "mystery," the task of the illustrator is comparatively easy. But when the author enters into details, and describes with care what he wishes to impress on the readers, the labour of the draughtsman rises in proportion. The artist has to be careful to follow all the points brought forward by the writer, and to see that each detail is subordinate to the whole. When the author is precise, the illustrator has to be general; when the writer is vague, the artist is free.

For these reasons the failure of the Buss plates was not so much owing to the failure of artistic power as to the sentiment of the writer being missed. The expression fails to satisfy the reader who has just read the description.

V.

ONE of the chief attractions of "Pickwick," and a secret of its popularity, is the singular *flavour* of its descriptions. This is really extraordinary, and denotes a rare power, and a vivid dramatic sentiment. The characteristic costumes, old-fashioned and effective, which enter into, and colour the story, the bits of description of Old London, legitimately helping on the narrative, the admirable painting of such things as inn life in country towns, coaching, with a hundred other touches, all add to the charm. There are some places, however, which live again for us, as they did sixty years ago, with a singular and effective vitality, such as Rochester and Bath. The colours here are "laid" with some of the tranquil grace of Miss Austen: there is little personal description, and in every movement and every touch we are conscious of that peculiar note of its own which distinguishes every place, and gives it a special charm, though but few possess the gift of discovering or describing it. It is much the same in the case of painting. We often turn to a collection of "Views of the Cathedrals of

England," either engraved or photographed, and hich seem to us so many imposing buildings of merit, and of many varieties; yet who has not felt, after a visit say to Salisbury or Canterbury, that he has hitherto had little idea of the charm of the building? It is the peculiar *tone* of the place, its surroundings, its relation to the town, its skies and colouring that is wanting. No pictured "elevation" of Salisbury Cathedral can furnish an idea of the fane itself, with its acute spire and peculiar tint, its strange air of solitariness, its retired close. But the painter, Constable, has pierced to the true note, and his fine picture brings before us the whole poetry of the scene, the airy, hovering clouds, the peculiar greens of the place, the relation of the trees and skies to the central object. It is the same with these old-fashioned, slumbering towns, round which still hover old and ghostly glories.

Rochester, and the neighbouring Chatham, is but little changed from the Pickwickian days. The old High Street has still a tranquil "snoozing" air, with its overhanging houses; and the old inns look very much as they did when the coach drove up to the Bull Inn with Mr. Pickwick and his friends on the outside. If we visit Rochester, we feel, as Sam says, that "we have knowd him afore," so perfectly has the tone been caught in the story. We have exactly the same sensations as

the party had, when we are set down, arriving as
strangers at the snug "Bull." While dinner is
getting ready there is no excitement, but still
pleasure of a curious kind. As we dine we hear
Mr. Jingle asking the waiter :—

"Devil of a mess on the staircase, waiter,"
said the stranger. "Forms going up—carpenters
coming down—lamps, glasses, harps. What's
going forward ? "

"Ball, sir," said the waiter.

"Assembly, eh ? "

"No, sir, not Assembly, sir. Ball for the
benefit of a charity, sir."

Three of the guests secure tickets. "Mr. Tracy
Tupman and the stranger entered the ball-room.

"It was a long room, with crimson-covered
benches, and wax candles in glass chandeliers.
The musicians were securely confined in an
elevated den, and quadrilles were being systema-
tically got through by two or three sets of
dancers. Two card-tables were made up in the
adjoining card-room, and two pair of old ladies
and a corresponding number of stout gentlemen
were executing whist therein."

The room is still shown, and how curious is the
feeling of looking at one of these rare hotel ball-
rooms ! The " elevated den " is still there.

Many years ago, in the lifetime of the author,
when staying at Gadshill, I walked betimes on

one Sunday morning, into the old town, where, for the moment, I seemed to become one of the Pickwickians. Everything was redolent of the story. The pleasant green lanes, rather than roads, rose up and down: occasionally I encountered a gig, and a stray waggon or van. There was to be a race or a fair on the Monday, and here was a two-wheeled cart, the proprietor of which walked by his vehicle in a Sunday cloak made out of the gauzy and dappled oilcloth which served as his roulette board. After three or four miles, the great river and the bridge came in sight. And there, as the spectator stood upon the bridge, was a striking view indeed. Pressing on, I entered the little old town, which seemed a snake-shaped street with old rustic inns and posting yards, and a few ancient framed houses, their thin old bones and joints well looked to, and kept as fresh as paint could make them. Everything was as bright and clean as a Dutch town, even to the one policeman who, having little to do, began an affable conversation. Taking another bend, the little old town showed me its well-rusted Queen Anne Town Hall with yellow stone corners, and a high French roof, and a delightful old clock, that hung out a great way over the street, in a mass of florid carving. Behind was a niche and a flamboyant statue of a naval officer, in gauntlets, pointing probably to the French, the

G

brave old Admiral Sir Cloudesley Shovel.
Further on was a low edifice, unmistakable in
character, with a portico and pillars, the Theatre
Royal, with some faded bills, which I approached
to read with interest. I found that, say, "Mr.
George Jenby," the eminent character actor and
vocalist, was to give two nights in this,

HIS NATIVE TOWN.
Being assisted by
Miss Mary Jenby (of the London concerts),
Miss Susan Jenby (of the London and suburban concerts),
Mr. William Jenby (who was of no concerts at all),
and by
The infant, Marie Jenby.

I wished the Jenby family all success, for I
was worked into sympathy with their efforts, by a
pathetic quotation subjoined to the Bill, that

As the hare whom hounds and horns pursue,
Pants to the spot from where at first it flew,

so had worthy Jenby and his family come to
ask support from his "native town" [1] As was
to be expected the host of Gadshill was delighted
with this little touch.

Among the agreeable books written on the
places described by Dickens, Mr. Langton's

This quaint little Rochester playhouse, which had an extraordinary Pickwickian air, has long since ceased to "function,"
and has been altered into some institution, a Conservative
club, I believe.

account of Rochester and the author's associations with it, is the most interesting. As we said, this subject seems to have a sort of fascination, and we find writers of all sorts and conditions return-ing again and again to it. Connected himself with Rochester and Chatham, this gentleman has related some interesting particulars of Dickens's youth, showing also how he delighted to enshrine in his writings all his early and most cherished associations. It will be recollected that a retired spot " behind Fort Pitt " at Chatham was selected as the scene of Mr. Winkle's duel. This place, it appears, was the favourite ground for settling disputes that arose between the four schools of the town, to one of which Dickens had been sent, and with which he was no doubt familiar. The scholars at these seats of education were described in a popular distich, as :—

> Baker's Bull-dogs,
> Giles' cats,
> New Road Scrubbers,
> Troy Town rats.

Dickens was at Giles' Academy.

Rochester with its inn, the latter minutely described, figures in one of the " Sketches by Boz," called " The Great Winglebury Duel." It was strangely entitled " The Blue Lion and Stomach Warmer," and had its " elegant and commodious " assembly-rooms. The tale is further curious as an anticipation of certain portions of Pickwick, there being a duel to come off, while a young lady, Miss Manners, visits the mayor, just as Miss Withersfield did Mr. Nupkins. The boots of the Blue Lion is placed on guard over one of the combatants, as Sam was over Mr. Winkle.

There is also another account of the scenes described by Dickens, a special "Pickwickian Pilgrimage," by an American, Mr. Hassard, and written in a very genial spirit. For this gentleman Rochester and the opening scenes had most attraction.

There is no doubt that this vivid conjunction of known localities with the characters has imparted a living force and a new interest to the story. It has made the Pickwickians live, move, and have their being in a very extraordinary degree. Dr. Slammer's second gave the clearest directions to the unhappy Winkle. "You know Fort Pitt; turn into the field which borders the trench, take the footpath when you arrive at an angle of the fortification, and keep straight on." "Following these instructions, we find ourselves in a rather lonely region of open meadow, with a clump of trees in the distance, much less secluded than it was in Mr. Winkle's time, for the houses are in full view."

The youthful and brilliant writer had taken stock of the manners and society of the place where he had been a boy, and from what we know of one specimen, it is likely that all the

characters were drawn from life. Slammer, the
" peppery" doctor, was sketched from a Dr. Sam
Piper, whom an old friend and brother officer
describes as "a worthy, honest, single-minded
man of the old school, given to swearing and other
peculiarities, who was one of the ' characters' of
Chatham upon my first going there in 1836. He
belonged to the Provisional Battalion of Chatham
in days long ago. Upon the occasion of ' Pickwick' being published, and the allusion to the
Rochester Ball, with Slammer's name, the latter,
in the first instance, ' naturally' thought of
calling out the author, and, on second thoughts,
of prosecuting him for libel. His true friends,
however, strongly advised against this step."
Looking over some papers lately, this reminiscent
gentleman found a letter of his ancient comrade,
which is quite in the " Slammer" style :—

"New Hill: March 17, '58.

" You, the two undermentioned officers, are
hereby required to attend at my house, to-morrow,
Thursday, at six o'clock, to meet only Dr. and
Mrs. ——, also to masticate and wash down your
food with good and wholesome wine. In neglect
of, or disobeying this order, you are liable to be
sworn at.

"Gentlemen, yours sincerely,

"SAM PIPER." [2]

[2] This was communicated to me by General Kent, an old
friend of Dr. Piper's brother officer.

The model for the " Fat Boy " was also supplied
from Chatham, and the tradition there—as I
have heard from several sources—is, that he
was one James Budden, whose father kept the
Red Lion Inn.   He used to assist in the bar, as
Mr. Kitton tells us, " his remarkable obesity attracting general attention ; but it is probably
doubtful if he possessed the other remarkable
characteristic—that of going to sleep in all sorts
of places and attitudes.   He acquired an establishment of his own in High Street, Chatham,
where, on more than one occasion, he was honoured by Dickens's presence as a guest."   In one
of the " Sketches by Boz," entitled " Mr. Minns
and his Cousin," there is a Mr. Octavius Budden
(a retired corn-chandler), and his wife and son,
who are said to have been members of the same
family.   Captain Budden was lately owner of
Gadshill.

It may be added that Dickens was partial to
Kentish names.   Upwich, the greengrocer juryman, was named after a little town in that county,
and Mrs. Pott's " body-guard " possibly received
hers from the Goodwin Sands.

The walk to Cobham, a charming bit of Kent, is
described in " Pickwick : "—

" A delightful walk it was : for it was a pleasant
afternoon in June, and their way lay through a
deep and shady wood, cooled by the light wind

which gently rustled the thick foliage, and enlivened by the songs of the birds that perched upon the boughs. The ivy and the moss crept in thick clusters over the old trees, and the soft green turf overspread the ground like a silken mat. They emerged upon an open park, with an ancient hall, displaying the quaint and picturesque architecture of Elizabeth's time. Long vistas of stately oaks and elm-trees appeared on every side: large herds of deer were cropping the fresh grass; and occasionally a startled hare scoured along the ground, with the speed of the shadows thrown by the light clouds which swept across a sunny landscape like a passing breath of summer.

" 'And really,' added Mr. Pickwick, after half an hour's walking had brought them to the village, ' really, for a misanthrope's choice, this is one of the prettiest and most desirable places of residence I ever met .with.' Having been directed to the Leather Bottle, a clean and commodious village ale-house, the three travellers entered, and at once inquired for a gentleman of the name of Tupman.

" 'Show the gentlemen into the parlour, Tom,' said the landlady."

It may be added here that there is a dreadful tragedy also associated with Cobham Park. A well-known painter of the day came down with his father, and, decoying him into the woods murdered him. He fled to the Continent, but

was captured and confined for life in an asylum,
where Mr. John Forster often saw him on his
visits of inspection.

A delightful walk which we took recently,
starting from breezy Gravesend, up by Windmill
Hill, thence across field-paths the whole way to
Cobham, and from Cobham on to Rochester—a
stretch of about ten miles—kindled afresh these
Pickwickian recollections to an extraordinary
degree. The district is in itself a charming
specimen of what may be called the snug Kentish
scenery, with its mixture of sober greens and
mellow, well-ripened brick colour; its sylvan
lanes, low woods, and hop-poles stacked effectively in pyramids. Cobham has a peculiar grace
of its own, an air of shelter and antique retirement. The stately Elizabethan pile, Cobham
Hall, with its cheerful red towers and innumerable
chimneys and gables, is the centre of the whole.
As we stood and looked, the memories of a walk
many years old rose up, when the genial author
himself led the way, and did the honours of his
country in showing all the choicest and most attractive bits. We see him trudging on before, in
the earnest, straightforward fashion he did everything, delighted with what he had seen a hundred
times before. We stand now as we did then, at
the entrance of the great lime-tree avenue, across
which a chain was mysteriously stretched, the

noble owner, as he explained to him, having to deny himself the use of this approach to gratify the prejudice or superstition of his lowly neigh-bours. This privilege he was allowed to enjoy on one occasion only—that of his own obsequies—when his remains were to be borne in state down the tabooed avenue to its final resting-place. The village adjoining had a charming, nestling air, a little gently winding street of quaint red-brick houses, old inns chiefly; at the furthest end of which, after passing " The Ship," and of course " The Darnley Arms," stood the modest " Leather Bottle."

A pretty, compact, white little tenement it is, with a sign swinging over the door, portraying Mr. Pickwick, his hands under his coat-tails, and the inscription, " *Dickens' Old Pickwick Leather Bottle Hotel.*" There is an overhanging, well-tiled roof, a lamp over the door, little shuttered windows at each side, and a general air of cosi-ness; luncheons, dinners, we are told, are "ar-ranged on the shortest notice," and it is " all among the cherries, apples, and hops," and also "clean and commodious (vide *Pickwick*); Cobham, Kent, opposite the Church and College, the favourite resort of the late Charles Dickens," an ambiguous but allowable exaggeration. There is " an Ordinary every Sunday at half-past one, at 2s." each, and the telegraphic address is " Pick-

wick Cobham." Entering, we find a snug little
bar, and, some good ale being drawn, the landlord suggests that it should be quaffed in "the
Pickwick room," to give it the suitable flavour.

From the chronicle, which is with us, we learn
that "A stout country lad opened a door at the
end of the passage, and the three friends entered
a long, low-roofed room, furnished with a large
number of high-backed, leather-cushioned chairs
of fantastic shapes, and embellished with a great
variety of old portraits and roughly-coloured
prints of some antiquity. At the upper end of
the room was a table with a white cloth upon it,
well covered with a roast fowl, bacon, ale, and et
ceteras." And there it is still; the passage, and
the door at the end of the passage, and a charming old room of some size, very low, and with a
sort of framed ceiling, its yellow walls grimed
with the smoke and steam of a hundred "ordi-
narys." There are the old, high-backed chairs, no
doubt bought in Rochester to add "local colour"
and to correspond with the text—an old portrait of
the teaboard-pattern, with an ancient clock, engravings and photographs of "Boz." From the
centre there used to hang a bottle or gourd; but
the "Leather Bottle" is clearly our old friend
"the Black Jack," now found in museums. It
is pleasant to find after over fifty years everything
corresponding so exactly and so naturally. The

"Leather Bottle," however, had a narrow escape of being burnt down, a few years ago.

Four or five miles trudging brought us to the river and to the noble view of Rochester, with its castle and church, and to the three bridges which cross it in such awkward companionship. On the right after crossing the bridge, we came to a large and mellowed chocolate-coloured building, with a long range of windows, an inn of importance, the old Pickwickian "Bull." A large gateway supported by two columns shows a huge courtyard within, and over the door is a solid "Royal Arms," with a little bull on the top of the lamp. But, alas! there is a sign that the "Bull" is faltering in its Pickwickian allegiance, or "wobbling," as politicians have it, for on each side of the gateway is a board with this inscription in gold characters :—

"LAWRENCE'S VICTORIA AND BULL INN;"

an intrusion, however loyal, which will assuredly end in displacing the older sign. We wandered in. On the right and left were the doors leading into coffee-rooms and offices, while down the yard were bowed windows and the "Assembly Room," overhead, supported on pillars. There was infinite accommodation in a spacious yard for post-chaises and gentlemen's private carriages of the old days. On the left, by the coffee-room, was the hall and flight of stairs—that flight, how

familiar it seemed ! For the moment we caught
ourselves saying, " Here Jingle actually stood and
bearded the peppery Dr. Slammer," just as we see
the pair in the etching. It was, indeed, exactly
as it appeared in those times, with a pleasant
flavour of very old fashion—a black japanned
clock standing at the top of the stairs, with
venerable carpets, and several landings. Somewhat timorously a demand was made to be shown
the ball or assembly-room ; but the spirit of the
request was understood, and, indeed, received as
flattering. We thought of the Pickwickians at
their dinner in one of the rooms below. A waiter
led the way, and threw open a door to the left,
close to the top of the stairs. There was the old
assembly-room, not very large, where some forty
or fifty could dance with comfort. There was an
air of faded old fashion about it ; its three spindly
glass chandeliers hanging in the centre, exactly
as they had lighted the august Clubbers and the
Hon. Mr. Snipe, as again for the moment we
firmly believed. At the end, only a foot or so
over our head, was a little attenuated railing or
balcony, with curtains drawn behind, in which
the musicians fiddle away to this hour.

"It was a long room, with crimson-covered
benches, and wax candles in glass chandeliers.
The musicians were securely confined in an
elevated den, and quadrilles were being systema-

tically got through by two or three sets of dancers.
Two card-tables were made up in the adjoining
card-room, and two pair of old ladies, and a
corresponding number of stout gentlemen, were
executing whist therein."

It was astonishing how exactly everything corresponded to this description, save that there
were circular rows of cane chairs instead of the
crimson benches. The waiter, alas! knew nothing of "Pickwick;" fancied some architectural
aim or purpose, and tried impartially to carry out
his guide or showman business. There were
dances, he said, often given here " in the season."
A curious, indescribable impression was left as
we surveyed this faded old chamber. One would
like to halt for the night at the Bull (or future
Victoria), for the old town is stored with attractions. The Town Hall and Corn Exchange are
fine crusted specimens of ripe brick; there are also
the memories of Edwin Drood, of the Minor Canon
Row, the Castle, and the Seven Poor Travellers.[3]

[3] There are other Pickwickian Inns—such as the Great
White Horse at Ipswich. It is evidence of the extraordinary
vitality of the story, that such works as Murray's Hand-
books, and the A.B.C. Railway guide, gravely record, as
if communicating a fact of actual historical interest, that at
this house (the White Horse), "*occurred* Mr. Pickwick's
remarkable adventure with the lady in yellow curl-papers,"—
while the Bull "*was honoured* by the visit of Mr. Pickwick." The inn-keepers themselves, in their advertisements,

Dorking, in spite of its two railway stations,
stands pretty much where it did fifty years ago,
and retains its air of pleasant rurality. The High
Street is as drowsy and old fashioned as the lover
of good old crusted rusticity could desire, while
the arrival of the " Dorking Coach " at mid-day
during the season, the bugle performing its fanta-
sias with a forced hilarity to impart a theatrical
effect, offers a counterfeit of the old coaching
days. There is an abundance of framed houses,
sound and in good working condition, in and
about the place; but the number of inns is
phenomenal. It has its White Horses, Black
Horses, Red Lions, Old Rams, Old Bulls, to say
nothing of Crowns, King's Heads, Bells, Wheat-
Sheaves and others. As it is, Wellers abound,
and on various boards and shop-fronts the name
meets the stranger's eye. The amateur's first
thought is to settle the identity of Mr. Weller's
inn, but claims are conflicting. A local guide-
book stoutly insists on the King's Head in West

quaintly invite attention to the fact "that Mr. Pickwick and
his friends had stayed at this house." Mr. Hissey asked the
landlord of the Great White Horse if this were not the hotel
Mr. Pickwick is supposed to have put up at. " Supposed ! "
was the indignant reply, " *I've the very carving knife and fork
he used when he was here : ivory mounted they are ; they go
with the hotel,* and were handed to me when I took it."
No other known work of fiction has imparted this extraordinary
feeling of reality.

Street; others set up the Three Tuns, about
the middle of the High Street, while a third
section are for the familiar Old White Horse.
It is disheartening, however, to find it contended
that Weller's inn was actually not in Dorking,
and that the candidate inn was scarcely pretentious enough to suggest a Marquis of Granby.

"The Marquis of Granby," we are told, " in Mr.
Weller's time was quite a model of a roadside
public-house of the better class, just large enough
to be convenient, and small enough to be snug.
On the opposite side of the road was a large sign-
board on a high post, representing the head and
shoulders of a gentleman with an apoplectic
countenance, in a red coat, with deep blue facings,
and a touch of the same blue over his three-
cornered hat, for a sky." All the now claiming
inns would probably repudiate the description
of "a roadside public-house of the better
class," even though complimented with being
" quite a model " in that category ; neither could
the White Horse or Three Tuns be correctly described as " roadside," nor would their position in
the High Street admit of the sign-board being
hung on the other side, which would be objected
to by tradesmen opposite. The White Horse
too, has more ambitious aims than the satisfying
the requirements of " convenience " merely, and
though snug enough, does not supply the " snug-

ness " that comes from smallness of accommodation. The King's Head, however, seems to have the fairest claim; the picture resembles it; and in a number of *All the Year Round*, in 1869, and which passed under Dickens' eye, it is stated that the King's Head was the inn intended.

The truth, however, is that the inimitable Charles, like a true artist, generalized, selecting a bit here and a bit there, and compounding the whole according to his wants. An American writer maintains that the " Markis o' Granby " lately standing at Esher, was intended. But alas! for such speculations, when Dickens was a child there was in Chatham a Marquis of Granby, kept by Thomas Weller, and this no doubt was in his mind. Sawyer is another Pickwickian name displayed here; there is even pointed out the actual locale of Mr. Wardle's shooting party, which Mr. Pickwick attended, it will be remembered, in a wheel-barrow. My friend Mr. Marcus Stone tells me that once, when he was walking with the author of " Pickwick " along the green lanes near Gadshill, a vegetable cart drove past, on which was the name " Weller." He remarked the coincidence. " Coincidence," exclaimed Dickens, " why, it is the man! " meaning that the name had been suggested by a shop in Chatham.

Desperate efforts have been made to identify the localities of Dingley Dell, Muggleton, and

Eatanswill, corrupted, we may presume, from Eat-and-swill. This latter town offered really nothing individual, and the election was of but a common type, many of which Dickens had witnessed. The author at the opening of chapter thirteen somewhat laboriously tries to show that he has no particular town in his eye:—

"We will frankly acknowledge, that up to the period of our being first immersed in the voluminous papers of the Pickwick Club, we had never heard of Eatanswill. We are therefore led to believe that Mr. Pickwick purposely substituted a fictitious designation, for the real name of the place in which his observations were made. In Mr. Pickwick's note-book, we can just trace an entry of the fact, that the places of himself and followers were booked by the Norwich coach; but this entry was lined through." From this we might be inclined to infer that the borough of IPSWICH was in Dickens' mind.

It may have been that Eatanswill was intended for EXETER, whither, in 1835, Dickens repaired "to 'take' the speech of Lord John Russell, in the midst of a lively fight, maintained by all the vagabonds in the county." An aristocrat, it will be recollected, was one of the candidates. It was here that he so humorously described his reporting under difficulties, two colleagues holding a handkerchief over his notes to keep off the rain.

H

The son of the author is inclined to fix on Town Malling as the original of Muggleton, it being always a great cricketing place. But the author gives a further indication which would be of help to those familiar with the politics of the time, that "Muggleton was an ancient and loyal borough, mingling a zealous advocacy of Christian principles with a devoted attachment to commercial rights; in demonstration whereof, the mayor, corporation, and other inhabitants, have presented at divers times no fewer than one thousand four hundred and twenty petitions against the continuance of negro slavery abroad, and an equal number against any interference with the factory system at home; sixty-eight in favour of the sale of livings in the Church, and eighty-six for abolishing Sunday trading in the street."

Mr. Frost, who travelled over Kent, visiting the various localities associated with Dickens, made what may be called a thoroughly scientific examination of these knotty points. Again it may be asked, does not this show how extraordinary is the hold which everything connected with "Pickwick" has on the public mind? He says:—

"Dingley Dell, if it is to be found at all, must be sought, therefore, east of the Medway, between the two lines of railway, and west of a curved line drawn from Judd's Hill to Paddock Wood, through Otterden and Staplehurst; and in that portion of Kent, though there may be many spots the seclusion and picturesqueness of which might suggest such a name as Dingley Dell, there is no town to correspond to Muggleton. All the localities mentioned by Dickens in his narrative of the Pickwickians' journey and their sojourns at Manor Farm must be regarded, therefore, as being equally with Mr. Wardle and the fat boy the creations of his fancy."

But it is BATH that, most of all, seems to live again in his pages. That stately city, always attractive, has now entered on a new revival of life, but cannot shake itself free from the old associations of Miss Burney, Miss Austen, and Dickens. How pleasantly quaint the names of the streets, the Parade, the Royal Crescent, the Circus, Queen's Square, Great Pulteney Street; with the Pump-Room, the Assembly-Rooms, the White Hart! The visitor, as he wanders about, thinks how appropriate it is that Mr. Pickwick and his friends should have lodged at the Crescent, and have joined with the Dowlers in taking the whole *suite* from Mrs. Craddock, the landlady. The great pump-room has or had a curious faded air of fashion, and is now, as then, " a spacious saloon, ornamented with Corinthian pillars, and a music-gallery, and a Tompion clock, and a statue of Nash, and a golden inscription, to which

all the water-drinkers should attend, for it appeals
to them in the cause of a deserving charity."

Then the Assembly-Rooms ; stately, well-de-
signed chambers, where there are forlorn concerts
and entertainments now given, and which seem
charged with the old glories. Once attending
these solemnities, I seemed to see the gay company
again, and in one of the little rooms could call up
the card-tables, and Mr. Pickwick seated at whist
with the terrible, feathered old ladies.

The scenes at this assembly, the glitter and
bustle and *va et vient*, are admirable ; witness the
little talk with Lord Mutanhed, in his " wed mail
cart," just of the length and complexion which
would occur in a crowded ball-room. Bantam
the M.C., is farcical enough, but excellent.

There have been some changes in the place
since the days of the Pickwickians. The White
Hart Hotel, which stood in Stall Street, appears to have been replaced by the present
Grand Pump-room Hotel. As already mentioned,
the White Hart was kept by Eleazer Pickwick,
who had been a post-boy at the Bear. The
old figure of the White Hart that used to be
over the entrance, is now, or was lately, to be
seen over the refreshment-rooms opposite the
Memorial Hospital. The waiters, Dickens tells
us, " might be mistaken for Westminster boys,"
from their costume—an allusion that must have
puzzled many. Mr. Peach explains that the

waiters then wore breeches and silk stockings, and the maids a peculiar, close-fitting dress.   This traditional costume of the inn was maintained almost to its closing in 1864.   Lord Lytton and Lord Beaconsfield, in their youthful days, were fond of patronizing the White Hart.

It was during Lord John Russell's candidature, in 1835, that Dickens was sent to Bath to report a dinner, at which the candidate was to speak. He stayed at the Bush Inn at Bristol, to which Mr. Winkle fled,—since pulled down.   One of his most spirited feats is connected with this trip, and proves that he would have been conspicuous in any walk of life.

" The report of the Bath dinner shall be for-warded by the first Bath coach on Thursday morning—what time it starts we have no means of ascertaining till we reach Bath; but you will receive it as early as possible, as we will indorse the parcel 'Pay the porter 2s. 6d. extra for immediate delivery.'   I need not say that it will be sharp work, and will require two of us; for we shall both be up the whole of the previous night, and shall have to sit up all night again to get it off in time.

" Pray direct to one of us at the White Hart, Bath, and inform us in a parcel *sent by the* FIRST COACH *after you receive this*, exactly at *what hour* it arrived.   Do not fail on any account."

Almost on the eve of his death, Dickens

wandered back to Bath, and it is curious to contrast the impression then left upon him, compared
with the jocund, almost riotous spirit of nearly
forty years before. "Landor's ghost," he wrote,
"goes along the silent streets here before me.
The place to me looks like a cemetery, which
the dead have succeeded in rising and taking.
Having built streets of their old gravestones,
they wander about scantly, trying to look alive,
a dead failure." These grim images scarcely
answer to our notions of the stately city.
Though the Bathonians were displeased at this
unfavourable description, they should find com-
pensation in the thought that it was in the house
No. 35, St. James's Square, at a birthday
dinner, the idea of "Little Nell" was first
conceived.

A pleasantly grotesque sketch is that of Bantam
as M.C., and though it may have been that Dickens
did not intend to portray the actual holder of
the office, he could not have been ignorant that,
for this very reason, it would be considered as a
portrait. The office was held at the time, and
until 1849, by Colonel, afterwards General Jervois,
who later was appointed Governor of Hong Kong
We could scarcely fancy Mr. Bantam filling such
an office. Further, Mr. Peach of Bath, who recalls
Colonel Jervois, writes that he cannot perceive the
slightest resemblance or verisimilitude to Jervois.

The George and Vulture, as we know, was Mr. Pickwick's favourite house when he was in town, and he was perpetually arriving there or departing thence. The name has a quaint, pleasant ring, and also illustrates forcibly the changes of social life. Now-a-days no one in Mr. Pickwick's position would dream of putting up at a place with a sign, though there are still some old houses left in Holborn, such as The Old Bell, and in the Borough, which are comfortable inns of the country pattern. A pilgrimage to the George and Vulture is the duty of every ardent Pickwickian; and the hostelry in question will be found near Lombard Street, close to the Bank of England.

This old tavern, as we now see it, closes up the end of a small court, with dull-coloured walls, and grimed bricks; an archway leads under or through it to the street beyond; while flanking it is the new and palatial-like building just constructed for the Berlin Bank. It has been said that this is not the veritable old "George;" but there stands the old house, with the name and title; and its hotel-like air. Now it is a city chop-house, with a narrow, squeezed and tortuous entry, and the low ceiling and "boxes" are to be seen through the dingy panes. In the face of these facts, the burden of proof seems to lie upon the objectors.

Perhaps the most interesting of these Pickwickian inns, is the old one in the High Street,

Borough, the White Hart, which till lately tottered
on in a very crazy state, in company with its fellows
of the same pattern, up and down the street, the
King's Head, the Queen's Head, and others.   It
is interesting, even on other grounds, to pay a
visit to these relics of a bygone style of travelling,
and at some hour of the day there is generally to
be seen some American stranger, often standing
in the centre of the yard, and looking up at the
ruined galleries.   There is almost a firm faith
that a real Pickwick, Wardle, and Perker stood
there over fifty years ago, questioning Sam ; such
has been the vitality of the story.   It is astonishing that some of the great railway companies had
not secured it as a "Goods Depôt," the general
final stage ; but there it stood, decayed and
abandoned.

A very interesting and learned work has recently been published, on the " Inns of Old Southwark," by Messrs Rendle and Norman, in which
is set out the whole history of the White Hart,
which is an extraordinary one, dating from the
time of Jack Cade.   The antiquarian authors
declare that not a word could be added to
Dickens' perfect description.   " The sober his-
torian who wished to describe faithfully the place
as it was, could not do it better, if so well.
Dickens has filled in particulars evidently from the
life.   In only one little detail does he deviate

from strict topographical accuracy. The galleries were on three sides of the yard instead of two, as he states." . . . "Till September, 1884, the old galleries were let out in tenements, and the presence of the inmates gave life and movement to the scene. Here every afternoon might be seen a solitary omnibus which plied to Clapham, the last descendant of the old coaches. The inner yard is now finally closed."

It will be recollected that after his excited interview with Dodson and Fogg, Mr. Pickwick, turning into Cheapside from Cornhill, asked his servant where he could obtain a restorative. "Second court on the right-hand side," was the reply, "last house but vun on the same side the way. Take the box as stands in the first fire-place," &c. This turn is Freeman's Court, nearly opposite Bow Church, a dark little flagged passage, and the "last house but vun" is now old Burton's coffee-house.

Another Pickwickian inn which has not suffered the least change is the "Spaniards" on the top of Hampstead Hill, not far from the Jack Straw's Castle, where "Boz" and his friend had so many pleasant "shoemakers' holidays." We can see the tea-gardens, with their bowery alcoves, where Mrs. Bardell and her friends enjoyed themselves, and, for the moment, can almost fancy we see the very spot where Mr. Jackson pointed the party out to the bailiff. This impression of reality is as extraordinary here as in other spots, and I fancy is owing to the author's perfect instinct of appropriation. He fitted his characters exactly to the localities and *vice versâ*. No other place would have suited the scene so perfectly.

It was from the Bull Inn, Whitechapel, that Mr. Pickwick started for Ipswich, on a coach driven by his servant's father. This was in the old days the regular point of departure for coaches going north-east. The old inn is still, or was very lately, to be seen, not much altered, and was visited by Mr. Hassard.

The Golden Cross, at Charing Cross, whence the Pickwickians started on May 13th, 1827, by the Rochester coach (and there is something Defoe like in this particularity of date), is now an important and decorous family hotel. But for some years after the date of the journey it was the great starting-point for the coaches, and displayed a sign. We can see still the outline of the very low archway which invited Mr. Jingle's warning :—

" Terrible place—dangerous work—other day —five children—mother—tall lady, eating sandwiches—forgot the arch—crash—knock—children look round—mother's head off—sandwich in her hand—no mouth to put it in—head of a family off—shocking—shocking."

The Great White Horse Inn, Ipswich, is still
what it was, and dates, Mr. Hissey says, from the
sixteenth century. "It is a building of many
passages and staircases; the courtyard is grass-
covered, with a fountain playing and ferns
around." A friend of the present writer lately
visited it, and was much struck with the low,
large chambers and rambling passages, where
the guest would lose his way, exactly as Mr.
Pickwick did.[4]

Recently the writer made a careful search in the
squalid purlieus of Clare Market, for the tavern
frequented by Perker's clerk, Lowten. "At
the back of the New Inn," I found a couple of very
ancient well grimed-taverns, close together and
not unpicturesque. Either would "serve." One is
The Old George the Fourth, a strange tottering place
propped over the street, and thus making a sort
of arcade, on wooden columns; near it is the
sombre, desolate-looking Black Jack, even yet
more decayed and grimed, the name almost
illegible, the windows admitting little light.

---

[4] This lady—a true Pickwickian—has had a number of
photographs taken of the old hostel, which are now before me,
and give an excellent idea of the place. To Mr. Hissey this
old doggrell was repeated:—

> "The White Horse" shall kick "The Bear,"
>   And make "The Griffin" fly,
> Shall turn "The Bell" upside down,
>   And drink the "Three Tuns" dry.

There is, however, an actual Magpie and Stump
to be seen in Fetter Lane. It is minutely described by the author, in his graphic fashion.

"In the lower windows, which were decorated
with curtains of a saffron hue, dangled two or
three printed cards, bearing reference to Devonshire cyder and Dantzic spruce, while a large black
board, announcing in white letters to an enlightened
public that there were 500,000 barrels of double
stout in the cellars of the establishment, left the
mind in a state of not unpleasing doubt and uncertainty as to the precise direction in the bowels
of the earth in which this mighty cavern might
be supposed to extend."

The extraordinary propriety in nearly all
instances of Dickens's selections of localities was
never better illustrated than by his choice of
"Lant Street, Borough," as the place of residence
for a medical student. There is something even in
the name, and still more in the dingy forlornness
and air of shabbiness and abandonment which it
now offers. This vivid impression he had gathered
from his own dismal juvenile recollections, and
which he sometimes transfers to his readers,
for, as we know, Dickens, when a boy, lodged
in this street at the time his father was imprisoned
in the Marshalsea. The house stood on part of the
site now occupied by the Board School adjoining
No. 46. "A back attic was found for me at the

house of an insolvent-court agent, who lived in
Lant Street, in the Borough, where *Bob Sawyer*
lodged many years afterwards. A bed and bed-
ding were sent over for me, and made up on the
floor. The little window had a pleasant prospect
of a timber-yard; and when I took possession of
my new abode, I thought it was a Paradise."

This opinion of his boyhood seems to have been
somewhat changed fifteen years later, when Mr.
Robert Sawyer had taken up his residence in the
locality. " There is an air of repose about Lant
Street, in the Borough, which sheds a gentle
melancholy upon the soul. A house in Lant
Street would not come within the denomination
of a first-rate residence, in the strict acceptation
of the term ; but it is a most desirable spot
nevertheless. If a man wished to abstract himself from the world, to remove himself from
within the reach of temptation, to place himself
beyond the possibility of any inducement to look
out of the window, he should by all means go to
Lant Street."

This exactly describes the tone and aspect of
Lant Street at this hour, its air of waste, lonely
dinginess, and shabby gentility. On the right as
we go down, there is a row of houses, such as
are seen in country towns, with very narrow,
prim-looking doors, all of the same pattern, but in
sound if shabby condition. Here was certainly

Mr. Sawyer's apartment; on the other side is a row of a much meaner sort, and where, it is to be feared, the little boy lodged, in the old disastrous days. Part of the street, close to the High Street, has been levelled, and a Board School has been erected. It is a depressing place altogether.

The Pickwickian Pilgrim will own that Goswell Road, the former Goswell Street where Mr. Pickwick lodged, is unsatisfactory in its power of reviving Pickwickian memories. We imagine—nay, require a dull, comfortable-looking, old-fashioned, retired street; but, instead, find a busy, noisy thoroughfare, a long hill crowded with tramcars and omnibuses, given over to shops rather ill formed, and suggesting a street in some manufacturing town.

VI.

ONE of the most attractive sides of "Pickwick" is the complete picture it offers of an old English state of manners which has now disappeared or faded out. These characters and incidents belong to the state of society that then existed—nay, are its product. Thus the slow and deliberate mode of travelling by coach, the putting up at inns, enforced a sort of fellowship and contact, and led to ready acquaintanceship and to a display of peculiarities. The same conditions of travel, too, promoted a species of adventure, often not without its farce. Now, with the various changes has come an orderly uniformity, reflected in the dramas of our time, which contrast as strongly with the old boisterous humour of the ancient farces. In country houses, cut off from regular contact with the metropolis, simple, unsophisticated characters such as were found at Dingley Dell were not at all improbable. Mistakes in double-bedded rooms, cordial acceptance of adventurers and impostors, like Captain Fitz-Marshall picked up at an assembly rout, elopements, duels, were, as can be seen from the newspapers of the time, ordinary incidents enough.   The vivid yet unaffected style in which these now abolished incidents are brought before us is extraordinary.   Nothing could be more perfect as a complete picture than the account of the Fleet Prison, the fashion of life there, the singular characters, their reckless originality ; yet all contributing entertainment as they forwarded the strict " business " of the piece.   We know as much of the Fleet as if we had resided there for months.   As we have shown, our author caught the whole flavour of Bath, with its assemblies, master of ceremonies, footmen, &c., so that even now a visitor for the first time finds himself in a manner familiar with it, and feels the peculiar tone of dignified old fashion which had been described to him.

It might seem paradoxical to say, that one reason for the extraordinary vitality of the book is found in so much of it being drawn from transient events that were then exciting public attention, and going on about the author ; such as the state of the prisons, the general corruption at elections, the violence of counsel, and various follies of fashion ; with sketches of not a few foolish people, and their " fads."

At the time " Pickwick " was appearing the treatment of debtors was attracting much attention, and the House of Commons had been ordering returns.   In the month in which the first number appeared, the "warden" of the Fleet wrote to the

Times to deny that "he was aware that a guinea and a half was often paid for a room;" or that four or five persons were crammed into a single apartment. These guarded denials may have attracted the young author's eye; he had besides his own dismal recollections.

As we stand at Ludgate Circus, looking to St. Paul's, we shall see facing us, on our left, in Farringdon Street, an imposing Congregational Hall. This, with the buildings adjoining, stands upon part of the ground once occupied by the "Fleet" prison. It stretches back to the ground, or to a portion of it, now occupied by some large printing offices. A long blank wall, with a small central block of entrance, ran along the street. Mr. Ashton, who has written an account of the place, has given a plan; but do we not know it better than any plan could show it? and could we not find our way to the coffee-room flight, or to the racquet-ground?

Pierce Egan, in his "Life in London," described Tom and Jerry being taken by their friend Bob Logic, just as Mr. Pickwick was, to "a whistling shop." It was customary not to ask for drink, but to whistle, which was understood as an order. The "Fleet" was finally closed about 1842, and a few years after the appearance of the story, the prison was sold and levelled to the ground. It was curious, too, that the pathetic history of the

chancery prisoner should have been more than
justified by a piteous tale which came out at an
inquest held on a poor woman who was for years
confined in the Queen's Bench prison. It was
related that, after this long immurement, she had
died from fever brought on by anxiety and hope
deferred. Imprisonment for debt was not prac-
tically abolished until 1864. Many years later
Dickens described the interior of another prison,
the Marshalsea, of which he had many painful
memories. This was done in his later manner,
when he had completely changed his style, and it
would be interesting to compare the effect of
the descriptions of the two places. It must be
said the later account is not nearly so effective
as the first, though infinitely more minute and
elaborate. It is often a mistake to imagine that
the most detailed " inventory " of a place conveys a perfect idea of it ; a few bold, vigorous
strokes will be far more effective. The Marshalsea
is painted almost laboriously, but somehow the
Chiverys who are "on the lock" and the collegians,
and the scene of the signing of the address in
Mr. Dorrit's room, have an artificial air, beside
the masterly picture, done with a few bold, natural
strokes, of the precious trio, the butcher and his
friend, and the parson, whose noisome room in the
Fleet Mr. Pickwick came to take. The squalor,
the meanness consequent upon imprisonment

for debt, the white walls and long galleries, described with a sort of pride to Mr. Pickwick when he was introduced: "this is the coffee-room flight;" the bare background of the lodge, lit up, into which Mrs. Bardell was brought, all have an extraordinary, life-like air.

In "The Old Man's Tale of the Queer Client," the author described what he had seen in his childhood :—

"In the Borough High Street, near Saint George's Church, and on the same side of the way, stands, as most people know, the smallest of our debtors' prisons, the Marshalsea. Although in later times it has been a very different place from the sink of filth and dirt it once was, even its improved condition holds out but little temptation to the extravagant, or consolation to the improvident. It may be my fancy, or it may be that I cannot separate the place from the old recollections associated with it, but this part of London I cannot bear. Want and misfortune are pent up in the narrow prison; an air of gloom and dreariness seems, in my eyes at least, to hang about the scene, and to impart to it a squalid and sickly hue."

The tragic story that follows is certainly a reminiscence, as is also the scene at the funeral.

We find that, not only in the Pickwick Club, but in other productions written about the same

time, our author exercised much good-humoured
satire on the subject of learned societies and their
" Transactions." In the " Mudfog Papers," which
he wrote when he was editor of *Bentley's Miscellany*,
there is much ridicule, carried out in a very elaborate way, of the scientific meetings at Mudfog,
with specimens of the papers read, discussions by
Professors Dosey and Wheazy, not, it must be said,
in his lightest manner. The opening chapter
of " Pickwick," it will be recollected, contains
persiflage of the same kind, with a special ridicule
of the " letters " which many such societies
attach to their names. Later on came the well-
known discovery of the stone with inscribed
characters, which some of the profane insisted on
interpreting as Bill Stumps, &c. This persistent
satire of one subject, it is likely enough, was
excited by some more than ordinary exhibition of
absurdity; and I find that the period in question
was marked by a sort of rage for founding new
societies. Within half a dozen years had come into
being the Geographical Society, the United Service
Institute ; the Harveian Society, the Entomolo-
gical, Statistical, Numismatic and Ornithological
Societies. But the society that seems specially to
have excited his satire was the British Association,
founded in 1831, and whose progresses about the
country are so ludicrously paraded in the Mudfog
Papers. The " Pickwick " opening chapter seems
to have been intended to ridicule this now popular

association.   In this way many a pleasant passage in the story, when made thus intelligible, becomes doubly acceptable.

Thus some reference of the kind was clearly intended in the second page.   "The travelling members were to correspond with the society, and requested to forward, from time to time, authentic accounts of their journeys and investigations, together with all tales and papers, which local scenery associations may give rise to."   Dickens was fond of this sort of *machinery* for his works, and tried to adapt it to Master Humphrey's Clock. But in "Pickwick" it was found too pedantic and constraining a process, and he almost at once abandoned it, though occasionally the original notion seemed to recur ; as when he would present Mr. Pickwick making notes of his day's proceedings, or collecting tales. Mr. Snodgrass also made records ; "we frankly say that to the note-book of Mr. Snodgrass we are indebted for the particulars recorded in this and the succeeding chapters." This was but a cramping, roundabout process after all. The novelist has the privilege of being invisibly present to witness the serious or humorous turn of events ; but it was difficult to imagine that, for all such shrewd observations and droll comments, we were indebted to Mr. Snodgrass's diary. " The Pickwick papers are our New River Head. The labours of others have raised for us an immense reservoir of facts.   We merely lay them on."

It is curious indeed to note the escape we have had of what might have been failure, owing to the adoption of a forced style, based on this sort of humour.   The established magazine treatment of the time was a kind of subdued burlesque, aiming at the description of serious matter in a tone of mock gravity, but which after a time became fatiguing.   The account of the club discussion at the opening is in this formal manner, a good illustration of which is the conceit of the letters " C.M.P.C." put after every name, again and again explained in a note to mean " *Corresponding Member of the Pickwick Club.*"   This was, at the time, a form of humour. So with the rather formal headings of the chapters, such as, " *How the Pickwickians made and cultivated the acquaintance of a couple of nice young men belonging to one of the Liberal Professions, &c. ; *" while another chapter, " *Records a touching act of delicate feeling, achieved and performed by Messrs. Dodson and Fogg,*" which has a laboured air.   But the whole antiquarian element was an inconsistency.   The " Bill Stumps his mark " incident, as every one will recall, was treated in a comedy spirit in the " Antiquary," where we all recall the old Monkbarns expatiating on the inscribed stone with the four letters :—

A.D.L.L.

which he interpreted *Agricola dicavit libens lubens*, but which, as the Bedesman explained, meant " *Adam Drum's lang ladle*." There is also a story told of a hoax played off on a brother antiquary, by Steevens, who had a tablet engraved with Saxon characters, and exposed in a broker's shop, where it was discovered, and purchased by the credulous virtuoso.

Few things have been so often quoted as the apologetic explanation of the expression 'a Pickwickian sense.' This happy phrase was suggested by "the parliamentary sense," by which orators in the House of Commons protested they meant nothing offensive. Not long before Sir Robert Peel had called Mr. Hume to account for some language of the kind, and the latter had made some lame explanation, which Dickens may have had before him.

One of the author's original ideas was certainly to find material in the lighter absurdities of the day, illustrated by Jingle's anecdote of Ponto's sagacity. This was no doubt one of Seymour's pictorial suggestions, and the author seemed to excuse its introduction in a note withdrawn in later editions:—

" Although we find this circumstance recorded, as a singular one in Mr. Pickwick's note-book, we cannot refrain from humbly expressing our dissent from that learned authority; the stranger's anecdote is not one quarter so wonderful as some of Mr. Jesse's 'Gleanings.' Ponto sinks into utter insignificance before the dogs whose actions be there records."

The subject of this little hit was the well-known naturalist, who, like Mr. Pickwick's original, later lived at Richmond, and was one of the lights of the pleasant society of that place.

The incidents described at the Eatanswill election, the locking up and pumping on voters, the upsetting them into ponds, and such disorders, had been occupying public attention only a year or two before. Much time in Parliament was taken up investigating such excesses, and the cases of Ipswich and Norwich, and Stafford particularly, had caused many scandals. It is impossible not to admire the judicious tone he adopted in dealing with these points, a satirical, half-sarcastic description—for, as in the instance of the Fleet, he rarely speaks in his own person, but lets his personages and incidents speak for themselves.. Stiggins, and others of his character, he despatched and ridiculed with a hearty relish, that showed how keenly he felt. In later works he revived the type several times in the persons of Snawley and Chadband. It is likely that in early life he had suffered from one of these sanctimonious impostors, and it is probable that his father and mother may have been partial to such persons.

The elaborate sketch of Stiggins, which is, however, exaggerated in some portions—witness his drunkenness at the public tea, when he must have lost his character—is on the whole admirable; and his scene with the widower and his son, and his gradual doubtful approaches, capital. A scrupulous person, shocked at the " profanity " of the sketch, wrote six years later to remonstrate; and the author explained his design, which was to show " how sacred things are degraded, vulgarized, and rendered absurd, when persons who are utterly incompetent to teach the commonest things, take upon themselves to expound such mysteries, and how, in making mere cant phrases of divine words, these persons miss the spirit in which they had their origin." " I have seen a good deal of this sort of thing in many parts of England. . . . That every man who seeks heaven must be born again, I sincerely believe. *That it is expedient for every hound to say so in a certain snuffling form of words to which he attaches no good meaning,* I do not believe." This is a capital comment.

Mrs. Leo Hunter, a delightful character in its way, seems to have been sketched from life, and there is little doubt was intended for an enormously rich, "lion-hunting" lady living in Portland

Place, but who eventually became poor. The fancy *fête* at "the Den" was a curious illustration of social manners—fancy dresses being worn in broad daylight. These, too, were the days of the "Annuals," "Talismans," "Winter's Wreath," "Books of Beauty," which were filled with verses from noble and genteel amateurs, often as ridiculous as the "Ode to the expiring frog."

Here too will be noted the tall figure of Mr. Pott as a Russian, with his knout. In the early plates there was an absurd likeness in the nose and face to Lord Brougham, but in successive impressions a shaggy beard was added, and the whole disguised. Dickens, no doubt, did not wish it to be thought that he was ridiculing one who was his and Forster's friend.

It may be added here, that Gad's Hill Place formerly belonged to Mrs. Lynn Linton's family. Old Weller, according to her recollection, was well known on the road between London and Rochester, bearing the name in the flesh of " Old Chomley," and who was at once recognized by the neighbourhood as the original. Indeed all his best, most spirited characters were inspired by his own recollections : "Pickwick" is stored with such. Stareleigh, Buzfuz, Snubbin—Pott beyond question, though unidentified, with the other characters we have mentioned.; to say nothing of Micawber, Skimpole, Boythorn, the Cheerybles, and many more.

It may be doubted if Jingle and his follower Job are as successful characters as the rest. They rather belong to the stage, and Jingle's utterances seem meant for the footlights, from their peculiar form; neither is the character quite original, though useful in conducting the narrative, as through the story he draws out and plays upon the Pickwickian weakness and credulity. Charles Mathews the Elder, had a favourite figure in his entertainment, one Major Longbow, who told Munchausen stories much in the same style. One of the Major's favourite tales, was that of the lady in India burnt by some accident, and whom the husband called in his servants to "sweep up." This may have suggested Quanko Samba and his fate. Again, we find, that a year or so before, Lemaitre had brought Robert Macaire and Jacques Strop to London. The grotesque devotion of the latter to his master no doubt furnished hints to Dickens, who must have seen the piece. Still there is great art in presenting Jingle as an "agreeable rattle," with nothing repulsive. The buoyant humour of the writer carries him along. In reality Jingle was a common *swindler*, yet we never think of this harsh term in connection with him.

For his many life-like sketches of "limbs of the law," he must have drawn on his own memory. Nothing can be more varied, more distinct, than

these various types.   On leaving school he was
for a time in the office of Messrs. Ellis and Blackmore, Solicitors of Gray's Inn.   Indeed Mr. Kitton
says that Mr. Blackmore, the junior partner,
afterwards recognized several incidents that
occurred in this office and also some of the
characters.   He had a fellow-clerk named Potter,
who was partial to theatricals, whom Mr. George
Lear,. who was one of Dickens' fellow-clerks,
fancied was the original of Jingle.

VII.

So buoyant and tumultuous is the spirit in
which the story is carried on, that the author
often falls into some oddities and incongruities
which, according to the old stage phrase,
he "bustles through" by sheer force of good
spirits. Thus, at starting he got his dates confused, the proceedings of the Club preparatory
to the expedition being put in the year 1817.
This may have appeared too far back, so a
little further on we have the year 1827, which
was the proper starting-point of the Odyssey.
But when Mr. Jingle was on the coach going to
Rochester, it will be recollected he described his
writing a poem on "the revolution of July."
"Present? think I was! fired a musket, fired
with an idea," &c. Extrication here was literally
hopeless; it would be absurd to alter the date of
the whole story for the convenience of a little
anecdote. So the lively author took the most sensi-
ble course, left it as it was, adding this jocose note
in later editions, "A remarkable instance of the
prophetic force of Mr. Jingle's imagination: this
dialogue occurred in the year 1827, and the
Revolution in 1830."

When Dodson and Fogg served their notice on Mr. Pickwick, the author may have had this mistake in his mind, and dated it 1830. It was evident, however, that it had occurred only a few months after the party had started on their tour in 1827 ; so the date had to be put back to that year.

Our pleasant author, always one of the most scrupulously accurate in all that concerned his "proofs," made a few little slips in the course of his work. This is not surprising in what was so *gigantic* an enterprise from the vast number of characters, incidents, names, relations, localities, with a hundred other things which had to be kept in view. The result were some oversights of a pleasant sort, and which we note here, not from any foolish wish of detecting blemishes, but to increase the sense of humorous enjoyment. In the first edition there was a list of *errata*, which is entertaining in its way :—

P. 1, line 9, *for* 1817, *read* 1827.

P. 185, line 25, *for* 1830, *read* 1827.

P. 202, line 30, *for* 1830, *read* 1827.

P. 278, line 40, *for* " the elder Mr. Samuel," *read* " the elder Mr. Weller."

P. 342, line 5, *for* " S. Weller, Esquire, senior," *read* " Tony Veller, Esq."

P. 541, line 12, *for* " Sun Court, Cornhill," *read* " George Yard, Lombard Street."

These little slips are characteristic.

In chapter 28, when he is describing the

marriage festivities at Dingley Dell, he portrays
the old lady, Mr. Wardle's mother, seated at
the top of the table "with her newly married
daughter on one side." This was of course her
granddaughter. In chapter 27, we find Sam
speaking of his father's second wife as his
"mother-in-law," meaning thereby his "step-
mother." Even the printers occasionally nodded,
as we find two "chapter 28's," one of which is
distinguished by a star.

Not unnaturally he sometimes found himself con-
fusing the two Wellers. But a more curious mistake
was the making Mr. Pickwick give his London
address to Mr. Winkle, senior, as the "George
and Vulture," in "Sun Court, Cornhill," instead
of George Yard, Lombard Street. The same mistake occurs also in chapter 30, when "Mr. Jackson bent his steps direct to Sun Court, and
walked straight into the George and Vulture."
Sun Court was, however, not far off.

Another mistake of dates is found in the account
of the visit to Mr. Pott's house, who, in 1827,
orders a file of the *Gazette* for 1828 to be brought
up to him. "Here," says Charles Dickens the
younger, "Mr. Pott falls into the same sort
of prophetic mistake as that to which the author
calls attention in the case of Mr. Jingle in the
footnote to chapter 2, which was added in later
editions."

"Mr. Pickwick's adventures began with his departure from Goswell Street, 13th May, 1827, and the Eatanswill Election evidently took place in the same year. Messrs. Dodson and Fogg's first letter to Mr. Pickwick was dated August 28th, 1827, and was necessarily written after these events."

There is one form of mechanism in the management of his story for which the author had a strong *penchant*, namely, the introduction of an occasional tale. This was too often contrived *à propos de bottes*. A coach is upset in the snow, and the travellers have to sit round the inn fire; or Mr. Pickwick opens a drawer as he is going to bed and finds a MS.; or in the commercial room some one relates a " Bagman's Tale;" or there is some one on a bridge who gives him a story to read at his leisure, or Sam relates another which Mr. Pickwick takes down and edits. Through the course of " Pickwick " we meet no less than a dozen of these tales. One is inclined to suspect that they were unused magazine stories lying by the author, with which he filled in his number, if time failed or inspiration flagged. But the truth is, Dickens always had a fancy for this old-fashioned device. His introduction to " Master Humphrey's Clock " he made a sort of miscellany for short stories; and in the numerous " Christmas Numbers " of *Household Words* and *All the Year Round* he reverted to his pet idea, and showed much ingenuity in devising machinery or "framework" for the same purpose. Some of the "Pickwick" stories, however, we would not willingly part with, notably the ghostly mail-coach legend, which is highly original, and even in a sort of keeping with the narrative.

Some of the feats of walking, described in these memoirs, are indeed of an extraordinary kind. Thus it is somewhat astonishing to read that, "after dinner they met again, *after a five-and-twenty mile walk*, undertaken by the males at Wardle's recommendation, to get rid of the effects of the wine at breakfast," an amazing feat considering that some of "the males" were elderly, stout, and plethoric. But it is exactly what the genial author himself would have thought a trifle under such circumstances. These unconsidered statements were after all only proofs of the buoyancy and enthusiasm of his narrative, and no one pauses to consider the incongruity. Again, when Mr. Pickwick took out the Legend of Prince Bladud, to read before going to bed, we are told expressly, " he lighted his bedroom candle, that it might burn up well by the time he finished"—odd evidence, by the way, of the inferior chandlery of the day—but when, with many yawns, and "a countenance expressive of the utmost weariness," he had got to the end of the story, " he lighted his

K

chamber candle," already, as we were told, alight. When the mistake was laughingly pointed out to the gifted author, he refused to credit it.[1]

Another singular incident for which no explanation can be given was the conveying of Mrs. Cluppins with Mrs. Bardell to the Fleet prison and there locking her up ; for on this lady Messrs. Dodson and Fogg had no claim whatever, and they left the other members of the party, such as Mrs. Rogers, unmolested. Mrs. Cluppins would have had good grounds for an action against those astute gentlemen.

In the obstreperous scene at Bath, when Mr. Winkle, in his dressing-gown, was shut out into the street, the landlady had seen from the drawing-room window Mr. Winkle "bolt" into Mrs. Dowler's sedan chair. She then rushed to call Mr. Dowler, shrieking " that his wife was running away." Now that gentleman had to come

It was Mr. Charles Kent who made the discovery. He pleasantly describes Dickens' burlesque indignation, vehement denial, and half astonishment at the idea even of such an oversight. " No ! No ! NO ! " he exclaimed. An appeal was made to the book itself. We can see the twinkle in his eye, and the simulated comic fury with which he made as though he were about to hurl the volume at his friend. Then, rushing to the top of the steps that led down into the garden, he called to some of his family who were walking there, " Come ! Come ! Come up quick ! " to show them the discovery. The mistake was certainly of an amusing kind, but he never amended it.

from his bedroom, and throw up the window, " yet the first object that met his gaze was Mr. Winkle bolting into the sedan chair." It may be added here, that the arrangement of this scene was the subject of much consultation between artist and writer; there were many figures to be brought in, and Mr. Pickwick was to have thrown up the window on the story above, which would have placed him too high. "Phiz" writes, " Shall I leave Pickwick where he is, or put him under the bedclothes? I could not carry him so high as the second floor." The author replied, " Winkle should be holding the candlestick above his head, I think. It looks more comical, the light having gone out. A *fat* chairman, so short as our friend here, never drew breath in Bath. I would leave him where he is, decidedly. Is the lady full dressed? she ought to be.—C. D."

On arriving at old Wardle's after the accidents on the road, and after a glass of cherry brandy, we have a curious specimen of the manners of the time; for we are told of the party " being joined by Mr. Tupman, who had lingered behind" to snatch a "kiss from Emma" (the maid), for which he had been duly rewarded "with sundry pushings and scratchings," an extraordinary proceeding on the part of a very stout, elderly gentleman who was a new guest, and had barely entered the house. The Pickwickians too had been on the

road the whole day, had had a long, weary walk of
at least ten miles, and yet were offered no refresh-
ment, save a glass of cherry brandy ; after which
they were at once set down to a game of cards
until supper came.   These are traits of social life.

Sometimes, in his pleasant exuberance, the
author forgets an element or incident, in his description, and introduces something that appears
inconsistent with what has gone before.   Thus,
when Mr. Pickwick is found in the garden of Miss
Tomkins' Ladies' School at Bury St. Edmund's,
and admitted to the house, he is locked up in " a
closet in which the day-boarders hung their
bonnets and sandwich-bags."   Yet further on we
read :—" Mr. Pickwick sat down in the closet,
beneath a grove of sandwich-bags, and awaited
the return of the messengers," &c.   In the
middle of the night the sandwich bags would be
at the day-boarders' homes.

When Mr. Pickwick was on the bridge at Rochester, he encountered "dismal Jemmy," who had
read the story of the stroller to the party the night
before.   Not content with this, Jemmy made a
proposal, " Would you communicate it to the club,
of which you have spoken so frequently ? "   " Certainly," replied Mr. Pickwick, " if you wished it ;
and it would be entered on their transactions."
" You shall have it," replied the dismal man.
" Your address ? "

Here was of course promise of another tale, which it was not convenient to introduce at the moment. It is amusing to find that the author altogether forgot this engagement until the close of his story, when he found an adroit excuse. As Mr. Pickwick was saying farewell to Jingle, he finds that " Jemmy " turns out to be Job Trotter's brother, who had emigrated to America. " That accounts for my not having received the ' page from the romance of real life,' which he promised me one morning when he appeared to be contemplating suicide on Rochester bridge, I suppose," said Mr. Pickwick, smiling. This was the best that could be done under the circumstances.

When the ice broke under Mr. Pickwick, he sank completely under the water, and disappeared for some time, which had to be accounted for by his saying, "that he fell upon his back." Why Mr. Allen and his friend should during the crisis, have consulted seriously about bleeding the company generally, is not clear.

At the Raddle supper party, when the hot water was ordered up, it will be remembered that the landlady had ordered the fire to be raked out. "You can't have no warm water," said the girl. But at the beginning of the night, the "first instalment of punch in a white jug " was brought in, and after supper " another jug of punch was put on the table; it had been ready made in a red pan." This might be an oversight, or it may be that punch had then a stricter and more limited sense, meaning the " materials " simply.

There is a slight anticipation of Sam's mode of illustration, in the extraordinary, original speech addressed by the ostler to Mr. Pickwick, when about to drive to Dingly Dell. " Shy? he wouldn't shy if he was to meet a waggon-load of monkeys, with their tails burnt off." The scene where Sam is writing his valentine under the easy criticism of his father, suggests the well-known one in " The Rivals," where Acres is writing his challenge. Actors nearly always introduce a " gag," which they may have borrowed from Mr. Weller ; "addressing the same lady " being *malaproped* into " undressing." We find the same idea in Sam's letter. "I feel myself ashamed, and completely circumscribed in a dressin' of you." A careful study of this admirably drawn character will show that at the opening the author had not quite grasped its capabilities. It was only after two or three numbers' progress that he found himself developing his happy varieties of humour and illustration, which ripened as he went along. Sam at the " Old White Hart " was rather a flippant and even uncongenial person, and his answers pert rather than humorous. We wonder, too, how the son of the proprietor of a flourishing inn, and so

superior in his gifts, should have found himself
reduced so low as to accept the post of "boots"
in a borough inn. But it is likely that Weller
senior, his inn, and his widow were after-
thoughts suggested by Sam's successful development.

It may be noted, to show that Sam's character
was then not quite fixed in the author's mind,
that he probably intended to make him more
of a vagabond; for we find the impatient landlady calling him from one of the galleries,
"Where's that lazy, idle—Why, Sam—oh! there
you are!—why don't you answer?" And the
Boots did answer pertly enough, "Wouldn't be
genteel to answer till you'd done talking." Here
was still the "wagginer's boy," undeveloped till
he took service with Mr. Pickwick.

As "Pickwick" was itself full of odd allusions
and originalities, so it was destined to be associated
with a chain of still more curious coincidences.
What could be more singular than that the
author should have become, many years later,
most intimate with a family of Wellers, one
of whom married his brother? Another of the
ladies married Mr. Thompson, and became the
mother of Lady Butler, the artist. Weller is an
invaluable, effective name. A more direct suggestion of the name is found in the fact that his
nurse's name is said to have been Mary Weller.

The name, therefore, under all the varied conditions, seemed almost to invite his selection.

As regards the "origin" of Sam Weller,[2] it is said that there was a popular actor *tempore* "Pickwick," named Sam Vale, who performed Simon Splatterdash, in an old piece of Beazley's, the theatrical architect, called, "The Boarding House." There is certainly a suggestion in the name, and Sam Vale seems like Sam "Veller." In the farce, the servant of the Boarding House is represented as interlarding his conversation with metaphorical illustrations, such as :—

"Let every one take care of themselves," as the jackass said when he danced among the chickens.

"I am down upon you," as the extinguisher said to the rushlight.

"Come on," as the man said to the tight boot.

"Where shall we fly ?" as the bullet said to the trigger.

"Sharp work for the eyes," as the devil said when a broad-wheeled waggon went over his nose.

"Why, here we are all mustered," as the roast beef said to the welsh rabbit.

"Nibbled to death with ducks," as the worm said to the fisherman.

---

[2] People now bearing this name seem to like to christen their children Samuel ; and not long since, at a concert, we heard a young postman, announced as "Mr. Samuel Weller," troll forth a song.

These specimens, it will be seen, are of a rude and vulgar type, and cannot be put beside the sagacious and apt utterances of Sam.

Stiggins might well have held the elder Weller in a sort of holy horror, and have been frightened away from the inn; for Mr. Weller attacked him no less than three times in the course of the story; first when he assailed the shepherd, giving him two or three for himself and then " two or three more for the man with the red nose ; " then at the Brick Lane meeting, when he drove Stiggins into a corner, and danced round, " tapping him " on the head ; to say nothing of the last assault, when he kicked him out, and held his head in the trough.

It might have been a question in Mr. Calverly's set of questions, " Who first used the expression, ' Life isn't all beer and skittles,' and on what occasion ? " It is to Sam we owe that oft-quoted proverb, though a little altered in the use, but which few suspect that he uttered. " It's a regular holiday to them," he said in the Fleet, " all porter and skittles." It has been objected, however to Sam, that in his anxiety to display his sagacity, the author credited him with more knowledge than he could have had opportunity of acquiring. Not many will recall his own account of himself; he was " a carrier's boy at startin', then a wagginer's, then a helper, then a Boots, now he's a gen'l'man's servant." This sort of rustic

education, and familiarity with horses, shows that
it may have been intended to make him a sort of
element in the "sporting" direction; but the
truth is we do not think of Sam in such a connection, and the passage may be accepted as an
oversight, like Jingle's share in the French
Revolution of 1830.

The objection, however, to Sam's knowledge
of all kinds, is not well founded.   There is a vast
deal of knowledge of the *names* of things, without actual knowledge, which quick and sagacious
observers pick up.   Such is Sam's allusion to
"the perpetual motion."   Not to be thus justified,
however, is his acquaintance with Mr. Sterne's
Sentimental Journey. "No man," he says, "never
see a dead donkey 'cept the gentleman in the
black silk smalls, as know'd the young 'ooman
as kept a goat, and *that* wos a French donkey."
Here we see he knew not only the "dead ass"
of Nampont, but the passage where Mr. Sterne
describes his own dress; and also "Maria of
Moulines"!   This is astounding in the *ci-devant*
"wagginer's boy."   It must be said, however,
that plates of these interesting scenes were often
seen in the shop windows, and the inquisitive
might have been attracted by the one in which
the dead donkey figures.   So with his speech on
disappointed men, who he says, "if they were
gen'lmen you'd call 'em *misantropes*."   Occasionally Weller senior indulges in his son's peculiar

form of metaphor, as when he tells him he will be wiser when he is married, " but vether it's vorth while goin' through so much to learn so little, as the charity boy said ven he got to the end of the alphabet, is a matter of taste." We find Sam also anticipating Mr. Crummles' prodigy, and calling a boy " an infant phenomenon."

It was said by several writers that in some points his humour was founded on, or suggested by, that of Washington Irving, whose little tale of the " Stout Gentleman " was named as being his model. No doubt he vastly admired the American writer, and it may be admitted that the machinery of " The Sketch Book" and " Bracebridge Hall," which was original enough, and conveniently offered a mode of " setting" short tales in a romantic frame, was before his mind. For both writers scenes of affectionate enjoyment and revelry in old mansions had a kind of fascination. But the humour of Irving was of a very mild, tempered character: he had little fertility; in fact comparison on this point is almost ludicrous.

Mr. Ward, in his account of Dickens, notes the amount of feasting and enjoyment of victuals and drinking through the work. But as he says truly, Dickens " loved merely the paraphernalia of good cheer, and talking about wassail bowls and good punch; in practice he was most abstemious."[3]

---

[3] This we can testify from our own experience, and there was something quaint in this contrast of precept and practice.

In a conversation with his father, Sam Weller accuses him of " prophesying away like a red-faced Nixon," which provokes Mr. Weller to ask, " Who wos he ? " and he is answered, without much filial feeling, " Never mind who he wos—he wosn't a coachman, that's enough for you." The inquiring reader will also naturally ask " Who wos he ? " This " red-faced Nixon " was a mysterious allusion enough ; but lately, in a bookseller's catalogue, we came upon the following, which explains it : " Nixon's Cheshire Prophecy, with the prophecy at large. Coloured folding frontispiece representing Nixon "— probably with " a dab " of carmine on his cheeks.

Count Smorltork, one of Mrs. Leo Hunter's guests, is drawn in a few touches, and the dialogue between him and Mr. Pickwick is perfect in its appropriateness and humour—such is his reply to the former's courteous remark, " Politics comprises in itself a subject of no inconsiderable magnitude," " Poltic surprises in himself, ver good." This foreigner was modelled on Prince Puckler-Muskau, who only a year or so before had travelled through England, paying visits to the nobility and gentry, furnished with a note-book, the contents of which filled out his volumes. This hurried scampering over the country brought him much ridicule, and by jesters of the poorer sort he was dubbed " pickled mustard."

Sam's odd story of the "buttered muffins," is excellent, and dramatically told, particularly in the conversation between the doctor and the patient. This propriety in the short sketches, where the writer completely disappears, is one of the best things in the book. A story nearly similar is found in Boswell, where we are told that "Mr.——, who loved buttered muffins, but durst not eat them because they disagreed with his stomach, resolved to shoot himself, and then ate three buttered muffins before breakfast, knowing that he should not be troubled with indigestion." This unfortunate gentleman had two pistols; one was found lying charged upon the table by him after he had shot himself with the other. Sam's friend had eaten three shillings' worth.

The worthy Hain Friswell's comment on this is characteristic, and would have "arrided" the writer himself: "That appetite must indeed be morbid which is willing to purchase a solitary gratification, such as eating buttered muffins, at the expense of life itself!"

Cricket at this time had not developed into a science, and hence we meet with some odd technical phrases connected with the game. The fielders are called "scouts," who were to "look out" in different parts of the field. What was more odd, there were two bowlers, one for each wicket, which we may suppose was the custom at the time.

VIII.

FROM an eminent Counsel, Mr. Bompas, Q.C., I have received this interesting and amusing letter in reference to the original of the learned Sergeant Buzfuz, in the memorable " Trial :"—

"I am the youngest son of Sergeant Bompas, and have never heard it doubted that the name Sergeant Buzfuz was taken from my father, who was at the time considered a most successful advocate. I think that he may have been chosen for the successful advocate because my father was so successful ; but I have never been able to ascertain that there was any other special resemblance. I do not remember my father myself ; he died when I was eight years old, but I am told I am like him in face. He was tall (5 feet 10 ins.) and a large man, very popular and very excitable in his cases, so that I am told that counsel against him used to urge him, out of friendship, not to get so excited. A connection of mine who knew him well, went over to hear Charles Dickens, sen., read the trial scene, to see if he at all imitated him in voice or manner, but told me that he did not do so at all.

I think, therefore, having chosen his name as a writer might now that of Sir C. Russell, he then drew a general type of barrister, as he thought it might be satirized. If I can give you any other information, I will gladly do so. My father, like myself, was on the Western Circuit, and leader of it at the time of his death. I had a curious coincidence happen to me once. A client wrote to apply to the court to excuse a juror on the ground that he was a chemist, and had no assistant who understood the drugs. It was not till I made the application, and the court began to laugh, that I remembered the Pickwick trial. I believe the application was quite *bonâ fide*, and not at all in imitation of it.

" Yours faithfully,

" JOHN BOMPAS."

" Mr. Justice Stareleigh," writes Mr. Croker, "is an admirable likeness of an ex-judge, who, with many admirable and valuable qualities of head and heart, had made himself a legitimate object of ridicule by his explosions on the bench." This is quite true; for the little judge, as is well known, was a sketch from life, being the portrait of the oddly named Mr. Justice Gazelee, a name which is clearly suggested by Stareleigh. In his readings, Mr. Dickens chose for his model, as he himself assured me, the cavernous, sepulchral tones of " old

Rogers," whom he could take off to the life.[1] It is curious that the judge should have resigned his office in 1837, the very year in which the "Trial" appeared. I have always heard that Serjeant Talfourd revised "Bardell v. Pickwick," and had drawn Dickens' attention to some existing legal absurdities.

"It is generally believed," goes on Croker, "that the counsel in 'Bardell v. Pickwick' are portraits, but we have tried in vain to discover more than a very faint resemblance in either of them, and Serjeant Buzfuz's speech is certainly not in the manner of the gentleman supposed to be intended under the name. It is simply a clever quiz on a style of oratory which was finally quizzed out of fashion by Lord Brougham." He adds, however, that the sketch of the judge might also apply to Lord Tenterden, whose precision in keeping witnesses to the point was illustrated by his question to a young counsel at dinner: "Would he have venison?" The reply being that he was going to take some boiled chicken, the Judge said, "That is not an answer to my question, sir."

A portion was a satire on the *cause célèbre* of "Norton v. Melbourne," in which heavy damages

[1] Sir Stephen Gazelee was a Judge of the Court of Common Pleas for fourteen years, having the reputation of being a very "painstaking, upright judge, and in his private capacity a worthy and benevolent man." He died in 1839.

had been sought. The counsel for the plaintiff, Sir W. Follett, laid much stress on three scraps, or notelets, of the most harmless kind addressed to Mrs. Norton. The exaggerated tone of his speech suggests many points of the learned serjeant's.

Thus he very gravely urged that " the letters showed a great and unwarrantable degree of affection, because they did not begin and end with the words ' My dear Mrs. Norton.' " And he added that " it seems there may be latent love like latent heat in these productions," which is one of the points of the serjeant—" A mere cover for hidden fire," &c. The signature too, " Yours, Pickwick," is like " Yours, Melbourne." He proceeded :—

" These three notes relate to his hours of calling, but there is something in the style of these trivial notes which leads at least to something like suspicion. Here is one of them ' I will call about half-past four. Yours.' There is no regular beginning to the letters ; they do not commence with ' My dear Mrs. Norton,' as is usual. Here is another of the notes. ' How are you ?' Again, there is no beginning, as you see (' which is in itself suspicious,' said Serjeant Buzfuz).

" The third runs thus :—' No house to-day. I shall call after the Levée, about four or half-past. If you wish it later, let me know. I shall then explain about going to Vauxhall.' These are the only notes which have been found. They seem to impart much more than the mere words convey."

The whole description of the trial of *Bardell* v. *Pickwick* seems conceived in the best spirit of satire; and it can be even better appreciated by members of the legal profession, or by those accustomed to attend courts of justice. Exaggerated as the points may seem, the exaggeration is perfectly legitimate, and the farcical instances offered stand for a whole class. Thus the highly illogical reason given by the judge for the accuracy of his note of Mr. Winkle's name is a "common form," and often witnessed at trials. "What's your Christian name?" "Nathaniel, sir." "Daniel? Any other name?" "Nathaniel, sir—my lord, I mean." "Nathaniel Daniel, or Daniel Nathaniel?" "No, my lord, only Nathaniel, not Daniel at all." "What did you tell me it was Daniel for, then, sir?" "I didn't, my lord." "You did, sir," replied the judge, with a severe frown. "How could I have got Daniel on my notes unless you told me, sir?" This appeal to "my notes," as though they must be independent testimony, has been often heard in courts.

Another formula offers when Mrs. Cluppins is giving her evidence. "When I see Mrs. Bardell's street door on the jar."

" On the what ? " exclaimed the little judge.

" Partly open, my lord," said Serjeant Snubbin.

" She *said* on the jar," said the little judge, with a cunning look.

" It's all the same my lord," said Serjeant Snubbin.

The little judge seemed doubtful, and said " he'd make a note of it."

It is not the practice now, by the way, for the judge or counsel to ask witnesses their names, this formula being gone through by the officers of the court.

By a sort of hyper-criticism, Mr. Winkle's and Sam Weller's examinations have been objected to as unprofessional, no counsel being allowed to cross-examine their " own witnesses," unless they prove themselves " hostile."

No professional man can ever tire of Serjeant Buzfuz's speech, which, as a piece of large and comprehensive satire, is as good in its way as James Smith's imitation of Scott in the " Rejected Addresses." In a small compass the hackneyed points, so invariably enforced in a trial for "breach" are gathered together and put in the most humorous fashion, and yet with an air of *vraisemblance* that seems to carry conviction.

After a few words as to the tremendous responsibilities which rested on him,—

" You have heard from my learned friend, gen-

tlemen," continued Serjeant Buzfuz, well knowing
that, from the learned friend alluded to, the gentlemen of the jury had heard just nothing at all—
" you have heard from my learned friend, gentlemen, that this is an action for a breach of promise
of marriage, in which the damages are laid at 1510*l.*
*But you have not heard from my learned friend, inas-
much as it did not come within my learned friend's
province to tell you,* what are the facts and circumstances of the case. Those facts and circumstances, gentlemen, you shall hear detailed by me,
and proved by the unimpeachable female whom
I will place in that box before you." Again,
" She placed in her front parlour-window a written
placard, bearing this inscription—' Apartments
furnished for a single gentleman. Inquire
within.' " *Here Serjeant Buzfuz paused while
several gentlemen of the jury took a note of the document.*

" *There is no date to that, is there ?* " inquired a
juror.

" There is no date, gentlemen," replied Serjeant Buzfuz; " but I am instructed to say that
it was put in the plaintiff's parlour-window just
this time three years."

Who that has attended a trial has not heard the
intelligent juryman's question, to the full as absurd
as the one quoted, " *There is no date to that, is
there ?* " wishing to display his intelligence ; with

the friendly gravity of the counsel, who treats it *au grand sérieux.*

Excellent and natural too is the mode in which the learned Buzfuz is beguiled by Sam.

" Now, Mr. Weller," said Serjeant Buzfuz.

" Now, sir," replied Sam.

" I believe you are in the service of Mr. Pickwick, the defendant in this case. *Speak up, if you please, Mr. Weller.*"

" I mean to speak up, sir," replied Sam; " I am in the service o' that ere gen'l'man, and a wery good service it is."

" Little to do, and plenty to get, I suppose ? " said Serjeant Buzfuz, with jocularity.

" Oh, quite enough to get, sir, as the soldier said ven they ordered him three hundred and fifty lashes," replied Sam.

" *You must not tell us what the soldier or any other man said, sir,*" interposed the judge, " *it's not evidence.*"

This delightful hit has always received deserved admiration, being a happy satire on the system of dealing with " secondary evidence " at trials. Yet technical as the allusion is, at the Readings it was always received with a roar. It is actually quoted in a legal text-book, " Taylor on Evidence." It is astonishing that the reader should have added to the little judge's speech, " unless he be present in court and dressed in full regimentals."

This really took away the point, as such a condition would not make the evidence admissible. The remark about the "warming-pan," is a specimen of that sort of lawyers' nonsensical comment, which has absolutely no meaning whatever, but is carried off by a sort of undisguised plausibility. "*Don't* trouble yourself about the warming-pan!" words spoken very slowly and with an air of indignant surprise. Then the burst: "Why, gentlemen, who *does* trouble himself about the warming-pan?"[2]

Admirably caught, also, is the tone of the examination of witnesses, and the perfectly professional style of counsel. "And you listened, I believe, Mrs. Cluppins." "Beggin' your pardon, sir, I would scorn the haction." When Mr. Winkle was being questioned, we are told that Mr. Skimpin inclined his head to listen with great sharpness to the answer, and he glanced at the jury as if to imply that Mr. Winkle's natural taste for perjury would induce him to give some name that did not belong to him."

The charge of this learned judge, though short, is not the least effective portion of the satire.

[2] Not long since I heard a London preacher, expatiating on the advantages of prayer, to be gained with little exertion, use this illustration:—"In fact, as Sergeant Buzfuz said to Sam Weller, in the trial of Bardell *v.* Pickwick, there is little to do, and plenty to get."

Who that has "sat on a jury," after being bewildered by long and intricate details, has not
been enlightened by the judge announcing, with
an air of scientific discovery, that, "It is for *you,*
gentlemen, to decide. If you accept the testimony of the plaintiff's witnesses—why, then," &c.

"Mr. Justice Stareleigh summed up, in the old-
established and most approved form. He read as
much of his notes to the jury as he could decipher
on so short a notice, and made running comments
on the evidence as he went along. If Mrs. Bardell were right, it was perfectly clear that Mr.
Pickwick was wrong, and if they thought the evidence of Mrs. Cluppins worthy of credence, they
would believe it; and if they didn't, why they
wouldn't. If they were satisfied that a breach of
promise of marriage had been committed, they
would find for the plaintiff with such damages as
they thought proper; and if, on the other hand, it
appeared to them that no promise of marriage
had ever been given, they would find for the
defendant with no damages at all."

In this view a distinguished counsel, who
heartily appreciates his "Pickwick," has given me
his "advice and opinion" on the Trial :—

"I have no doubt," he writes to me, "that if
now tried, it would be held there was no case to go
to the jury, and the plaintiff would be non-suited.
But it could not arise now, because now both par-

ties can be examined in a breach of promise case;
but even if a plaintiff swear to a promise in such a
case, it must be to some extent corroborated. The
reason that were the case now tried (assuming the
parties could not be examined) it would be held
that there was no case, is because when the facts
proved are equally consistent with two states of
fact (i.e. of there having been, or not having been a
promise), they are held not to be evidence of either.
Dickens must have seen and appreciated the absurdity of the law as it stood before parties could
be examined, and worked up very cleverly the ambiguous position, which, whilst quite consistent
with no promise, might be held *by a Jury* to prove
them; and I daresay that in those days many a
verdict was obtained without any sounder foundation of fact or law to rest on.   There is a story told
of a gentleman who, having been sued on a forged
bill of exchange, instructed his attorney to defend
on that ground, and found when the day of trial
came, that his counsel got up and expressly admitted
that his client signed the bill.   He then, however,
produced a witness to prove that he was present
when it was paid, and also proved a forged
memorandum purporting to be signed by the
plaintiff, stating that he could not find the bill,
but would return it to the defendant when signed."
All this sort of thing has now ceased to exist, with
' the *merits* ' on what are called suits are now

tried, but with as much perjury as before. So also is it notoriously in the Divorce Court."

Passing from " the Trial," we find an allusion in the speech delivered by Mr. Pickwick at his club : " But this he would say, that if ever the fire of self-importance broke out in his bosom, the desire to benefit the human race in preference effectually quenched it. *The praise of mankind was his Swing;* philanthropy was his insurance office. (Vehement cheering.)"

Now what was his " Swing "? From the "Annual Register," and other usual works of reference, we find that a year or so before, there were many burnings of hayricks and farm produce which were set down to a sort of genuine personage called Swing. For everything Swing was accountable. Hence the sort of proverbial " your Swing." [3]

Dickens was a profound admirer of Washington Irving's writings, and I have little doubt that the name of Winkle was suggested to him by that writer's powerful tale of Rip Van Winkle. It is no common name. His natural wish to secure realistic effect made him resort to the most familiar channels for the selection of his names. Lowten the clerk, Wardle, Dowler, Trotter,

[3] But here, again, it has been discovered that "Swing," thus alluded to, oratorically, in 1827, did not begin his hayrick burning until 1832 or 1833 !

Clarke, Allen, Martin, all appear in the report of
the Duke of York's notorious trial : and in Huish's
account of " Orator " Hunt I have found something very like Dodson and Fogg, in the name of
the firm of Dawes and Fogg.[4]

[4] To prove the faithfulness of the Pickwickian types and
how they recur, I will quote here the sketch of the eccentric
Sergeant Arabin, given by the late Sergeant Robinson, in his
agreeable " Recollections."   Judge : " Well, witness, your name
is John Tomkins." Witness : " No, my lord, John Taylor."
Judge: " Ah, I see, you are a sailor, and you live in the New
Cut." Witness : " No, my lord, I live at Wapping." Judge :
" Never mind your being out shopping. Had you your
watch ? " &c.

IX.

Mr. Forster, the last of the old well-grounded
school of critics, and who had a personal
share in the revising of Dickens' writings,
did not rate "Pickwick" so highly as its
successors. While sharing the general admiration for its humour, spirit, and characters, he
held that in form and treatment it fell short
of the highest standard. The wish was indeed
often expressed, "Why not write another
'Pickwick'?" to which only a writer of experience could give an answer. The novelist is
passive, and must write as he is inspired, or
has material. Had he yielded to this pressure,
there would have been a second "Pickwick"
indeed, but which might have been only a replica
or imitation of the first.

In all good spirited story-telling I believe that
"the note" of every character is taken from
life. No author, great or small, can do anything
worth notice, without being thus assisted.
There is a vulgar notion that it is enough to transfer
the original character, bodily and coarsely, to the
book, but this is a journeyman's idea. The copy

in the hands of a skilful artist may not be in the least like the original, and yet suggestion may have produced the character. Some one in real life offers eccentric forms of speech or manner which the writer may altogether alter for something more effective, though the form may be left. The very manner of viewing things may be borrowed, though the application be different. Late in life our author found himself evolving characters from his imagination, which were not so true to nature as the old types.[1]

And here arises a curious reflection connected with this wonderful book, that it is almost the only one that has informally registered and recorded the social life and manners of its era, This is done in a vivid, but unofficial way. It would almost need notes and a regular commentary to explain the curious bygone allusions and customs, the well-known personages who are sketched, and the events then exciting public interest, and which he turned to profit for his story.

[1] There is hardly a writer who has not drawn from life—that is in the way I have described. Some turn of speech has furnished a suggestion or inspiration, and the invention went to work on this basis. I am convinced that the great masters of fiction have always worked in this way. "My father," says Mrs. Ritchie of Mr. Thackeray, "scarcely ever put real characters into his books, though he, of course, found suggestions among the people with whom he was thrown."

The influence of Seymour had extended even beyond sporting characteristics. His coarse, broad style of humour, and necessary exaggeration, insensibly directed the composition of the early numbers. Costumes and manner had to be unduly and farcically emphasized : as where Mr. Snodgrass is shown seated at the club, " poetically enveloped in a mysterious blue cloak with a canine skin collar," or where Mr. Pickwick is described as " having traced to their source the mighty ponds of Hampstead, and agitated the world with his theory of Tittlebats." This sort of thing boded a sort of Pangloss or a fresh Dr. Syntax on his tour. What was meditated was no doubt farcical and boisterous adventures, accidents and embarrassments arising from unsophisticated enthusiasm, of which the " Bill Stumps " incident was a faint adumbration. There was already a successful venture of the same kind, which to a certain degree had taken the town, viz. the adventures of " Tom and Jerry," and their friend " Bob Logic," who travelled about London and other places in search of adventure. The lowness and vulgarity of this production is incredible, and puts it beyond criticism; but it had prepared the public to welcome something that turned upon peripatetic adventure. It is curious to think of the different forms which fiction has at times assumed; how at one time, as in the case of Jane

Eyre, it seeks for characters of strong mental emotion ; at another can tolerate only stirring adventure, with sieges, battles, and rescues ; at another vehement love-making. At the present moment it is not likely that any writer would be tolerated who sent off a party of his heroes, by rail and road, to travel through England in search of adventures. Of course the social arrangements of the time were more adapted to this sort of excitement than now ; for travelling was a more serious business then, and the remote parts of England were a *terra incognita* to many.

Within a very short time the better spirit of comedy overpowered the Seymour style of burlesque ; and Mr. Pickwick gradually crystallized into his most amiable shape. Nay, we might almost say that the incidents in which he figured actually seem to have moulded and developed the better side of his nature, precisely as such influences would operate in real life. The writer who works under inspiration, often becomes an unconscious instrument, in the hands of his character, is swayed by the events which he has himself created.   Identifying himself with his own personages, and "feeling" them thoroughly, he finds himself unconsciously bettered, like a living person. Mr. Pickwick himself, when winding up his course, confesses that this process had gone on in his case, and that he was "a wiser and

better man" from all he had experienced. Nothing
better shows the complete change in the treatment
of Mr. Pickwick than the passage quoted from
his note descriptive of Chatham. "It is truly
delightful to a philanthropic mind to see these
gallant men (the soldiers) staggering along
under the influence of an overflow both of
animal and ardent spirits. . . . . Nothing can
exceed their good-humour. . . . One of them had
been most grossly insulted in the house of a publican.
The barmaid had positively refused to draw him
any more liquor, in return for which he had
(merely in playfulness) drawn his bayonet and
wounded the girl in the shoulder. And yet this
fine fellow was the very first to go down to the
house next morning and express his readiness to
overlook the matter and forget what had occurred."
This strain, meant for humorous burlesque, is
quite inconsistent; for it either represents
Mr. Pickwick as favouring drunkenness and
violence, or as laughing at it. These trifles, it may
be repeated, are not pointed out by way of any
disparagement, but to show how the irresistible
power of the author carried him through everything. In this spirit it may be further noticed
that in Mr. Pickwick's awkward scene with Mrs.
Bardell, Sam was in the passage; but at the
trial Mrs. Cluppins deposed that she was on the
stairs, having found the door "on the jar."

The Pickwickians too seem to have noted the compromising situation at the same moment as Mrs. Cluppins, so she must have been surprised in the act of listening, much as " she scorned the haction."

Mr. Pickwick, in the earlier portions of the work, occasionally displayed a violence that was extra-ordinary. Thus, when Jingle tossed the licence to him at the White Hart, " he hurled the inkstand madly forward, and followed it up himself." He also, it will be remembered, struck the person in the Fleet, who had taken his nightcap, a smart blow in the chest, and invited him to " come on."

We find his bosom friend Tupman, resenting the epithets " fat " and " old " applied to him, about to inflict chastisement on his person, and Mr. Pickwick again challenging him to " Come on." Once more, when the testy Dr. Tappleton declared that he would pull every man's nose in the company, " He rushed forward with fury in his looks, and fire in his eye. His hand was upon the lock of the door ; in another instant it would have been on the throat of Doctor Payne of the 43rd, had not Mr. Snodgrass seized his revered leader by the coat-tail, and dragged him backwards.

" ' Restrain him,' cried Mr. Snodgrass, ' Winkle, Tupman—he must not peril his distinguished life in such a cause as this.'

" ' Let me go,' said Mr. Pickwick.

" ' Hold him tight,' shouted Mr. Snodgrass."

In his first scenes with Dodson and Fogg he clenched his fist, so that those gentlemen thought he was about to assault them. He was also not without difficulty restrained from assaulting the same " Firm " on at least two other occasions.

In the plate which introduces the Club at their meeting will be noted the intensely sporting character of the whole, further emphasized by a collection of fishing implements, rod, basket, fowling-piece, &c., laid down ostentatiously, and it must be said rather inappropriately, on the floor, in front of the table. The prints hung round the room display " sporting " subjects of horses, and over one of the windows is a stag's head. The cover shows Mr. Pickwick asleep and fishing in a punt down at Putney, whose church we descry.

It is sad to have to admit that the correct Mr. Pickwick set a bad example in one respect, and exhibited himself on two or three occasions in a state of deplorable inebriety. Thus on returning after the cricket match, he was seen in the kitchen, " his hands in his pockets, leaning against the dresser, shaking his head from side to side, and producing a constant succession of his blandest and most benevolent smiles ;" and when it was suggested that " he should be carried to bed," vociferating that " no living boy should

M

carry him." At the same house, at the shooting party, he indulged in cold punch to such a degree that "he expressed a strong desire to recollect a song which he had heard in his infancy, and, the attempt proving abortive, sought to stimulate his memory with more glasses of punch, which appeared to have quite a contrary effect; for, from forgetting the words of the song, he began to forget how to articulate any words at all; and finally, after rising to his legs to address the company in an eloquent speech, he fell into the barrow, and fast asleep, simultaneously."

On the occasion of going to the country to see Mr. Winkle, sen., this amiable being, again, drank so much cold punch and other liquids as to become mellow and affectionate. And it is curious evidence of the tone of the times that these constant excesses seemed to be considered quite matters of course, and a harmless weakness in this eminent man. Mr. Ben Allen was always in a state of hopeless "fuddle." He and his friend Sawyer, it may be added, went to Bengal, where, as we are told, they had the yellow fever fourteen times, though the malady is usually confined to the West Indies.

Returning now to Sam Weller, we find that the general appreciation of Sam Weller seems to rest on the ingenious and apposite

illustrations with which he used so often
to enliven his discourse, such as, "As the
soldier said when they ordered him, &c."
This form is in truth rather a farcical one, and
its constant repetition belongs more to a
fashion in vogue upon the stage, where it is
thought necessary to insist on such a "note" of
character, and the audience expects that such
peculiarities must be exhibited in almost every
expression that is uttered. In real life so fertile a gift of illustration would be impossible,
and require an amount of ability and knowledge and reading, as would have been beyond
the opportunities of a person like Sam, whose
early education had been that of a waif and
stray. This sort of metaphorical spirit is also
rather inconsistent with his eminently practical
character, and in fact formed an opportunity for the exhibition of the author's own
lively and exuberant powers, showing, as we said,
an amount of ability somewhat of the school of
De la Rochefoucauld. Granting even that a person
in Sam's station had this particular and irresistible
turn, the illustrations would have been of a more
homely cast, and would have been occasionally
inappropriate or halting; for the valet mind is of a
peculiar cast, singularly loose and inaccurate in
its appreciations. This criticism may seem far-
fetched, and perhaps crotchety; but it is really

urged in favour of what is otherwise an admirable
character drawn with the finest and broadest
touches.

In the case of every favourite character, as it
is also in the case of every story, after the first
tumult of popularity, a sort of revision of
judgment often takes place. Some works lose,
or grow in favour. The truth is, it is only
really good, large work that will last ; all artificial
forms of humour, and surface peculiarities furnish only temporary entertainment. Some sort
of process of this kind has been going on steadily
since Dickens' death. His first work, "Pickwick,"
may be considered to be advancing in favour, and
has roused a new interest and favour. The
popularity of the various characters are affected
in the same way. Sam Weller—once the universal
idol for his " modern instances," seems now
to offer a rather antique form of wit, and to be
free and smart, rather than humorous. These
" Wellerisms " have been collected and published
as a gathering of wise sayings and proverbs, with
an introduction by Mr. Charles Kent. But
on the other hand, the appreciation of Sam's
real sagacity and sound good sense, exhibited on a
hundred occasions ; his shrewd observation ; his
appropriate view of every situation that presents
itself ; his capability on all occasions ; his pleasant
replies, and stories, always ready ; his unflagging

good-humour; his spirited share in any conversation that was going on, has grown and ripened. So with his fidelity to his master and his friends, and his many amiable qualities. These are the sterling points of character and treatment which will last, like the characters of Fielding, being independent of the manners and eccentricities of a generation that passes away, and which cannot change with a new one.

The dialogue in this book has much of that double charm which is the attraction of Goldsmith and Sheridan in their comedies. The business of the situation is carried forward, while at the same time entertainment is provided by unexpected turns, and humorous associations. A good specimen is when Mr. Pickwick is first introduced to his unattractive bedroom in the Fleet. The situation is this. The turnkey wished to make the most of what he had to offer, and in return desired to enlist the feelings of the persons who were to enjoy his favours. With what few yet skilful touches is the scene presented!

" 'There,' said Mr. Roker, holding the door open, and looking triumphantly round at Mr. Pickwick, 'There's a room!'

" Mr. Pickwick's face, however, betokened such a very trifling portion of satisfaction at the appearance of his lodging, that Mr. Roker looked for a reciprocity of feeling into the countenance of Samuel Weller, who, until now, had observed a dignified silence.

" ' There's a room, young man,' observed Mr. Roker.

" ' I see it,' said Sam, with a placid nod of his head."

Could any reply be more significant ?

" ' You wouldn't think to find such a room as this in the Farringdon Hotel, would you ? '

" To this Mr. Weller replied with an easy and unstudied closing of one eye, which might be considered to mean, either that he would have thought it, or that he would not have thought it, or that he had never thought anything at all about it, as the observer's imagination suggested."

And here should be noted Dickens' happy fashion of lighting up, as it were, and enriching a trifling incident of this kind with a grotesque speculative comment, which seems to impart the notion of character or thought.   Another would have said merely " winked," and left it to speak for itself.   Mr. Weller then inquired where was the individual bedstead that Mr. Roker had so flatteringly described as " an out and outer."

" ' That's it,' replied Mr. Roker, pointing to a very rusty one in the corner. ' It would make any one go to sleep, that bedstead would, whether they wanted to or not.'

"' I should think,' said Sam, eyeing the piece of furniture in question, with a look of excessive disgust, ' poppies was nothin' to it.'

"' Nothing at all,' said Mr. Roker.

"' And I s'pose,' said Sam, ' I s'pose the other gen'l'm'n as sleeps here *are* gen'l'm'n ? '

"' Nothing but it,' said Mr. Roker. ' One of 'em takes his twelve pints of ale a day, and never leaves off smoking, even at his meals.'

"' He must be a first-rater,' said Sam.

"' A 1,' said Mr. Roker."

This short dialogue brings everything before us, and is better than a page of description. It will be noted that the patron of the bed is not daunted by the disparagement of the article, but rallies with spirit to its support. There is a world of meaning in Sam's phrase, "I should think poppies was nothin' to it."

It has been said sometimes, by way of rather disparaging praise, that the merit of the book lies in its unflagging spirit and boisterous fun, to the exclusion, as it were, of wit and of the higher sort of humour. But with the vivacity and high spirits there is wit, and wit of a very genuine kind ; such as old Weller's remark when Sam was condoling with him on the loss of Mrs. Weller the second, " Vell, sooner or later we must all come to it, one day or another."

" So we must, Sammy."

"There's a Providence in it all," said Sam.

"Of course there is," said his father, with a nod of grave approval. "What 'ud become of the undertakers vithout it, Sammy?"

This Sterne might have put in "Tristram Shandy" with credit. Mr. Weller said it with a perfect sincerity, yet what a grotesque image!

The scene at the end of the story between old Weller and Mr. Pickwick is in the best style of the best comedy, and really offers a fine dramatic interest, from the various situations it offers. The delicacy and good feeling shown by the rough father, and his son, are only the least of its merits. Mr. Weller, sen., wished Mr. Pickwick to take charge of his money, and pressed it on him, believing that he was in want of it, for "that 'ere *conviction*," so he considered the verdict in the civil action. He had himself arranged to undertake the nervous duty of opening the matter to Mr. Pickwick, but was left unassisted by his son. His impatience at this desertion, and his relief when aid is given, is excellent. "This here money," said Sam, "he is anxious to put someveres, vere he knows it 'ill be safe; if he keeps it, he'll go a lendin' it to somebody, or droppin' his pocket-book down a airy, or making an Egyptian Mummy of hisself in some vay or another."

"Wery good, Samivel," observed Mr. Weller, in

as complacent a manner as if Sam had been passing the highest eulogiums on his prudence and fore-
thought, " wery good." An admirable original
stroke worthy of Fielding. The money being forced
on the reluctant Mr. Pickwick, who agrees to take
care of it, the latter seizes the opportnnity to
speak to the father about his son's marriage. The
change that follows shows true knowledge of
character. Much flattered on being told his
advice was desired, Mr. Weller listens to the
proposal; and most natural is the process shown
in his reception of it. When Mr. Pickwick tells
him that the young woman is attached to his
son, he takes it as a sort of warning : " It's
nat'ral," he said, after some consideration, " but
rayther alarmin'. Sammy must be careful—careful that he don't say nothin' to her, wery careful
that he ain't led away in an innocent moment, to
say anythin' as may lead to a conviction for breach.
You're never safe vith 'em, Mr. Pickwick, ven
they vunce has designs on you." This view he
naturally fancied must be acceptable to Mr. Pickwick, and the sketch is true comedy. When
he is at last brought round, there is another
most characteristic turn. Sam being called
in, his father felt that he was now associated with
Mr. Pickwick in the purpose which he had
before opposed, and he puts on a special dignity
in consequence.

"Your father and I have been having some conversation about you," said Mr. Pickwick.

"*About you*, Samivel," said Mr. Weller, in a patronizing and impressive voice, and this tone of dignity he maintained, supporting Mr. Pickwick in enforcing his views. A fresh turn is Sam's touching exhibition of fidelity when he positively declines to leave his master. Nothing is more unaffectedly natural than his declaration, "Wery good. If you vant a more polished sort o' feller, vell and good, have him; but vages or no vages, notice or no notice, board or no board, lodgin' or no lodgin', Sam Veller as you took from the old inn in the Borough, sticks by you, come what may; and let everythin' and everybody do their wery fiercest, nothin' shall ever perwent it." The perfect truth and appropriateness of this touching speech is surely one of the reasons for the affection in which Sam has been always held. The whole scene is one of infinite art, and should be studied by every writer who would learn how to deal with character.

Dickens seems to have been conscious that this rustic training scarcely harmonized with Sam's speeches; for he makes his father tell Mr. Pickwick later on, that he let him "*run in the streets*, when he was wery young." Few, save Pickwickian students will recall, that he introduces allusions to other members of his family, besides his father.

That he had a brother; an uncle who drank himself to death; that his mother's name was Clarke: these matters being dropped naturally and carelessly, as they would be in real life, and not officially announced by the narrator. Another "hand" would have told us, "Mr. Samuel Weller was Mr. Weller's son by his first wife, whose name was Clarke; one of his brothers had not turned out very well, and having become addicted to strong liquors, &c." It is astonishing how the other mode adds to the *vraisemblance*.

What really captivated the public and fixed Sam for ever in the affections of the people, was this perfect fidelity to his master, shown always in the most practical way, and without the least affectation. The contrast to his often farcical behaviour shows the highest art, and the mode in which this fidelity is testified is exhibited in the most natural and unexpected style. One is inclined to believe that in the drawing of such natural scenes, and spontaneous dialogues there must be a sort of *inspiration* to secure an effect; utterances and turns of speech seem not to be devised, but suggested to the writer as by another. When it was proposed to Sam by his master that he should not attend him in the Fleet, a less skilled observer would have made him offer objections or entreaties; but how natural that he should adopt a sort of imprac-

ticable *surliness* and even insolence, but still the
insolence of wounded attachment!

"Now I'll tell you wot it is, sir," said Mr.
Weller, in a grave and solemn voice. "This here
sort o' thing won't do at all, so don't let's hear no
more about it."

"I am serious, and resolved, Sam," said Mr.
Pickwick.

"You air, air you, sir?" inquired Mr. Weller,
firmly. "Wery good, sir. Then so am I."

Thus speaking, Mr. Weller fixed his hat on his
head with great precision, and abruptly left the
room.

"Sam!" cried Mr. Pickwick, calling after him,
"Sam! Here!"

This much-admired character has been naturally
claimed by contending districts, eager for the
honour of having engendered such a credit to
humanity. We have seen what are the preten-
sions of Sam Vale; but there lately reached me
from the country, this modest plea for an old and
almost forgotten local character.

"It may be interesting to you to know that Sam
Weller was 'Boots' at the 'Bull' Inn, Sittingbourne. I lived at Sittingbourne from 1829 to
1841. The 'Bull' was a very comfortable commercial inn, and it was kept by a Mrs. Hogben.
The Boots was called 'Bob,' and I think that his
surname was Erenden, but I cannot be sure.

'Bob' was a very pert and flippant person, rather what we called a wag. I remember the man well, for he used to bring the dinner beer to our house daily. We always looked out for Bob, and he was pretty certain to have a joke ready for us youngsters, and especially for our maid-servant. My parents and other relations who lived at Sittingbourne at that time, never had any doubt that Dickens had met 'Bob' and put him into 'Pickwick' as Sam Weller. I can now see 'Bob' coming into the house and marching through to the kitchen with the beer, with his tall hat on one side and with the cheeky cut. I have no doubt that Dickens stayed at the 'Bull' when at Sittingbourne. The 'Bull' was a very snug, comfortable house. The time from 1829 to 1841 was, as you may know, the very hey-day of the coaching and posting time."

Mr. Jerdan, the well-known critic and editor of the *Literary Gazette*, was accustomed to claim some share in the development of Sam Weller.

"I was so charmed," he writes in his autobiography, " with the creation of Sam Weller, that I could not resist the impulse to write to the author expressing my admiration, and counselling him to develop the character largely—to the utmost." No doubt this encouragement, coming from so important a critic had its effect. When the story was finished and the event was to be cele-

brated by a dinner, Jerdan was thus warmly
invited by the author, " I depend upon you above
everybody."

It will be recollected that Sam describes in
humorous fashion his father's arrangement with
an election committee for upsetting a number of
voters whom he was to bring down on his coach.
Here Dickens had in view the very corrupt borough
of Great Yarmouth, where extraordinary modes of
dealing with voters were rife. There were no
less than 800 non-resident voters who had to be
brought from a distance, and Mr. Langton states
that the tradition of a casualty thus described,
prevails in Yarmouth to this day.[1]

Tupman, according to the American, Dr. Shelton
Mackenzie, was thought to be sketched from
a certain Mr. Winter, a stout and elderly
" Buck," noted for his attentions to the other sex:[2]

A description of a groom he had in Devonshire terrace
recalls Sam Weller :—"' 'I vent to the club this mornin', sir,
There vorn't no letters, sir.' 'Very good, Topping.' 'How's
missis, sir?' 'Pretty well, Topping.' 'Glad to hear it, sir.
My missis ain't very well, sir.' 'No!' 'No, sir, she's a goin',
sir, to have a hincrease very soon, and it makes her rather
nervous, sir; and ven a young woman gets at all down in sich
a time, sir, she goes down wery deep, sir.' To this sentiment
I replied affirmatively ; and then, he adds, as he stirs the fire
(as if he were thinking out aloud), 'Wot a mystery it is ! Wot
a go is natur ! '" (*Vide* Mr. Roker's speech.)

[2] We find a family "The Tupmans," in Miss Austin's
" Emma."

and Mrs. Bardell, it was said, was drawn from a buxom Mrs. Anne Ellis, who kept an eating-house close to Doctors' Commons.   This, however, seems carrying the "realism" of the story a little too far, as Mrs. Bardell is of a very general type. At the same time it is certain that for a versatile writer, a simple hint, as it were, supplied from real life or character, a casual encounter in train or omnibus, will furnish the basis of a regular character.[3]

[3] Mrs. Lirriper, the lodging-house keeper, was thus accidentally suggested, and the author told me that he could have filled out the character to proportions suited to one of his regular stories.

X.

THERE is something at once pleasing and interesting in the way in which the author has enshrined his earliest recollections in his work: thus securing a sort of vitality and inspiration. These little touches we meet everywhere, and might escape the ordinary observer. They seem, however, to have been more directly for his own satisfaction, by way of record, or reminder of some old association. Thus one of the cricketers at the famous Dingley Dell match was Mr. Struggles, whom Mr. Langton identifies as an old schoolfellow of the writer's—whose name was Stroughill—pronounced Struggle. The Boarding House at Bury St. Edmund's, the scene of Mr. Pickwick's grotesque adventure, is called Westgate House, and there is now, or was a few years back, a school for young ladies, bearing the same name. One of the most painful passages in his childhood was associated with Warren's Blacking, and in " Pickwick " and in many other of his works, there are allusions to this sore point, to the poet who was kept to celebrate the article in "poetry," the whimsicality of the recollection overpowering the more dismal associations.

The vivacious chronicle of "Pickwick" is so closely associated with the rather limited stock of public pleasure, that we must look with a sort of affection on the places of what Elia would call its "kindly engendure." The first portion was written in Furnival's Inn, a number or so at Chalk in Kent, and at Broadstairs, and the last part in Doughty Street. The old Furnival's Inn, a picturesque mass of low-roofed, heavily-eaved, shaggy-browed brick, facing Holborn, was removed nearly a century ago, and the present tame, uninteresting structure substituted. Entering through a low, tunnel-shaped archway, we find ourselves in a retired square with a general tone of dinginess, in the centre of which is a statue of the late Mr. Peto, of contracting memory, who looks forlorn enough. Behind him is an hotel with a cheerful-looking coffee-room—"Wood's Hotel," which has a snug, old-fashioned air enough. No doubt the Wardles and other countrified folk of our time, when they come to town, repair to Wood's Hotel, and are "entreated" comfortably.

Here it was that the young and brilliant "Boz," then in the first flush of his prosperity, and working on the *Chronicle*, took rooms. Lately the books of the old Inn were laid open before me by Mr. Price (of the firm of Messrs.

N

Rose, who manage its business), and in one of them I read :—

No. 13.   THREE-PAIR BACK.

Mr. Charles Dickens.

Came Christmas, 1834.................. £35   5   0
Paid.

The door of No. 13 is squeezed into a corner of the square, on the right as we enter; and its steep darkened stair leads up to his modest rooms, almost at the top, now occupied by Mr. Slagg. It consists of a suite of three small chambers. He lived a year at No. 13, the "three-pair back," and thence shifted his quarters to No. 15, the house which now displays one of the tablets of the Society of Arts. This little change has not been hitherto known. Now we find a new account opened :—

No. 15.   THREE-PAIR FLOOR SOUTH.

At £50 a year.   For three years certain.

From Christmas, 1835	£35	15	0
On Jan. 3, 1837 .... *paid*	50	0	0
Nov. 20 .... „	37	10	0
May, 1838 .... „	25	0	0
Dec., do. .... „	12	10	0
Feb. 11, 1839 .... „	25	0	0

Such was his little account. He was married in April, 1836, and removed to a house in Doughty Street in February, 1837; so that for two years he was paying rent for two separate establishments.

No. 15 is on the right, nearer the archway, and is of more pretentious character. Not long since this set was in possession of the lively writer who signed himself "O. P. Q. Philander Smiff." There is no change since " Boz's " time, even to the smooth, brass-bound rail on the stone stair. It is notable that next to the Inn, outside, stands one of the few genuine old Pickwickian taverns left in London—Ridler's—with its low coffee-room and bow windows of the pattern of the destroyed Saracen's Head. There are not half a dozen of this type of tavern in the metropolis now.[1]

Looking from Mecklenburgh Square—long the residence of one of " Boz's " own merry men, the genial Sala—towards the pleasant Gray's Inn Gardens, whose trees can be seen waving over their wall, we find a compact, tidy-looking street, of small two-storied houses, all of the same pattern, and yclept Doughty Street. It is protected against waggons and heavy traffic by a bar, though

---

[1] The present proprietor of " Wood's," Mr. Whaley, when I furnished this little sketch of Furnival's to the *St. James's Gazette*, with natural pride, put in a claim for his Hotel, which it is pleasant to recognize :—" I may state that he occupied the sitting and bed-room, Nos. 58 and 59, immediately over the entrance of Wood's Hotel, for a period of six months ; and it is not long since the old waiter died who attended to Charles Dickens and who had great pride in showing the rooms to the visitors of the hotel, informing them that he had the pleasure of attending to Mr. Dickens's wants."

a board at the top announces a gracious dispen-
sation in favour of the tenants by the lord of the
soil, " Sir James Doughty Tichborne, Bart,"—
that is, between certain hours. It was in 1837
that Dickens came here, to No. 48. I felt a
curiosity to see the interior where the last half of
" Pickwick" and the first of " Oliver Twist "
were written. There were " Apartments to let "
which had a very Bardell-like air. A sort of
" little marchioness " came to open the door, and
positively refused admittance; but a second
attempt was successful. It was a comfortable
tenement, and more spacious than it appeared
outside, with a roomy stair and moderate hall.
A " lodger," practising the piano in the parlour,
kindly admitted the curious intruder, and, not
without pride, did the honours. The back room
—a rather contracted but snug chamber, giving
on a small yard or garden—had been the novelist's
study. As one looked on the whitened wall, the
faint lean stucco and skimpy mantelpiece, and
other furnishings, one could imagine those bright
intelligent eyes gazing upwards, seeking the
images of Sam, and Winkle, and the rest. The
walls of the stair display the old marble paper of
his time, grimed to a mahogany yellow. There is,
it seems, a general tendency in all the adjoining
houses to set up as Dickens's own house, and
hesitating lodgers are often influenced by being

artfully told " it were his very room that you're now a-standin' in."

The chronology of " Pickwick," as it may be termed, is one of the most curious phenomena in fiction—it is so mysteriously disposed. Yet it has a sort of interest of its own, and the amazing spirit and genius of the writer—as in the case of Shakespeare—seems to triumph over the technicalities of time and space. The earlier incidents follow so naturally and in such gay profusion, that we seem to have been living with the Pickwickians for years : whereas, on strict examination, it will be found that only a few weeks have passed over : thus suggesting the Eastern fairy tale of the man who dipped his head into a tub of water, when he passed through a long life, was married, had children, was sold into captivity, &c., all before he drew his head out again ! The innumerable incidents of the early portion, or more than a third of the book, all took place within a period of three weeks ! Yet during that short span we have lived with, talked with, listened to and grown as familiar with these characters, as if we had known them all our lives.

Allusion has been made to the curious changes in dates made by the author, in successive editions —somewhat hurriedly it must be said—with a view of extricating himself from a particular embarassment. These, however, did not oure the difficulties, and, as often happens, were only the cause of fresh confusion. What added to the embroglio, was the minute and natural way in which dates were set down for every proceeding, which adds an extraordinary air of vraisemblance and reality to the whole. We would not part with this, even to gain perfect symmetry and correctness.

The narrative commences with the meeting of the Club, when the travelling party was commissioned, as it were. Here is the sequence of events, with their dates :—

1827.

May 12. Meeting of the Club.
  „   13. The start—Arrival at Rochester—The Ball.
  „   14. Winkle's Duel.
  „   15. The Review.
  „   16. The Drive to Manor Farm.
  „   17. The Rook Shooting, and Cricket Match.
  „   18. Jingle's Disclosure to the Spinster Aunt.
  „   19.
  „   20. }The Plot.
  „   21.
  „   22. The Elopement.
  „   23. Arrival of Wardle and Mr. Pickwick at the "White Hart."
  „   24. Return to Manor Farm.
  „   25. The "Leather Bottle."
  „   26. Return to Town.

On the 25th, at the "Leather Bottle," Mr. Pickwick stated that the Eatanswill Election was to take place " in a few days "—say within three—which brings us to the day before :—

May 28. Scene with Mrs. Bardell.
  „ 29. Departure for Eatanswill.
  „ 30. The Nomination.
June 2. The Election.

It is at this point, when everything was going so smoothly, in almost diary-fashion, that we find our author, of a sudden, taking a leap forward of some two years. For Mr. Pott, it will be remembered, to amuse Mr. Pickwick, directs " Jane " to bring him " the file of the *Gazette* for eighteen hundred and twenty-*eight*," thus set out at length. The file was of course for the year preceding the one in which it was called for, which last must have been 1829. But to resume our chronological table :—

June 5. "Third morning after the Election"—Visit from Mr. Leo Hunter.
  „ 6. Mrs. Leo Hunter's Party.
  „ 8. Bury St. Edmunds.
  „ 9. Adventure at the Boarding School.
  „ 10. ⎫ Mr. Pickwick confined to his bed.
  „ 11. ⎭
  „ 12. Reads aloud the Story of the Parish Clerk.
  „ 13. Arrival of Winkle and Tupman.

Here our chronology again grows confused. Winkle and Tupman remained at Mrs. Pott's, we are told, for " two days after the breakfast at Mrs. Leo Hunter's," that is during the 8th and 9th,— on the morning of the 10th, Mr. Pott's display of jealousy took place, and at noon the departure of the two Pickwickians, who reached Bury that

evening.   Our author makes the day the 13th.
But this is a trifle to what follows.   While they
are at dinner, Dodson and Fogg's "notice of
action" arrives, dated August 28th, 1830, an
advance of another year.   It seemed likely that
this date was fixed on to reconcile events with
Jingle's allusion to the revolution of 1830,
though the two incidents were too close to each
other to cure the matter.   At any rate, even if we
ignore the year, we have to jump from June 13
to the 1st of September, fixed by "the commencement of the shooting season."

Sept. 1. The Shooting Party.
  ,,   2. "Thursday"—Mr. Pickwick goes to London.
  ,,   3. "Friday"—Interview with Dodson and Fogg.
  ,,   5. Ipswich—Adventure in the Double-Bedded Room.
  ,,   6. Scene with Nupkins.
  ,,   7. Return to Town.
  ,,   8. }
  ,,   9. } Sam's Visit to Dorking.

At this point our chronology again becomes
wild.   The party separated for a "short time,"
each going home, to "prepare" for a visit to
Dingley Dell at Christmas.   These preparations,
however elaborate, could not engross more than
two or three weeks at most—say even a month
—which would bring us to the middle of October.
But our author wished to get to his Christmas
festivities at once, or had no adventures ready
to fill up the interval.   So we find the four

Pickwickians starting on December 22nd, " in the year of grace "—mark this—" in which these, their faithfully recorded adventures were undertaken and accomplished " ! Thus we are wonderfully put back again from 1830 to 1827 ! But to resume :—

Dec. 23. Trundle's Wedding.
 ,,   24. The Gabriel Grub Story.
 ,,   25. Christmas Day—Introduction of Bob Sawyer.
 ,,   26. Return to London.
 1828.
Jan. 8. "Ten days or a fortnight after his Return," service of *subpœna* by Jackson.
 ,,   9. Visit to Perker.
 ,, 10. Bob Sawyer's Party ("the Invitation was given at Dingley Dell for Thursday Fortnight.")
Feb. 13. Sam's Valentine.
 ,, 14. The Trial—*Bardell* v. *Pickwick*.
 ,, 16. Departure for, and arrival at Bath, "to stay two months."
 ,, 17. Ball at the Assembly Rooms.
 ,, 20. Mr. Pickwick moved to the Royal Crescent.

Mr. Pickwick, we are told, returned to town at the expiration of the first week " in Trinity Term "—which would have fixed his arrival at about June 24th. He had thus remained *four* months at Bath.

June 27. "The third morning after his Arrival," Arrest of Mr. Pickwick.
July 24. Arrest of Mrs. Bardell.
 ,, 25. Mr. Pickwick leaves the Fleet Prison.

He had thus been confined not a month. Yet we are assured that " for *three* long months he remained shut up" in the prison. Again it must be said, that these little oversights are not pointed out with any view of disparaging what is not to be disparaged, but as a sort of entertainment. Nay, we would rather have them with us than not, or than a precise, mathematical or pedantic adherence to all the formalities. The writer himself would have assuredly given one of his hearty and jovial laughs, were they pointed out to him.

July 22. Arabella Allen married to Winkle.
  „   26. Mr. Pickwick goes down to Bristol.
  „   27. Goes to Birmingham.
  „   28. At the Saracen's Head, Towcester.
  „   29. Returns to Town.
August 1. At Osborne's Hotel, Adelphi.

Here our author makes one more *demivolt*, and speaks of "the healthy, fine *October* mornings." For "a week" Mr. Pickwick was busy engaging the house at Dulwich, which he announces, forgetting "the fine October mornings," when on

August 8. the Dinner at Osborne's.

On this occasion, he declares that he had "devoted the greater part of two years" to his adventures. It will have been seen that the time covered was just one year and three months. Putting aside the trivial oversights which it has been an agreeable pastime to point out, it may be said that in no other work of fiction can be found so natural, and probable, and even consistent an arrangement and sequence of events.

It is recorded that an eminent composer writing an opera for his family, amongst whom there was a member who could not sing, contrived a part in which not a note was required, but in which he had periodically to give a yawn, or monosyllable, we forget which, and which was contrived to fit in with the measure. Something after this principle, there is one utterly silent character in "Pickwick"—as a friend has pointed out to me—who figures prominently, taking his regular part in the drama, marries one of the young ladies, and yet from the first to the last page never once opens his mouth! Here is another "puzzler" which might have been "set" at Mr. Calverley's examination, and we will venture to say that few readers could find the answer off hand. This silent personage was Mr. Trundle, Wardle's son-in-law, whose marriage was celebrated with such festivities. Even on this occasion it is not recorded that he returned thanks for the bride—though Mr. Pickwick's speech is given in full.

"The Bagman's Story" somewhat reflects the influence of Washington Irving—and there is one of his stories, "The Adventures of my Uncle," which has something—but a very little something—ot the same cast. "Gabriel Grub," however, may have been written in imitation of that remarkable legend of "Rip Van Winkle;" and the return of Gabriel after ten years, and his drunkenness are suggested by similar points in the American author's story.[2]

[2] The scene of this story is laid in "an old abbey town in this part of the country," which we identify by the illustration as St. Albans. Dingley Dell is thus shifted from Kent to Hertfordshire. In an old book, called Angelo's "Picnic," there is a place described, called "Dingle Dell." It may be added that M. Magnus's "blue" spectacles become "green" after a few pages, a droll oversight.

XI.

THE most dramatic and genuine scenes in "Pickwick" are the legal ones. We have only to think of the number of the figures, and the nice and perfect fashion in which they are discriminated, the distinctness with which they present themselves to the memory, to acknowledge the wonderful knowledge and observation displayed by our author. We may name Dodson and Fogg, the scheming attorneys; Mr. Pell, a delightful type of the low practitioner; Jackson, Lowten and the other clerks; Justice Stareleigh and the counsel in the famous trial; Perker, the family solicitor. All these were suggested by his own experience and familiarity with the business. Every touch is put in with a rich variety, and every turn and point of character is legitimately connected with professional influences and habits. There is nothing out of place or out of keeping; though the *Edinburgh Review* wrote, on the appearance of "Bleak House," that "his legal knowledge was only that of attorney's clerk, and that he could describe the swearing of an affidavit correctly, but nothing more"!

Dodson and Fogg are delightful in their perfect naturalness, even to the refined and subtle and most original strokes by which their knavery is exhibited. As when Mr. Pickwick in his innocence appeals to the candour and good feeling of the firm : "You will permit me to assure you that I am a most unfortunate man, so far as this case is concerned," how characteristic is Dodson's mode of meeting the point ! " The writ, sir, which commences the action was issued regularly. Mr. Fogg, where is the *Præcipe* book ? . . . Here is the entry. Middlesex *Capias*. Martha Bardell, widow, *v.* Samuel Pickwick, Dodson and Fogg for the plaintiff. August 28th, 1830. All regular, sir, perfectly." This " regularity " was their mode of acting fairly. The incident suggested itself, not long since, on my receiving a somewhat heavy " Bill of costs " from a firm of solicitors. On making some remonstrance, the senior partner of the firm wrote in defence of his charges, adding, " To show you how anxious I am to meet your wishes, my partner, on receipt of your letter, went through all the items of our costs, and I am glad to tell you, joins with me in thinking them moderate in the extreme." This appeal from one partner to the other is quite in the Pickwickian firm's style ; " Give me the *præcipe* book ; all regular ;" and shows how little exaggeration there is in Dickens' sketches. The scene

at the close, when the costs were being paid
in Perker's chambers, is in the best spirit of
comedy, and based on the profoundest knowledge of character. Their jocularity and offensive
familiarity is exactly what stupid villains would
assume must be accepted as complimentary.
" I don't think you are looking quite so stout
as when I had the pleasure of seeing you last,"
Dodson said " in an affable manner." And
later when they were going, " I hope," said
Fogg, softened by the cheque, " you don't
think so badly of us, Mr. Pickwick, as when
we first had the pleasure of seeing you." " I
hope not," said Dodson, with the high tone
of calumniated virtue; " Mr. Pickwick now
knows us better, I trust. I beg to assure
you, sir, I have no vindictive feelings for the
sentiments you thought to express of us," &c.

Any one who has ever met such of the
common practitioners as furnish their services at
the Police Courts, will own to the truth of the
sketch of Mr. Pell, with his taste for rum-hot,
his friendships, and his repeated references to the
lucky circumstance that they had come to him,
and not fallen into the hands of some other
practitioner. When he describes the compliments
his " noble friend " was in the habit of paying
him, we have a delicate touch of character :

" You flatter me, my lord," he said. " Pell, if I

do, I'm damned." Mr. Weller objected to this
phrase, seeming to think it inconsistent with the
dignity of the personage, and conveying, perhaps,
a doubt of the narrative. " Go on, sir, he said.
"No, sir, I will *not* go on. You have reminded me,
sir, that this conversation was private, private and
confidential. Gentlemen, I'm a professional man.
It may be that I am a good deal looked up to in
my profession. It may be that I am not. Most
people know. I say nothing. Observations have
already been made in this room injurious to the
reputation of my noble friend. You will excuse
me, gentlemen, I was imprudent." The natural,
grave way in which this is put carries off what
would otherwise be far-fetched and verging on
burlesque. Indeed all the scenes with the
coachmen, when Mr. Pell exhibited his boastings,
become plausible enough, as we think that this
practitioner knew well he was dealing with open-
mouthed, simple-minded men who were awed by
their contact with the law and one of its instru-
ments.

Dickens' art was shown in his way of indicating
a character by broad outlines with a masterly
reserve, just *touching* on the special peculiarity
and leaving it to the reader to fill in the rest for
himself. Take, for instance, the character of
Magnus, with whom Mr. Pickwick travelled to
Ipswich. There is nothing very marked in what

he says or does, his speeches have nothing very
peculiar : but somehow the impression is left that
we have met a very pretentious, foolish person,
who yet conveys the idea of one who makes
himself important.   There is a genuineness in his
confidences.   "Curious circumstance," he says,
"about these initials, sir; you will observe, P.M.,
post meridian.   In hasty notes to intimate
acquaintances, I sometimes sign myself "Afternoon."   This absurdity touches caricature, but
how natural when he adds, "It amuses my friends
very much, Mr. Pickwick."   When they arrive
at the inn, he asks, "Do you stop here, sir?"
"Dear me!" said Mr. Magnus, "I never knew
anything like these extraordinary coincidences.
Why, I stop here too!   I hope we dine together."
This is exactly the exuberant wonder and garrulity
of a frivolous man.   This may be contrasted with
the author's later or last manner, when such a
person would be fitted with a stock phrase, which
would be iterated, and the sense would be
conveyed by long speeches.

The same reserve is shown in Magnus' later
conversation.   "After sundry accounts of himself
his family, his business, and his brothers (most talkative men, have a great deal to say about their
brothers)," &c., he tells Mr. Pickwick he has come
down to propose to a lady.   "I think an Inn is
a good sort of place to propose to a single woman

in, Mr. Pickwick. She is more likely to feel the loneliness of her situation in travelling." An amusing speech, equal to whole pages of description.

It would be a difficult thing to decide, of all the characters in this varied gallery, which is the best drawn and most skilfully touched. In a story, it is but a small thing to present a character; no matter how effectively drawn, to be shown effectively, it must be itself part of the story, produce incidents and be itself developed by the incidents produced. This is what we see in real life, and indeed it is only by events and incidents that we learn what a person's character is. We see much of this in " Pickwick," where most of the characters are shown in action, and help on the story. Adopting this test, we should be inclined to pronounce Mr. Pott, the editor, not only the most amusing and original, but in every way the best drawn of the characters. He has many "sides," and is developed in a very remarkable way. Nothing is more entertaining than the contrast between his editorial ferocity, and his meekness to his wife, whose contempt for his newspaper is not the least of the good touches. His jealousy of Winkle is founded not on any particular regard for his lady, but because it furnishes the rival journal with a topic for ridicule. We almost see him in the flesh, and know him thoroughly, and read the portion that concerns him, much as we look on a good picture, with the sense of discovering something new every time. The incident of the war between the two newspapers is truly admirable and laughter-moving to a degree, and shows the profoundest knowledge of provincial press quarrels. In the lines to " A Brass Pot," is caught in a most accurate way the personality of such things ; and the leader beginning " Our obscure and filthy contemporary," with the one headed " Hole and Corner Buffoonery," are exquisite even in, their exaggeration. What a capital touch is the editor's reply to Mr. Pickwick, " Is the Independent still in being ? " " The Independent, sir, is still dragging on a wretched and lingering career, abhorred and despised by even the few who are cognizant of its miserable and disgraceful existence : stifled by the very filth which it so profusely scatters ; rendered deaf and blind by the exhalations of its own slime; the obscene journal is rapidly sinking," &c. " Having delivered this manifesto (*which formed a portion of his last week's leader*)," &c.

How truly founded on human nature is this ludicrous journalistic animosity, will be seen from a specimen which turned up in the most casual way, and had not to be sought for. It will be agreed that it rather goes beyond the two Eatanswill organs in scurrility.   It is taken from the *Andover Standard* :—

" That Thug of Journalism and Judas Oracle (thanking thee for the word) *The* ——, the latest of the gutter efforts of the Metropolitan Radicals in the newspaper line, is a stain on this country's face, and a blot in the writing of her name.   The only possible redeeming feature of this pot-house swaggerer is its utility in showing to what depths of crapulous deviltry a mercenary mind can sink in lickspittling to the thievish and rowdy interests of a " political" faction whose orb if for a moment it feebly sparkled into publicity has now set again for ever before the risen sun of Unity.   For the benefit of our Hants readers, the common decency of whose homes is happily unpolluted by the invasion of this and kindred evening rice-wrappers, we may say that its policy at the first sight has the look of being rather fresh.   The Hibernian editorial heart of this halfpenny slobbery, would-be-Bowery-style of literary street-walker, loves to bleed over the fiendish inhumanity of the institution of property, the ' absurd old-maidish respect ' which so awkwardly seems to exist towards social law and order.   *Certes*, if Swift's ' hospital for incurables ' were now open, at least one City scribe might qualify with undoubted success for a certificate of admission as the finest single-handed liar of the season.   But this sort of tin-thunder and

fustian, high-falutin gets tame and ineffective with
the lapse of days, since this journalistic Roscius
apparently only owns one shirt, which he wears
white on Mondays, turns into striped cambric with
a ha'porth of blue crayon on Tuesday, intersperses
with red on Wednesday, and so forth. We have
seen a strayed copy or two lately exposed for sale
on an Andover counter. It is the duty of respectable folk to boycott criminals, fools and
traitors, though this will hardly be necessary in
this case within our own walls, on the principle
that vermin by instinct leave a sinking ship,
and because in this Division the rotten raft of
Radicalism has to-day hardly a stick left peeping
above the waters of oblivion."

The whole picture of life at Bath is filled
in with many perfect touches, and furnishes a
further proof of the author's admirable art in
making distinct and perfectly individual species
of the same genus. Footmen and servants
generally from their office, offer little that is
distinct; they are usually servile enough in
following the traditions of their kind. Yet who
does not think with delight of the specimens offered
here in such brilliant profusion, and touched in a
Hogarthian spirit of comedy! This again gains
strength from the appropriateness of the situation,
for Bath was the fitting locale for the humours of
the footman-world. One reads with wonder, akin

to pleasure, the gaiety, the spirit, the broad strokes with which these amusing beings are sketched. It will hardly be believed that there are some seven or eight of these gentry exhibited, all more or less distinct and amusing. Need we name Mr. John Smauker a quaint character, with his fox's-head snuff-box, and explanation of the "killibeate" which, read for the thousandth time, always moves a smile.

Another scene unpretending in its way, but which is most original, and which we recall with delight, is that of the arrival of Mrs. Cluppins and the Raddles' for tea at Mrs. Bardell's. This amounted to no more than a party in a cab or fly, driving up, and mistaking the hall door. Yet what a display of character and human weakness !

"Stop at the house with a green door, driver," said the heavy gentleman.

"Oh! You perwerse creetur!" exclaimed one of the vixenish ladies. "Drive to the ouse with the yellow door, cabmin."

"Upon this the cabman, who in a sudden effort to pull up at the house with the green door, had pulled the horse up so high that he nearly pulled him backward into the cabriolet, let the animal's fore legs down to the ground again, and paused.

"Now vere am I to pull up?" inquired the driver. "Settle it among yourselves. All I ask is, vere?"

"Most wotes carries the day!" said one of the vixenish ladies at length. "The ouse with the yellow door, cabmin."

"But after the cabriolet had dashed up, in splendid style, to the house with the yellow door: "making," as one of the vixenish ladies triumphantly said, "acterrally more noise than if one had come in one's own carriage"—and after the driver had dismounted to assist the ladies in getting out—the small round head of Master Thomas Bardell was thrust out of the one pair window of a house with a red door, a few numbers off.

"Aggrawatin' thing!" said the vixenish lady last mentioned, darting a withering glance at the heavy gentleman.

"My dear, it's not my fault," said the gentleman.

"Don't talk to me, you creetur, don't," retorted the lady. "The house with the red door, cabmin. Oh! If ever a woman was troubled with a ruffinly creetur, that takes a pride and a pleasure in disgracing his wife on every possible occasion afore strangers, I am that woman!"

"While this dialogue was going on, the driver was most ignominiously leading the horse, by the bridle, up to the house with the red door, which Master Bardell had already opened. Here was a mean and low way of arriving at a friend's house!

No dashing up, with all the fire and fury of the animal; no jumping down of the driver; no loud knocking at the door; no opening of the apron with a crash at the very last moment, for fear of the ladies sitting in a draught; and then the man handing the shawls out, afterwards, as if he were a private coachman! The whole edge of the thing had been taken off; it was flatter than walking."

If we analyze this sketch, it will be astonishing how much is introduced,—the conjugal dispute, the cabman's disgust, the ludicrous caracoling up to the wrong house: the real person in fault laying the blame on another, and the comic final approach in an ignominious way, in which lurks a sort of moral as to a fable. And all arising out of a cab driving up!

The judicious mode in which Mr. Pickwick's adventure in the double-bedded room is treated is dramatic, and natural to a high degree. In other hands it had become a boisterous farce; here it is comedy. All through, there is the hint of its being a serious and even distressing situation, whose gravity is not even disturbed by that ludicrous touch of Mr. Pickwick putting on his hat "over his night-cap, like one of the old watchmen." Capital comedy too is his disregard of this costume, in his chivalrous wish earnestly to explain matters to the lady.

What a ludicrous image is often called up

by a single touch! As when Mrs. Raddle was turning out Bob Sawyer's guests. "You ought to be ashamed of yourselves," said the voice of Mr. Raddle, "which appeared to proceed from beneath *some distant bedclothes.*"

A hundred other little instances might be selected, to show the wit, humour, and gaiety of the author. As when Nupkins hesitated to see the Pickwickians alone : " He was a public man, and he turned pale at the thought of *Julius Cæsar and Mr. Percival.*" So Mr. Weller senior, on Stiggins, who, he said, " gives out as he's a persecuted saint, and says he hopes the heart of the turncock as cut the water off 'll be softened and turned in the right way, *but he rayther thinks he's booked for something uncomfortable.*"

This is as exquisitely funny as it is unexpected,—founded too in human nature. Then : " If I'd my way, Samivel, I'd just stick some of these lazy shepherds behind a heavy wheelbarrow and run 'em up and down a fourteen inch wide plank all day."

What shrewd observation is there in the remarks on the two simple phrases, " never mind," and " upon my word!"—the former uttered by Mr. Magnus in his quarrel with Mr. Pickwick ; the latter Mrs. Pott's adroit exclamation in a conjugal quarrel. The analysis of the inflection in both cases is an essay.

XII.

In its way one of the most satisfactory testimonies to the value and popularity of this work is the well-known (to the curious at least in such matters) examination paper, once "set" at Cambridge in the year 1857, by the witty Calverley. This humorist had a flavour of his own quite unique, much as Elia has, and his series of questions, like everything connected with the "Pickwick," is in itself an entertainment. The thing was gravely carried out in the regular examination hall, and there were a number of candidates. There is a singular quaint feeling as we read, and even the most profound student must feel his ignorance as he reads. A few of the more difficult questions will be found welcome.

"1. Mention any occasions on which it is specified that the Fat Boy was not asleep; and that (1) Mr. Pickwick and (2) Mr. Weller, senior, ran. Deduce from the expressions used, Mr. Pickwick's maximum of speed.

"3. Who were Mr. Staple, Goodwin, Mr.

Brooks, Villam, Mr. Bunkin, " Old Nobs," " Cast-iron Head," Young Bantam ?

5. Give, approximately, the height of Mr. Dubbley; and accurately the Christian names of Mr. Grummer, Mrs. Raddle, and the Fat Boy, also the surname of the Zephyr.

8. What Church was in the valentine that first attracted Mr. Samuel's eye in the shop ?

9. Describe the common " Profeel machine."

10. Describe the component parts of Dogsnose, and simplify the expression " taking a grinder."

16. State any incidents you know in the career of Tom Merton, butcher, previous to his incarceration.

17. Where was Mr. Weller's wife's will found ?

18. Show that there was at least three times as many fiddles as harps in Muggleton at the time of the Ball at Manor Farm.

20. Is there any ground for conjecturing that Sam had more brothers than one ?

23. " She's a swelling wisibly." When did the same phenomenon occur again, and what fluid caused the pressure on the body in the latter case ?

26. Give some account of the word " fanteeg," and hazard any conjecture explanatory of the expression " My Prooshian Blue " applied by Mr. Samuel to Mr. Tony Weller.

30. Who beside Mr. Pickwick is recorded to have worn gaiters ?

There is, we venture to say, a fine delicate humour here, worthy of the book. One of the
happiest and most puzzling is the question No.
20, as to Sam's having brothers. To be relished
also is No. 30, " Who besides Mr. Pickwick is
recorded to have worn gaiters ? " Who too could
say anything as to the identity of Messrs. Bunkin,
or Staple ? It is recorded that Mr. Besant obtained
the premium for best answering.

It is not so well known that at Oxford also
there appeared a *jeu d'esprit* of the same kind
but not nearly so witty, published many years
ago in a clever anonymous *jeu d'esprit*—entitled
" The Student's Guide to the School of *Litteræ
Fictitiæ*, commonly called Novel-Literature."
The passmen were required to take up the " Pickwick Papers."

" Give some account of the game of cricket as
played in the West Indies ; and describe an
imaginary match between any number of blacks
(including Quanko Samba) and an eleven, including Lillywhite.

" Collect passages which bear upon the theory of
' Widders,' as enunciated from time to time by
Mr. Weller, senior.

"Show how far the fundamental principles of the
British Constitution are exhibited in the account
of the Eatanswill election ; and apply specially
(1) to the freedom of the *press*, as manifested by

the local papers ; (2) to the freedom of *opinion*, as expressed in the language of the electors.

" Can you assign any probable grounds for the popular representation of Mr. Pickwick under the figure of an ' Aged Ram ' ?

" Give a succinct account of the trial, Bardell *v.* Pickwick; and estimate the influence exercised upon the minds of the jurors by (1) the eloquence of Serjeant Buzfuz; (2) the confusion of Mr. Winkle ; (3) the grammatical dogmatism of Mr. Weller, senior ; (4) the arrangement of Master Bardell's buttons.

" Can the fragments of the poetry in the ' Pickwick Papers ' be reduced to any system of classification ? If so—assign to their respective classes (1) ' The Ivy Green ; ' (2) the lines ' To a Frog,' by Mrs. Leo Hunter ; (3) the Goblin's song ; (4) the romance of Dick Turpin ; (5) the conclusion of Mr. Samuel Weller's love-letter.

" Show the beneficial effects of brandy-and-water physically, ethically, and socially; and illustrate by reference to the experience of Mr. Pickwick. State in round numbers how many glasses of this liquid Mr. Pickwick is recorded as having consumed.

" What data have we for supposing that the politics of Mr. A. Jingle were those of a Free-trader ?

" Compare the faculties of Medicine and Law as

treated of by your author ; and state how far
they severally affected the fortunes of Mr. Pickwick.

" Define ' alley tor,' ' alleybi,' ' commoney,'
' killibeate,' ' tap,' ' have-his-carcase,' ' a rig,' ' a
go,' ' reduced councils,' ' mizzle,' ' twopenny
rope,' ' small fire-arms,' ' flummoxed :' and explain (1) ' Fruits is in, cats is out ; ' (2) ' Dash
my vescoat ; ' (3) ' A reg'lar soft-headed, ink-
red'lous turnip ; ' (4) ' They're a twigging of you,
sir ; ' (5) ' You're a amicably disposed young
man, sir, I don't think.' "

The very Preface to " Pickwick," as it proceeded
on its prosperous course from edition to edition,
has a little history of its own. It seemed that
the work was so stored with vitality, and excited
such interest as it went along, that the author
had to come forward, as it were, speak, and
explain all that was connected, as " Elia "
would put it, " with its kindly engendure." There
were no less than three prefaces in succession :
and the variations and additions, set out in a
natural candid style, furnish some autobiogra-
phical details which add greatly to the interest of
the volume. The easy, unaffected mode, the
genial air of confidence with which the author
addressed his friends and readers, is akin to the
style shown in his letters ; and was always one of
the charms of this engaging character.

As the first Preface is not found in the later editions, the reader will be glad to have it here. It ran :—

" PREFACE.

" The author's object in this work was to place before the reader a constant succession of characters and incidents; to paint them in as vivid colours as he could command; and to render them at the same time life-like and amusing.

" Deferring to the judgment of others in the outset of the undertaking, he adopted the machinery of the Club, which was suggested as that best adapted to his purpose; but, finding that it tended rather to his embarrassment than otherwise, he gradually abandoned it, considering it a matter of very little importance to the work whether strictly epic justice were awarded to the Club or not.

"The publication of the book in monthly numbers, containing only thirty-two pages in each, rendered it an object of paramount importance, that while the different incidents were linked together by a chain of interest strong enough to prevent their appearing unconnected or impossible, the general design should be so simple as to sustain no injury from this detached and desultory form of publication extending over twenty months. In short, it was necessary, or it appeared so to the author, that every number should be, to a certain extent, complete in itself, and yet, that the whole twenty numbers, when collected, should form one tolerably harmonious whole, each leading to the other by a gentle and not unnatural progress of adventure.

" It is obvious that in a work published with a view to such considerations, no artfully woven or ingeniously complicated plot can with reason be expected.   The author ventures to express a hope that he has successfully surmounted the difficulties of his undertaking.   And if it be objected to the 'Pickwick Papers' that they are a mere series of adventures in which the scenes are ever changing, and the characters come and go like the men and women we encounter in the real world, he can only content himself with the reflection that they claim to be nothing else, and that the same objection has been made to the works of some of the greatest novelists in the English language.

" The following pages have been written from time to time, almost as the periodical occasions arose.   Having been written for the most part in the society of a very dear young friend who is now no more, they are connected in the author's mind at once with the happiest period of his life, and with its saddest and most severe affliction.

" It is due to the gentleman whose designs

accompany the letter-press, to state that the
interval has been so short between the production
of each number in manuscript and its appearance
in print, that the greater portions of the illustrations have been executed by the artist from the
author's mere verbal description of what he
intended to write.

" The almost unexampled kindness and favour
with which these papers have been received by
the public, will be a never-failing source of gratifying and pleasant recollections while this author
lives. He trusts that throughout his book no
incident or expression occurs which could call a
blush into the cheek, or wound the feelings of
the most sensitive person. If any of his imperfect descriptions, while they afford amusement
in the perusal, should induce only one reader to
think better of his fellow-men, and to look upon
the brighter and more kindly side of human
nature, he would indeed be proud and happy to
have led to such a result."

It will be noted what a pleasant vindication
is here of what is called the periodical form
of publication, which through his long course
he treated, as it were, on scientific principles.
Only a skilful hand and unwearied labour could
overcome the difficulty of furnishing a work, of
which each fragment should be full and complete
in its interest, yet which, taken as a whole should be

homogeneous in form, without having an air of
" scrappiness." Hence his efforts always to reach
a sort of *juste milieu*, and the restraint and
sacrifice of large portions which he thought sur-
plusage, with addition where he thought the
number was not " strong " enough. The happy
result is that the reader is hardly able to note the
joinings, and any one who makes the acquaintance of " Pickwick " for the first time will see few
signs that the work was issued in portions.

Not less interesting is his declaration that the
book was written as the demand for " copy "
arose, that is " from time to time almost as the
periodical occasion arose." This adds to our
wonder and admiration ; and we are told further
that it was under the inspiration of " the society
of a very dear young friend now no more." The
illustrator, as we are also told, showed equal
fertility and readiness, often dashing off his
sketches from mere description. One day would
often suffice for the drawing, and another for the
etching process. The last sentence speaks volumes
for the tender and unaffected nature of the young
author, when he declares that " he would be proud
and happy " if he induced a single reader to
look upon the brighter side of human life. This
is really an almost unique expression, and may
be contrasted with the practical purpose of the
average novelist, which is often to entertain or

make money ; and we may admire the manly
courage which prompted him to such a declaration,
as it was not unlikely to excite a smile of
incredulity.

Twenty years later, by which time the long
series of his best works had appeared, there
was issued a handsome Library Edition in post
octavo, two volumes being generally allotted to
each story. This involved the recasting of some
of the introductions ; the dedication to Talfourd
was withdrawn, and one to the " trusty friend,"
Forster, substituted, which however belonged
to the whole series. Never was there a happier
or more appropriate term than this, used in
his will when bequeathing his watch to this
true, steadfast, and lifelong friend and ally :
" This best edition of my books is, of right,
inscribed to my dear friend, JOHN FORSTER,
biographer of Oliver Goldsmith, in grateful re-
membrance of the many patient hours he has
devoted to the correction of the proof sheets of
the original editions ; and in affectionate acknowledgment of his counsel, sympathy, and faithful
friendship doing my whole literary life." This
tribute, as I can testify, was well deserved, for the
careful scrutiny and sanguine care of this friend
literally watched over every sheet of his works.[1]

---

[1] One of my most cherished possessions is a " long " set of

In this pleasant introduction he gratified the curiosity of his readers with, some interesting details as to the origin and composition of the work, thus following the example of Sir Walter Scott in the forty-eight volume edition of the Waverley Novels, one of the finest and most satisfactory of the kind ever issued.

Extraordinary as was the impression made upon the country by the story itself, more remarkable it is to follow out what may be termed the Pickwickian development, and the almost exuberant shapes in which it has manifested its influence. The reading world in foreign countries seems to have been fervently eager to share in the general hilarity, and it was translated into every language, even into those outside the regular group of familiar tongues. In France it has been several times translated :—

" Le Club des Pickwickistes, Roman Comique traduit librement par Madam E. Niboyet. 2 vols. 1838."

" Aventures de Monsieur Pickwick, traduit sous la direction de P. Lorain, par P Grolier. 1859."

There have been also German, Russian, Dutch, Danish, Hungarian and Spanish versions. Our

this edition of 1857—a fine, well printed one in octavo, which he called "the best"—which he presented to me, with an inscription in his own hand on the title-page, "*This set of my books to Percy FitzGerald—Charles Dickens.*"

old friend looks odd and outlandish enough in his foreign dress :—

"Udtog af Pikvik-Klubbens, efterladte Papirer, Frit oversat, af a Andresen, 2 Del. Kjbenhavn. 1881."

"Samuel Pickwick en Zijne Reisgenooten, C. Mensing, Schiedam. 1868."

"Die Pickwickier, oder Herren Pickwick's und der correspondirenden Mitglieder des Pickwick Club's Kreuz-und Quer-züge, Abentheuer und Thaten. Von Boz, mit Federzeichnungen nach Phiz."

The following appear to be Magyar and Swedish versions :—

"A Pickwick Klub, hátrahagyott iratai. (Kot 1-3). Pest. 1862."

"Klub Pickwickia, Przeklad z angielskiego. 2 toms. 1869."

"Pickwick Klubbens, Efterlemnade—Papper. af L. Malmgren. Stockholm. 1861."

The German translator was hopelessly mystified by the dialect and allusions, and seems to have been led astray altogether by Sam's pronunciation of particular words. Thus when he said, "Out with it, as the father said to a child when he swallowed a *farden,*" we find him translating this last word as "frog." More extraordinary is his version of Mr. Tuckle's direction, "Take the *biron* off," which is oddly rendered, "Take down

the *bell*." Even more wonderful is the rendering
of "I should get the sack, I suppose," which
becomes, "He would *foam like March beer*"!
Dickens, however, was destined to suffer yet more
severely from his translators, and many years
later wrote an indignant protest in his journal
against these distorters of his meaning, giving
also some ludicrous specimens. The truth was,
the foreign workmen found it impossible to deal
with the English *argôt*, and either made the
blunders we have seen, or turned the difficulty
by leaving the passages out. Whole paragraphs
and even pages are thus dealt with.

Singular and unusual proofs of popularity
were the imitations that poured from the Grub
Street presses, and which, strange to say, enjoyed
a measure of success; "The Posthumous Papers
of the Cadger Club." "The Posthumous papers
of the Wonderful Discovery Club, formerly of
Camden Town. Established by Sir Peter Patson.
With eleven illustrations designed by Squib
and engraved by Point." "The Posthumous
Notes of the Pickwickian Club. Edited by Bos.
132 engravings. 1839."

But the boldest of these rivals was Mr. G. W.
Reynolds, who brought out in regular numbers
"Pickwick Abroad, or the tour in France, with
forty-one plates by Alfred Crowquill. 1839;"
and "Pickwick in America." There was also

"The Penny Pickwick," which had a great sale.

As for the popular variations on the one Pickwick note, they were literally endless. There were:—"Lloyd's Pickwickian Songster. 1837." "The Pickwick Comic Almanac, 1838, with twelve comic illustrations by R. Cruikshank." "The Pickwick Collection of Songs, Illustrated. 1837." "Pickwick's Treasury of Wit, Dublin, 1840." 'Sam Weller's Favourite Song Book. 1837." "Sam Weller's Pickwick Jest Book," with illustrations by Cruikshank, and Portraits of all the Pickwick Characters. 1837." "Mr. Sam Weller's Scrap Sheet, with 40 wood-cut Characters."

It is remarkable that this work alone has received the compliment of being produced not merely at the lowest conceivable price, but at an absolute loss. Two or three years ago the hucksters' carts in Cheapside and other streets near the Mansion House appeared of a sudden laden with copies of "Pickwick." These were vended at the extraordinarily low price of a penny. This marvel of cheap production, well printed, on decent paper, consisted of some 200 pages, and contained on computation 350,000 words. It comprised seven sheets of twenty-eight pages each, and weighed some ounces. Messrs. Chapman & Hall issued a shilling "Pickwick," which was thought a marvel of cheapness; but the penny

" Pickwick " was astounding.   The force of cheapness could not farther go.   There was, however, a little bit of secret history connected with it. A Leeds firm of purveyors, " Goodhall, Backhouse and Co.," who were proprietors of a well-known sauce, " The Yorkshire Relish," whereof, we are assured, " six millions bottles are sold annually," was stimulated into this reprint by the hope of doing a good turn to their business. Half a million copies of " Pickwick " at a penny were printed, every page bearing at foot the name of some *spécialité* of the firm's, a baking powder, or it might be, mushroom ketchup. It need hardly be said that such a work could only be published at a loss.   The sixpenny Pickwick was vended at $4\frac{1}{2}d.$, which left a profit : so the publishers must have produced it at something under threepence.   A penny Testament was issued by a Bible Society at a loss, it costing them nearly twopence.   The penny Pickwick must have been issued at three-farthings, or possibly at a halfpenny.   On the back, or the cover, the enterprising proprietors had depicted *The Pickwick Club* discussing the merits of *Goodhall's household specialities !*   This curious book is now *introuvable*, and will by-and-by become a curiosity.

A work so dramatic did not of course escape the adapters.   There were some half a dozen plays founded upon it, of which the most successful was, "Sam Weller; or, The Pickwickians. A drama in three acts. By W. F. Moncrieff. 1837."

Then followed "The Pickwickians; or, The Peregrinations of Sam Weller."

"The Pickwick Club. A burletta in three acts. By E. Sterling. 1837."

"The Peregrinations of Pickwick. An acting drama. By W. Lemon Rede. 1837."

The most successful of these was Moncrieff's "Sam Weller," given at the Strand Theatre, and which had a great run; Hammond making a great success in "Sam."

"The Pickwickians" was the work of an actor and playwright, Mr. Edward Sterling, who still flourishes. There is a criticism of this performance written by Dickens or by Talfourd, in the *Examiner*, which must reflect the author's opinion. It is not known that Dickens at this time occasionally "did" theatrical criticisms for his friends, and there is a note of his among the Forster papers at Kensington, in which he speaks of his review of pieces at "Droory Lane," and the "'Delphi." Indeed, I am inclined to think, from the severity of the style and his known hatred of such piratical attempts, that this may have been of his writing. He speaks of "the modest address prefixed to the Play Bill in which he pays compliment to, and gives a eulogium of the author," apologizing for what the critic calls " his own sheer nonsense and vulgarity." Mr. Pickwick was "execrable, a third rate-actor in nankeen pantaloons, a high collar and a night-cap, with a narrow fringe of hair behind." The whole was nothing but " the boisterous pantomime of the half a dozen miserable performers of a minor theatre." He excepted from this censure two performers, Reeve's " Sam Weller," Hall as the elder Weller, " whose face, dress, and manner, were those of the old coachman to perfection. Dowton in his brightest day never played with more raciness."

" As it is, the house is crowded every night, and the audience have expressed ' unequivocal satisfaction,' notwithstanding that the burletta is some half-hour longer than a five act tragedy, and in spite of the execrable acting of Mr. J. Lee, who ' does ' Jingle and perpetrates certain scraps of mawkish sentimentality in the last act, which are eminently repulsive and disagreeable. Mr. Pickwick, at the termination of the last scene, tells them by way of congratulation that all they have to do now is to live and be happy, which we believe is all that most people have to do at any time, if they can only manage to accomplish it."

The version of " Pickwick " dramatized for the City Theatre was done by a wretched creature

who was under contract to furnish the management with seven melodramas for five pounds,
"to enable him to do which a room had been hired
in a gin-shop close by." There he was perpetually drunk, and did not fulfil his contract.
"Well," said our author, "if it has been the
means of putting a few shillings in the vermin-
eaten pockets of so miserable a creature, let him
empty out his little pot of filth and welcome."

Down to our time the taste for some theatrical
version of "Pickwick" continues unsatiated.
Under Mr. Bateman's management, an adaptation
was brought out, rather boisterous and hearty, by
Mr. Albery, with a view to set forth the quainter
side of Mr. Irving's talent as "Jingle." This
arrangement descended into farce instead of
comedy, and only the more pantomimic scenes
were selected, such as the elopement, with a
real horse and chaise, &c., in fact, rather suggesting Jeremy Diddler. Now Jingle is associated
with scenes of genuine comedy; and the ball at
Rochester would lend itself admirably to the stage.
It should be noted that so rich are Dickens'
stories in varied character, that a dozen dramas
could be made out of any one of them, according
to the point of view taken.

The "Trial" has had extraordinary popularity,
and is constantly being acted or read all over the
country. The reading has its traditions handed

down, and even its " gags." Mr. Toole excels as
the Serjeant, and has often selected the Trial for
his morning performances. Mr. James Fernandez
is, in our opinion, the best of the Buzfuzes. There
have been full half a dozen versions of the
Trial.

The musicians also have been busy with the
subject, and have " set " it as an opera. Such is
" The Great Pickwick Case, arranged as a comic
operetta. The words of the songs by Robert
Pollit, the music by T. Rawson, 1884."

The last of these is being presented as I write,
an operetta, styled " Pickwick," written by the
buoyant and versatile F. C. Burnand, with music
by Mr. Solomon.

In Mr. Burnand's writings there is often a
Dickens' tone, as in his " Happy Thoughts,"
where one situation at least is quite in the
master's style. I mean where the hero dreads
the effect of a boisterous friend's manners on a
prim and precise aunt, and is astonished to find
the new arrival's unceremonious proceedings regarded with favour and indulgence, while he
himself is dislodged.

Mr. Calverley might have put the questions,—
" Who was the Baker ? was he single or married ? did he marry ? with whom did he keep
company ? &c., the fact being that he was an
admirer of Mrs. Bardell's. Few Pickwickians

are likely to have noted this subtle allusion, from which " F.C.B." has extracted a story—much as the " third murderer " is speculated over by Shakespearian commentators.

And then the songs in " Pickwick,"—the " Ivy Green," the " Christmas Song." These have all been set and set again. The most popular was, of course, Henry Russell's, who voiced it at his entertainments with much energy. There were other settings, too, by Mrs. F. Dale, A. de Belcour, &c. Then Gabriel Grub was somehow transformed into a " Cantata seria Buffa " so lately as the year 1881, by George Fox. There was " A Song of the Pickwickians; or, Sam Weller's Adventures,"—all which reads wonderfully, and are amazing testimonies to the fruitfulness of the work.

XIII.

It is always an interesting question to settle, whether Dickens introduced a new individual style, that took the public by surprise, or whether he improved on what was in fashion. There were then in favour two kinds of story, one the " novel of fashionable life," utterly ridiculous in its descriptions of drawing-rooms, wardrobes, and exquisites, and of a sentimental cast: the other, a sort of rollicking, boisterous narration, in which Theodore Hook revelled. The latter descended to the middle classes and low life, taking the same view as Dickens, his descriptions being of the same kind, but with what a difference ! Hook could only see the vulgarities of this *couche sociale*, whether bodily or mental, but Dickens may be really said to have created a new style by supplying the refinements and graces of humanity to " low life," and making interesting what would otherwise be repulsive. There is, of course, no comparison for a moment between Hook's " pantomime rallies," in which the " fun " turns on practical jokes, such as the clown stealing legs of mutton, or the fall of a porter carrying crockery on his head.

The truth is, Hook presented only a series of tableaux of farcical, awkward accidents, blunders, &c., such as are seen in pantomimes, where the clown burns himself with a red-hot poker, or lies down at the door of a shop, so as to cause the tradesman to tumble over him.

As regards the likeness to older novelists, Mr. Whipple, the American critic, points out with much truth that "he revived the novel of practical life as it existed in the works of Fielding, Smollett and Goldsmith. Fielding delineates with more exquisite art, *standing more as the spectator of his personages*, and commenting on their actions *with an ironical humour and a seeming innocence of insight* laying bare their most unconscious scenes of action, and in every instance indicating that he understands them better than they understand themselves. Dickens' eye for the forms of things is as accurate as Fielding's ; but he does not probe so profoundly into the heart of what he sees, and he is more led away from the simplicity of truth by a tricky spirit of fantastic exaggeration."[1]

[1] Professor Minto has pointed out that, when a boy at Chatham Dickens devoured all Smollett's and Fielding's novels, with other

It is significant to find that almost all critics of established power and authority, pronounced strongly, " were dead against," as it is called, the new writer. They seemed to take him as belonging to " the irregular horse" of literature; he did not work according to the canons, and, exactly as in the case of the Bailiff scenes in Goldsmith comedy, his scenes were pronounced " low" and vulgar. A certain vivid power of depicting life was admitted; but this was owing to his flow of spirits. The *Edinburgh*, *Quarterly*, and *Westminster Review*'s, *Fraser's* and the *Law Magazine*, with others, took the same tone. In *Fraser* a bitter attack was made upon him, which may have been the work of Dr. Maginn or of a certain Mr. Coalpitts Child, who later published a pamphlet against the author and his story. Some allowance, however, must always be made for the hostile reception of what is novel, and the public has gradually to learn to admire. This has been the case in all reforms and novelties in literature, arts and sciences, with Wagner, Corot, Constable, Turner, Stephenson, and many more who have had to suffer from such grudging reception. As he grew into favour, the tone seemed that of Dr. John-

old novels in which humorous character is exhibited. This broad and racy school of fiction naturally influenced his taste.

son, who said of a writer growing popular, "I suppose, sir, *his* nonsense suited *their* nonsense."

A prophecy of a very "slashing" kind has been often, very unfairly, attributed to Mr. Croker, who has been ridiculed for an owl-like lack of sagacity, in saying of our author that "he has risen like a rocket and will come down like the stick." It is generally repeated that the reviewer had tried to extinguish the young author, just as he tried to demolish Lady Morgan, and so many others. The truth is that for Croker, it was really a favourable and appropriate notice; though fault was found: it is evident that he thought Dickens a young man of great talents. It is really the only review which deals successfully with Dickens' character as a writer; the comparison with Fielding, Smollett, and others, and the specimens furnished for comparison from Theodore Hook's novels, are interesting. It is only fair to give his "rocket" passage in full, which winds up the article, and it will be seen that the metaphor is used by way of serious warning :—" The fact is, Mr. Dickens writes too often and too fast; on the principle, we presume, of making hay while the sun shines, he seems to have accepted at once all the engagements offered to him, and the consequence is that, in too many instances, he has put forth in their crude, unfinished, undigested state, thoughts,

Q

feelings, observations, plans, which it required
time and study to mature or supply the allotted
number of pages with original matter of the most
commonplace description, or hints caught from
others, or diluted to make them pass for his own.
If he persist much longer in this course, it
requires no gift of prophecy to foretell his fate,
he has risen like a rocket, and he will come down
like the stick ; but let him give his capacity fair
play, and it is rich, vigorous, and versatile enough
to ensure him a high and enduring reputation."

Mr. Croker made one acute and far-reaching
criticism which no one else, as far as we know,
has given. He points out a certain distinction
between Fielding and other writers, and the
modern Dickens. " The former, when describing
' low ' company and habits, seemed to con-
descend, to take a superior air. They appear to
have apprehended that they would be assumed to
know this class too well. But Dickens moves as
easily and naturally amongst his favourite characters, and no more dreams of being accused of coarseness than a Wilson or Gainsborough would dream
of incurring such a penalty for placing a pig-
stye in a landscape. *This perfect good faith and
straightforwardness* on his part greatly enhances the
probability and effect of his delineations, and
there is moreover a healthy, manly, independent
spirit diffused over them positively refreshing."

Nothing could be more just or accurate than this, as all admirers of Dickens will admit, and his manly, cheery straightforwardness was as conspicuous in his dealings with his characters as it was in his dealings with real persons.

It is almost amusing to find a reviewer in the *Westminster* making an apology for preferring the new writer to the well-established favourite, Mr. Theodore Hook :—"While we acknowledge the pleasure which we have occasionally derived from Theodore Hook's writings, we cannot by any means place him on a level with ' Boz.' The latter stands to him in the relation of the writer of good comedy to one of broad farce. Even when they describe the same things, the style of ' Boz ' always presents a contrast of remarkable simplicity and truth to nature ; the humour is always less broad and more easy; there is an abundance of wit, of which the other gives no proof ; there is an absence of exaggeration, of coarseness, and of effort, and a constant indication of a kindly and refined feeling."

A writer in *Fraser* deals with our author's Preface unceremoniously enough :—" When he informs us that the same objection which the perusal of his pleasant scenes will draw forth have been made to the works of some of the greatest English novelists, we do not think he is aware of what the objections to *him* as a novelist are.

No critic objects to a series of adventures in which 'the scenes are ever changing, and the characters come and go like the men and women of the real world.' What the critical reader objects to is that whatever we may think of the ' *come-and-go* ' characters, the ' *standing* ' characters are not like men and women of the real world. Mr. Pickwick's first appearance is that of a vain old fool, gravely occupied in the serene investigation of frivolous trifles. His opening speech is in accordance with this worn-out opening burlesque." The critic then goes on to inveigh against the inconsistencies of the characters. Mr. Pickwick at the beginning is " *a mere ass* "(*!*)—" in the hand of Boz he commences as a bore—the same idiotic lump of blockheadedness, and yet ends as a sort of hero. Nothing can show more dignity and propriety than his speech to Mr. Nupkins, but this is not the Mr. Pickwick of tittlebat fame, who is rolled in a wheelbarrow into a pound, or who makes speeches out of the top of a sedan, or who is hailed by ironical epithets of 'that immortal man,' 'that heroic-moulded man,' and so forth ; but a gentleman who acts with decision, and speaks with sense, and after figuring with pathos at the Dulwich wedding, his countenance lighted up with smiles which no man or woman could resist."

"Is this the Mr. Pickwick," the critic asks,

" of the fight with the cabman, the hunt after the hat, the drive to Dingley Dell, the breakdown in the chaise of Jingle, the tender scene with his landlady, the hiding in the boarding school garden, the double-bedded room with the middle-aged lady, the court of Queen's Bench ? We rayther think not."

" The Pickwickians," he adds, " are not furnished with a single gentlemanlike accomplishment, or possessed of a single gentlemanlike feeling. As for honour, of pathos or common sense, it must be wholly out of the question."

This coarse strain of vituperation, it will be seen, is based on the old objection of the scenes and characters being "low." The bear should dance only to the genteelest of tunes.

One of the best, almost contemporaneous accounts, more valuable because reflecting the early impressions before familiarity had supervened, was in the *Dublin Review*. After saying that the success was more astonishing, because there was no regular story, " all the ordinary sources of interest are disregarded, there was little love, and less sentiment. Most of the characters are every-day people, saying and doing every-day things. Through the whole there was a distinct and clearly distinguishable personality. There is no mixing up of qualities, no repetition, as in Byron, of the same character in a new form.

He possesses the rare faculty of entering, even in the most minute and trifling details, into the feelings and pursuits of the various personages he portrays. *His personages never forget themselves.* It would be impossible, for instance, to confound the attorney's clerk and the city shopman, nearly as they might seem allied."

The writer in the *Edinburgh* gives this rather mixed judgment on the Pickwick characters :—

"Pickwick's companions, Winkle, Snodgrass, and Tupman, are very uninteresting personages, having peculiarities rather than characters, useless incumbrances which the author seems to have admitted hastily among his *dramatis personæ* without well knowing what to do with them. The swindler Jingle and his companion want reality : the young ladies are nonentities : the blustering Dowler and the M.C. at Bath are mere caricatures. The medical students are coarsely and disagreeably drawn."

This sort of free, severe criticism seems to us now almost profane. It is true enough that on rigid analysis, Mr. Pickwick's followers will be found to be selfish, cowardly and ridiculous persons : but, in defiance of all laws and customs of fiction, they excite interest, sympathy and amusement ; one of the most astonishing feats of the author.

"Wardle, though a tolerably good country

squire, is hardly a modern one; and it may be doubted if Mr. Weller, senior, can be accepted as the representative of anything more recent than the last generation of stage coachmen."

On the other hand, Mr. Pickwick is pronounced to be "a most amiable and eccentric combination of irritability, benevolence, simplicity, shrewdness, folly and good sense, *frequently ridiculous but never contemptible*." How nicely accurate is this distinction! "Weller is a character which we do not remember to have seen attempted before." "His legal characters also are touched, though slightly, yet all with spirit and a strong appearance of truth."

"Ludicrous circumstances are those which he touches most happily, such as the equestrian distress of Pickwick and his companions in pursuit of Jingle, and Pickwick's night adventures. Incidents richly comic and worthy of Smollett, and which are narrated with Smollett's spirit, without his coarseness."

XIV.

" PICKWICK," as was before pointed out, apart from its humour, is interesting as a picture of manners and social habits which have insensibly altered, and a regular commentary on the work, pointing out these changes, would be interesting. It will have been noticed that personal chastisement on the spot, even in the case of friends and acquaintances, suggested itself frequently as a satisfaction for grievance or offence. Mr. Pickwick, as we have seen, was often ready to resort to this prompt mode of vindicating himself, and other personages of the story were with difficulty restrained from pursuing the same method. We have already noted the tendency to duelling which recurs through the story. Mr. Winkle, timorous as he was, "went out" with Dr. Slammer, and was prepared to "go out" with Mr. Dowler. Mr. Pickwick was ready to meet Mr. Magnus. The scorbutic youth threatened to send a friend to a fellow medical student; Mr. Slumkey challenged Mr. Fizkin on the hustings; and Mr Sawyer wished to call out his rival. This shows how familiar then was this mode of settling differences in society. Mr. Winkle's appearance in the field did credit to his courage, and is rather inconsistent with his later behaviour: and the author is driven to account for it by a fanciful theory that the seconds often omitted to put bullets in the pistols.

Frequenting taverns, too, was an odd element in social life, and it would now seem strange to find a gentleman in Mr. Pickwick's position repairing to a sort of pot-house, like the "Magpie and Stump," and sitting down with the *habitués* of the place. No legal practitioner would now drink with his clients, in the style Mr. Pell was accustomed to do: and the mode of doing business adopted by Mr. Wilkins Flasher, who was betting with his friends, killing flies with a ruler, while the clients were waiting to sell their stock, would now seem extraordinary indeed.

Another remarkable change often noted in our time, has been the alteration in the standard of age. A young lady's "dear old thing" of fifty years ago, is now considered to be rather a "youngish" man. Mr. Pickwick was looked upon then as we would now look upon a hale and vigorous old person of seventy years old. Spectacles and gaiters were then the regular accompaniments of age. Yet his real age could have been no more than forty-five or fifty at the most. He tells us that he had not slided for thirty

years, and that he used to do so on the gutters
when a boy. In the same way Wardle is
described as " a stout old gentleman," apparently
between sixty and seventy. But, as Perker told
Jingle, Mrs. Wardle, " old " Wardle's mother,
was but seventy-two, which would make her son
at the most no more than fifty-three or four.   His
sister, the spinster aunt, was fifty according to
his statement, quite " a young thing," of our time.
At the Bath assembly we find the young ladies
dutifully coming to their mammas, engaged at
the card-table, to ask their approbation in the
choice of partners.[1]

It may be said that the choice of names in a story
is an *instinct*, and more depends on a well-chosen
name than would be supposed. An ill-named
character checks the author all through the story.
The old system of names expressing the nature of
the character, such as Lady Sneerwell, and Sir
Pertinax Macsycophant, has happily passed away,
as being artificial and unnatural.   Dickens very

---

[1] This the Miss Wugsby's did. Wugsby was a good name
for a colonel's lady, "Mrs. Colonel Wugsby," and nothing
could be better than "Miss Bolo" for a card-playing spinster,
Lady Snuphanuph—that is Lady Snuff-enough, was a little
far-fetched, as are one or two other names in the book ; such
as the "Slummintowkens,"—but in all the rest there is an
almost perfect appropriateness, particularly in the case of the
minor characters—such as Smangle, Roker, Pell, and "Mr.
Watty," the baffled insolvent who called on Perker so often.

seldom adopted it, though in his later works he is
fond of choosing, or compounding grotesque
names, betokening quaintness or oddity, and not
to be found in real life. But as we said, all the
Pickwickian names are good, with just a faint
suggestion of farce. This appropriateness is not
confined to the names merely. The reality of
the story is further emphasized by the strange
harmony of the places described with the scenes
and characters. Sir Walter Scott and others
used to usher in a chapter with a formal,
elaborate description of a landscape, castle, or
town, and the narrative was suspended while the
author thus exerted his imagination. But in
Pickwick this is done in the most natural way : the
place seems to grow about us; the characters, as it
were, describe it to us.

The smallest touch in the description of Bath
manners brings a whole scene before us. As when
Mr. Tuckle speaks of his bath chair :—

"Well, they tell me I am looking pretty
blooming," said the man with the cocked hat,
"and it's a wonder too. I've been following our
old woman about, two hours a day, for the last
fortnight; and if a constant contemplation of the
manner in which she hooks-and-eyes that infernal
lavender-coloured old gown of hers behind, isn't
enough to throw anybody into a low state of
despondency for life, stop my quarter's salary."

This brings before us the procession of chairs
—the old lady sitting up stiff and stately, and
thus displaying the hooks and eyes of "the infernal old lavender gown "—the wearing of the
same dress—the gorgeous, bright crimson livery
and cocked hat of the menial who was propelling
the chair for two hours daily. How quaint the
glimpse of the " valet mind," and how natural too,
he being likely to resent the monotony of that
hook-and-eye display.

In no way was the skill of the writer better
displayed than in surmounting the difficulty of
the extraordinary, anomalous authority assumed
by Mr. Pickwick over his companions. This was
akin to that of a schoolmaster over his pupils.
Winkle, indeed, who was of mature age, considered
Mr. Pickwick " as in some degree his guardian and
adviser," and Mr. Winkle, sen., reproached Mr.
Pickwick with not having looked after him pro-
perly. Tupman was an elderly bachelor, of nearly
the same age as his chief. Snodgrass appears to
have been about as old as his friend Winkle. Yet
Mr. Pickwick's direction was of the most arbitrary
kind; he spoke of the party as *" my followers "*
—he directed Sam to pursue Winkle—to lock him
up, and "knock him down " if he resisted. Mr.
Tupman, when about to assume the bandit's dress,
he overwhelmed with reproaches and ridicule on
the ground of an insult to his dignity, from his

appearing " in *my presence* in a two-inch tail." The only ground for this despotism was a commission from the club; but Mr. Pickwick was the club, and had virtually " commissioned " himself. Yet such is the art of our author, that these " doubts " do not occur to us for a moment. It seems the most natural thing in the world. We never question Mr. Pickwick's authority. The reality is such, that we accept it as the legitimate influence of a superior mind. The " Head of the party," as he is called, is quite in his place, ruling the trio that were under his command.

It has been often repeated that the humour of " Pickwick " is of a rough and boisterous kind throughout, which contrasts with the more refined style the author adopted later. However this may be, the book is stored with delicate strokes and shadings, which are likely to escape the reader in the general hilarity. Take, for instance, the deportment of Mrs. Rogers, that well named, dignified lodger, who had taken Mr. Pickwick's rooms.

" ' Why, Mrs. Rogers, ma'am,' said Mrs. Bardell, ' you've never been introduced, I declare! Mr. Raddle, ma'am; Mrs. Cluppins, ma'am ; Mrs. Raddle, ma'am.'

—" ' Which is Mrs. Cluppins's sister,' suggested Mrs. Sanders.

"'Oh, indeed!'" *said Mrs. Rogers, graciously;* for she was the lodger, and her servant was in waiting, so she was more gracious than intimate, in right of her position. 'Oh, indeed!'"

This "Oh, indeed!" is significant and appropriate, betokening a polite reserve and generality. Every succeeding remark of "Mrs. Rogers" is in the same spirit.

What *finesse* and originality, too, in Mr. Weller's remark on a suspicion of his son's going to be married, "to see you a dilluded wictim, *and thinkin' in your innocence that it's all wery capital.*"

Stiggins on the "moral pocket handkerchiefs"—happy term!—is admirable.

"'What's a moral pocket ankercher?' said Sam; 'I never see one o' them articles o' furniter.'

"'Those which combine amusement with instruction, my young friend,' replied Mr. Stiggins: *'blending select tales with woodcuts.'*"

This light touch may be compared with his later treatment of the same topic in "Bleak House," which is more elaborate and laboured, and, it must be said, not so effective. Others of these slighter strokes are mirthful to a degree, if not witty; such as the description of Jingle's licence: "having procured a highly flattering address from the Archbishop of Canterbury to his trusty and well beloved Alfred Jingle and Rachael Wardle, greeting." So with the description of Mr. Solomon Lucas' fancy dress warehouse—a capital name, by the way, for a Jew *costumier :—*

" His wardrobe was extensive—very extensive —not strictly classical perhaps, or quite new, nor did it contain *any one garment made precisely after the fashion of any age or time,*"—where note the ironical force of the word " precisely." Again :

" ' Well, if you come to that,' said Mr. Winkle, ' how dare you call me a serpent ? '

" ' Because you are one,' replied Mr. Potts.

" ' *Prove it, sir,*' said Mr. Winkle, warmly, ' prove it.' "

It is impossible not to laugh at this natural, but absurd challenge.

We should note, too, the *variety* of the forms of humour offered ; and the gay originality and sportiveness of his devices. Contrast with the invitation to "prove" that you are a serpent, the following happy stroke which touches another note altogether. When Mr. Tupman was about making his declaration to the spinster aunt in the arbour, in her agitation she " took up *a large watering pot* which lay in one corner, and was about to leave the place." There is something grotesquely funny, and yet natural, in this simple act. But with what unenforced humour the author heightens the absurdity ! She trembled, we are told, " till some pebbles which had accidentally found their way into the large watering pot, *shook like an infant's rattle.*"

The sly appropriateness of this metaphor to the spinster aunt, adds not a little to the drollery. Smollett could not have put it better, though not so delicately.

One of the slightest but most perfect sketches is that of Martin, the "long game-keeper." His description exactly fits with his utterances ; his appearance, actions and remarks are all in keeping. Given the notions of an ignorant sportsman, and the good-humoured contempt with which such are regarded by game-keepers, nothing could be better than the dialogue, which gives the quintessence of the whole situation.

"'I'll tell you what I shall do, to get up my shooting again,' said Mr. Winkle, *who was eating bread and ham with a pocket-knife.* 'I'll put a stuffed partridge on the top of a post, and practise at it, beginning at a short distance, and lengthening it by degrees. I understand it's capital practice.'"

This cutting slices of bread and ham with a pocket-knife somehow seems appropriate to a vain and complacent state of mind, and the words "get up my shooting again" are delightfully absurd.

Lisping characters of foolish exquisites have been often attempted in fiction; but their lisp soon becomes tedious. We have Sleary or "Thleary" in "Hard Times;" but there is nothing for a short sketch to be found anywhere so good as Lord Mutanhed at Bath. The art of our author is shown in presenting him with a sort of toad-eater, the Hon. Mr. Crushton, who extracts, as it were, his peculiarities; as when he asks, "had they seen his lordship's new mail cart."

" 'Gwacious heavens!' said his lordship, 'I thought evewebody had seen the new mail cart; it's the neatest, pwettiest, gwacefullest thing that ever wan upon wheels. Painted wed, with a cweam piebald.'

" 'With a real box for the letters, and all complete,' said the Honourable Mr. Crushton.

" '*And a little seat in fwont, with an iwon wail, for the dwiver,*' added his lordship. 'I dwove it over to Bwistol the other morning, in a cwimson coat, with two servants widing a quarter of a mile behind; and confound me if the people didn't wush out of their cottages, and awwest my pwogwess, to know if I wasn't the post. *Glorwious! Glorwious!*"

This sketch is almost perfect, for it shows the lisp to be a note of a mind that also lisps. The best stroke is the enthusiastic mention of the "little seat in fwont, with an iwon wail, for the dwiver," as though that were a novelty, and also the delightful and appropriate burst, " *Glorwious, Glorwious !* "

A touch worthy of one of the best old comedies is the scene in which Winkle relates the incidents of Pott's jealousy, which roused Mr. Pickwick's anger.

" ' Is it not a wonderful circumstance,' said Mr. Pickwick, ' that we seem destined to enter no man's house without involving him in some degree of trouble ? Does it not, I ask, bespeak the indiscretion, or, worse than that, the blackness of heart—that I should say so !—of my followers, that, beneath whatever roof they locate, they disturb the peace of mind and happiness of some confiding female ? Is it not, I say—''

At which moment Sam brings in Dodson and Fogg's notice of Mrs. Bardell's action, and Mr. Winkle " murmurs with an air of abstraction, ' Peace of mind and happiness of confiding females.' "

Another of the attractions of the book is the unexpectedness of the strokes, the sort of extreme surprise from contrast, which is the foundation of all wit. Thus when Mr. Pickwick fell into the water, we are told that " Mr.

Snodgrass and Mr. Winkle grasped each other by the hand, and gazed at the spot where their leader had gone down, while Mr. Tupman, by way of rendering the promptest assistance, and at the same time conveying to any persons who might be within hearing, the clearest possible notion of the catastrophe, ran off across the country at his utmost speed, screaming ' Fire ! '' with all his might.''

This " conceit " is as diverting as it is un-expected. The " shepherd " is described as always bringing to the Marquis of Granby " a flat bottle as holds about a pint and a half,'' which he filled regularly before going away. " And empties it before he comes back, I s'pose ? '' said Sam.

"Clean,'' replied Mr. Weller, "never leaves nothing in it but the cork and the smell, trust him for that, Samuel.''

Quaint and humorous as this figure is, how appropriate it is to the speaker, as is also Sam's happy phrase, " I'd give him somethin' as 'ud turpentine and beesvax his memory for the next ten years or so.'' Here is another short sketch. " The secretary was Mr. Josiah Mudge, chandler's shopkeeper, an enthusias-tic and disinterested vessel, who sold tea to the members.'' How farcical too, Bob Sawyer's preparation of the jorum of punch, where, how-ever, the farce is legitimate, as it arises out of the

deficiency in the household appliances. " Ordering in the largest mortar in the shop; stirring
up and amalgamating the materials in a very
creditable and apothecary-like manner."

The one tumbler was assigned to Mr. Winkle,
and how comic the picture that follows :—" Mr.
Ben Allen being accommodated with a funnel
with a cork in the narrow end, and Bob Sawyer
contenting himself with one of the wide-lipped
crystal vessels inscribed with a variety of ca-
balistic characters." When Sam knocked off
the sheriff's officer's hat, how fitting his protest, " Observe this, Mr. Pickwick, I have been
assaulted in the execution of my dooty by your
servant. *I'm in bodily fear.*" There is surely
wit in this importation of legal jargon as part of
ordinary conversation. So with the art of suggesting a whole character in a sentence, and at the
same time in the most humorous way. " In
proof of Bob Sawyer's being one of the funniest
fellows alive, he proceeded to give Mr. Pickwick
a long and circumstantial account how that gentleman once drank himself into a fever and got his
head shaved." Here there is the other inconse-
quence between the " fun " and the fever, with
the suggestion of what is the consequence of such
" fun " in past life. Pell's description of Mrs.
Pell: " Mrs. Pell was a tall figure, a splendid
woman, with a noble shape, and a nose, gentle-

men, formed to command, and be majestic.   She
was very much attached to me—highly connected
too—*her mother's brother, gentlemen, failed for
eight hundred pound, as a Law Stationer.*" About
this last touch there is a genuineness in the form
and phrase, the amount, and calling of the
bankrupt which supplies entire verisimilitude.
It is not a comic flight of the author's, but we
listen to Mr. Pell himself, who quite believes that
it is a real illustration of Mrs. Pell's gentility.

In short, taking all these varieties of humour,
where the simplest fact is made either to suggest
a trait of character or a humorous image, or to
help the story on in some way, or merely
inspire gaiety or a passing smile, we may say
there is no other work whose mechanism and
humour is so incessantly brilliant without
fatiguing.   We have not space to give examples,
but it could be shown that whereas most
humorists have but one method and process,
the "inimitable" has a score at command,
now touching broad farce, now humour, now wit,
now a "conceit," now images or metaphors.   And
this was a young man of three-and-twenty !

There are some allusions in "Pickwick" which
would escape the ordinary reader, which are associated with certain painful memories of Dickens's
childhood.   We find Mr. Weller, sen., declaring that
"no man ever talked poetry 'cept a beadle on

Boxin' day," an odd presentation of what was
then a familiar figure, and adding, " or Warren's
blackin.' " No one, alas! knew so much of
" Warren's blackin' " as the poor lad who spent
his weary days in pasting on the labels at No. 30
Hungerford Stairs, Strand. What torture he
suffered here, he said later, "was beyond his
powers to tell." In many of his works he introduces this topic of " advertising verses," as
though he liked to remind himself of having
escaped from such horrors. It has been noted
that he recurs to this topic in other of his stories,
as though it had a sort of fascination for him.

There is another significant allusion in Mr.
Roker's reminiscence of Tom Martin, the butcher
(there are three characters in the story named
Martin, the " long gamekeeper," the " surly man,"
and this butcher), and the passage is exquisitely
humorous, as an illustration of grotesque sentimentality :—

" ' Bless my dear eyes ! ' said Mr. Roker, shaking
his head slowly from side to side, and gazing
abstractedly out of the grated windows before him,
*as if he were fondly recalling some peaceful scene of
his early youth;* 'it seems but yesterday that he
whopped the coal-heaver down Fox-under-the-
Hill by the wharf there. I think I can see him
now, a-coming up the Strand between the two
street-keepers, a little sobered by the bruising

with a patch o' winegar and brown paper over his right eyelid, and that 'ere lovely bulldog, as pinned the little boy arterwards, a-following at his heels. *What a rum thing Time is, ain't it, Neddy?*' "

We may here note the term " street-keepers." This " Fox-under-the-Hill " was a tavern in the disorderly quarter just below the Adelphi Terrace, where the child Dickens was often glad to obtain a welcome glass of ale.

Another house well known to Dickens was the old White Horse Cellar, to this hour a great coaching centre.

Up to a few years ago the White Horse Cellar was familiar to every Londoner, and remained in almost exactly the state it was in Dickens's time. The white horse was over the door, and the whole presented an antique, rather dilapidated aspect. Within the last few years it was taken down, and a new, rather " palatial " (as it is called) edifice erected in its stead, where persons of high fashion resort for dinners *en partie fine*. Thus all our cherished Dickens memorials are departing one by one.

When Mr. Pickwick was so seriously providing for Jingle, Perker took a rather dubious view of the chances of his reforming.

" ' However,' he added, ' your object is equally honourable, whatever the result is. Whether that species of benevolence which is so very cautious and long-sighted that it is seldom exercised at all, lest its owner should be imposed upon, and so wounded in his self-love, be real charity or a worldly counterfeit, I leave to wiser heads than mine to determine.' "

This wise remark embodied a favourite doctrine of Dickens's, and which in one of his letters he truly urged should be the basis of real charity.

At this wedding scene there are some curious reminders of exploded customs, such as "taking wine" and "taking in" other persons, and the custom that still prevailed, of the "happy pair" remaining with their family. I have a strong suspicion that "Emma," one of "the girls" at Manor Farm, was originally designed for Sam; for the author introduces her on several occasions with an undue emphasis. Mr. Tupman had shown his admiration for Emma, and Emma admired Sam. Mary, however, is a much nicer girl, and we could not spare her, for she belongs to the Pickwickian party.

Smart, good-humoured girls of this pattern Dickens described with particular skill, and in this book we find quite a variety of the character. Such was the barmaid who treated Mr. Namby so contemptuously; Tom Smart's innkeeper, "a very plump and conformable person," and Emma and Mary aforesaid.

XV.

No one, as we learn from Dickens's "life," lived
so entirely in the company of his characters,
while he was writing their history and progress:
and to this faith in their reality much of the
inspiration and variety is owing. In fiction, as
in real life, character produces situations more
frequently than a situation will produce character ; but a skilled novelist will work in both ways.
Thus Dickens, pondering over, living and
travelling with his Pickwickians, saw what
situations could be engendered by their many-
sided dispositions ; and though quaint and original
situations would have been suggested to him,
independently of his characters, these were really
developed and moulded by the characters.
Stories and incidents are, of course, essential for
the true development of character, and "bring
out," as it is called, the various turns of humorous
idiosyncrasy. A good illustration of this distinction will be found in that masterly creation of
Macklin's, "The Man of the World," where a
single character, Sir Pertinax Macsycophant,
with its varied exhibitions, contains, as it were,

the whole story. The meanness, greed, un-
scrupulous wickedness, are necessary develop-
ments, and these qualities in themselves form a
story. In the same way the Pickwickian characters give rise in the most natural way to the
adventures in which they are concerned, and the
author found it impossible to dwell upon their
qualities, apart from some exhibition of them in
droll or humorous situations.

But the mere display of character, however,
divorced from the stimulant of action, generally
checks its development. It ceases to have
vitality, and becomes an anatomical study. This
can be illustrated in a very curious way by
an attempt which our gifted author later made
to revive his Pickwickian group. When "Master
Humphrey's Clock" first appeared, his idea was
to issue a sort of miscellany in weekly numbers,
at three half-pence each, and which was to contain
a number of short stories, by himself and others.
These were supposed to be found in the old clock,
and the model before him was clearly something
of the kind adopted by Washington Irving in the
Sketch Book and other works. After a few
numbers the plan was not found very attractive,
and when Gog and Magog and other narrators,
had told their stories, it occurred to him to
re-introduce Mr. Pickwick and the two Wellers.
Our old friend was invited to join the club of

story-tellers, and presently with much hesitation contributed his little narrative. This " Sequel to Pickwick," for such it was, was continued for some numbers, and was eventually found unsatisfactory, owing to the reasons given above, viz. that there was no story to kindle the writer's imagination, or to develop the characters. They had simply to talk. There is a great deal of conversation of a humorous cast between the Wellers, father and son, and a precocious child, Sam's son. There is an old housekeeper, to whom Mr. Weller is paying his addresses ; and evidently the author intended that, in the course of events, the retired coachman should venture on a third marriage with this lady. Fortunately the author had started his beautiful story of " The Old Curiosity Shop," which became so attractive to himself and to his readers, that he abruptly cut short the Pickwickian narrative, and left Mr. Weller senior in the midst of his courtship, the issue of which was never known.

He, however, supplied Sam with some stories in the old vein, but which, being introduced without much *apropos*, seem to lack the old spontaneousness. The author's heart was evidently not in the work, and his pen travelled languidly. These stories seem to exhibit the author's personality and humorous mode of looking at things rather than Sam's. They are introduced by a conversation between the father and son about a local barber, one Slitters, which it is curious to contrast with the old vivacious dialogue of " Pickwick."

Sam on offering to relate a story about a barber, in presence of Mr. Slitters, his father interrupted him, " Samivel, address your obserwations to the cheer, sir, and not to priwate individuals."   " An' if I might rise to order," said the barber in a soft voice, " I would suggest that barber is not exactly the kind of language which is agreeable and soothing to our feelings. You, sir, will correct me, if I am wrong, but I believe there is such a word in the dictionary as hairdresser."

" Well, but suppose he wasn't a hairdresser," said Sam. " Wy then, sir, be parliamentary and call him vun all the more. In the same vay as every genelman in another place is a *h*onorable, ev'ry barber in this place is a hairdresser. Ven you read the speeches in the papers and see as vun gen'lman says of another, ' the *h*onorable member, if he vill allow me to call him so,' so yer vill understand, sir, that that means, if he vil͏̈ allow me to keep up that 'ere pleasant and uniwersal fiction."

Now this is hardly recognizable as Mr. Weller's utterances; as we said, it is the author speaking in his own person. Sam's two stories are about barbers—one, named Jinkinson, an enthusiast

on the subject of his Bears and Bear's Grease, a
toilet article long since fallen out of fashion.
The barber, it seems, had " spent all his money in
bears, and run in debt for 'em besides, and there
they wos a growlin' avay down in the front
celler all day long and ineffectooally gnashin'
their teeth, vile the grease o' their relations and
friends wos being retailed in gallipots in the shop
above, and the first-floor window wos ornamented
with their heads, not to speak o' the dreadful
aggrawation it must have been to 'em to see a
man always a-walkin' up and down the pavement
outside, vith the portrait o' a bear in his last
agonies, and underneath in large letters ' Another
fine animal wos slaughtered yesterday at Jinkinson's.' "

When the " Old Curiosity Shop " was brought
to a close, our author again could not resist his
old penchant for some " machinery " or other for
introducing the next story. Accordingly Master
Humphrey has to find his way to St. Paul's, and
there lights on the MS. of " Barnaby Rudge "
up in one of the towers. This he proceeds to
read to the club. " Jack informed us softly that
Mr. Weller's Watch had adjourned its sittings
from the kitchen, and regularly met outside our
door," so they were invited to walk in and hear
the narrative under more comfortable conditions.
Old Pickwickians must have been surprised to

find their favourites, the coachman and his vivacious son, thus engaged. What Mr. Weller senior could have thought of his John Chester and the other humours of the piece can hardly be imagined. The idea of the pair even listening to so long a story, the reading of which must have taken months, is inconceivable.

The amiable and energetic author, always thorough in his literary work, held valiantly on to his favourite " framework " to the very last. When " Barnaby Rudge " was concluded, Master Humphrey dies, and Mr. Pickwick is again introduced to become his executor. Mr. Weller senior pronounces a sort of funeral eulogium over him : "And the sweet old creetur', sir, has bolted! Him as had no wice and was so free from temper that a infant might ha' drove him, has been took at last with that 'ere unawoidable fit o' staggers as we must all come to! Gone off his feed for ever. I says to Samivel, ' My boy, the grey's a goin' at the knees;' and now my predilection's fatally werified ; him I could never do enough to serve, or show my liking for, is up the great universal spout o' natur'." This, as was said, is more in Mrs. Gamp's vein than in Mr. Weller's. Winding up the whole, the author then tells us that the barber and the housekeeper are likely to make a match of it. For old Weller " had conjured his son,

with tears in his eyes, that in the event of his
ever becoming amorous again, he will put him in
a straight waistcoat until the fit is passed.   Such
was this resuscitation and disappearance of Mr.
Pickwick and his friends.   In due time, as we have
seen, the author felt they were but incumbrances,
and discarded the whole, just as he had discarded
the machinery of the Pickwick Club itself.

We can trace in the early " Sketches by Boz,"
many little hints, and characters to, which he
returned in " Pickwick," and worked into important figures.   Thus, in " The Tuggs' at Ramsgate " we find in Captain and Mrs. Captain Waters
an anticipation of Dowler and his ferocity, with
his captivating wife, while " Cymon " Tuggs,
like Winkle, is the object of the Captain's ven-
geance.   The hurried concealment of Cymon
behind the curtain and his discovery suggests Mr.
Snodgrass' detection at Osborne's Hotel in the
Adelphi.   Jones, in " Mr. Minns and his Cousin,"
has a story about Sheridan which he never can
succeed in introducing, like the guest at Bob
Sawyer's party.   Mr. Budden's speech, too, is
helped out—" with every feeling—every sentiment of—of" "gratification," suggested the friend
of the family, just as Jingle helps out the speech-
maker at the cricket match.   In " Sentiment"
there is a dancing party that, with the arrival of

the writing master and his wife, anticipates the doctor at the Rochester ball. "Horatio Sparkins," turns upon the same point as the incident of Jingle's imposition on the Nupkins'. In " Mr. Watkins Tottle" we have a minutely described account of a sponging house, where some of the characters are almost the same as those in " Pickwick." " Well, Mr. Willis," continued the facetious prisoner, addressing the young man with the cigar, " you seem rather down to-day. Never say die, you know." " Oh, I'm all right," replied the smoker, " I shall be bailed out to-morrow." Readers will recall the young man, in " Pickwick," who was under the same delusion, that he was to be " bailed out to-morrow." " The Christmas Dinner " is in the same key as the Christmas at Dingley Dell: there is the sketch of the old stiff grandmamma and the " poor relations:" and the old lady softens and relents just as old Mrs. Wardle does to her granddaughter. To these may be added the sketch of the cab-driver, who, on being tendered eighteenpeuce, assaults his fare, on the principle of having the worth of his money " out of him," even if he got six months for it. These, however, are all the merest indications and outlines: indeed, nothing is more remarkable than the contrast between these rather crude touchings and the firm, bold, and satisfactory delineations found in " Pickwick."

The author here found himself in the heart of his story, surrounded by figures that lived and moved, every movement suggesting some touch of character. Mere detached or separate sketches cannot supply this inspiration.

The frontispiece offers proof of the author's art and power of suggestion. As we know, it exhibits Mr. Pickwick seated, in his retirement at Dulwich, the faithful Sam beside him reading aloud. His old master listens with a placid benevolence. On the wall overhead is a picture of an old lady in spectacles, probably of the owner's mother. On the top of the cabinet are some helmets, and other objects of antiquarian interest. The curtains are drawn aside, to give us a view of this interesting interior ; while below there are two vignettes of Snodgrass and Winkle— the former humorously crowned with a wreath of bays, in allusion to his poetical tastes. Now the art of this scene, as we said, is in its suggestive power. The author had wound up his narrative ; yet he here contrived to project us forward, into the future, and furnish us with a happy picture of the retired life of his amiable hero : which is shown as being of a pensive, serious cast, contrasting with the humours that have gone before, and suitable to the evening of worthy Mr. Pickwick's life. We never look at this sketch without some feelings of

s

this kind : and the story seems to commence afresh.[1]

[1] A significant circumstance is connected with the title of this work. Familiar as it is, it is not every reader who can give it in its proper shape. Most commonly the book is spoken of as "The Pickwick Papers," often as " The Pickwick Club:" but the most familiar and best known shape is " Pickwick " simply. The true original form, however, is " The Posthumous Papers of the Pickwick Club,—Being a faithful Record of the Perambulations, Perils, Travels, Adventures and Sporting Transactions of the Corresponding Members." This rather laboured title the author discarded in his first complete edition, that of 1858, and it has since always stood as " The Posthumous Papers of the Pickwick Club." " Pickwick " pure and simple is the common and most acceptable form, a convenient generality which covers the adventures of all concerned—including Mr. Pickwick himself: as though it meant " the Pickwickiad." This change shows the hold the Book has on the affections of the public. In nearly all cases it is satisfied to accept the author's title as he gave it : and none of Scott's or Thackeray's have been in the least changed for popular use.

XVI.

THE Pickwick "mania," as some might call it — we might rather say the Pickwickian "*Fanteeg*," or extravagant appreciation—has reached an extreme point within the last two years. In 1889, a sale has taken place at Messrs. Sotheby's, the well-known auctioneers, when two trifling Pickwickian "lots" were "submitted to public competition." The first of these consisted of six sketches by the ill-fated Seymour, with two or three of his etchings, and the original of the author's letter to the artist, already quoted in this volume. The lot was described as "loosely arranged in five or six pages of a scrap book, and the entire could be comfortably stowed away in the waistcoat pocket." Seymour's drawings, as we have shown, are graceful and artistic : but their market value, as drawings, could not exceed a few pounds. A letter of Dickens ought to be procurable for a couple of pounds. The reader will be astonished to hear of what followed. Ten pounds was first offered : Mr. Quaritch and Mr. Stevens, the American Book-

seller, then began to compete : and the figure of
one hundred pounds was speedily reached.   It will
hardly be credited, that, at last, the coveted
little batch was secured by Mr. Quaritch
—acting, it is said, for a purchaser in
Paris—for the enormous sum of FIVE HUNDRED
POUNDS ! [1]   We hear of this with amazement, and

[1] The unpretending "lot" is thus described in the
catalogue :—

" This collection contains the *original* drawing for the first
illustration in Pickwick, representing that gentleman
'ADDRESSING THE CLUB,' which may be considered the
creation of that famous figure in fiction.   Also the original
drawings of 'THE PUGNACIOUS CABMAN,' 'DR. SLAMMER'S
DEFIANCE OF JINGLE," and 'THE DYING CLOWN.'   There are
besides, two drawings that were not published, one representing the incident of 'THE RUNAWAY CHAISE' and the other
'THE PICKWICKIANS IN MR. WARDLE'S KITCHEN.'   All these
drawings are beautifully finished in sepia with the exception
of the 'DYING CLOWN,' which is evidently the *first* sketch of
the subject.   That of 'DR. SLAMMER'S DEFIANCE' shows an
alteration in the attitude of the arm made at the suggestion of
Dickens."

With it was another Pickwickian relic, which brought 64*l.*:—

" Account of the origin of the Pickwick Papers, by Mrs.
Seymour, widow of the distinguished artist, who originated the
work, with Mr. Dickens' Version, and her reply thereto,
showing the fallacy of his statements ; also letters of her
husband's and other distinguished men, VERY SCARCE, *having
been suppressed, beautifully clean copy, in the original state
printed for the author, n. d.*

" This copy contains manuscript corrections by Mrs. Seymour,
a visiting card of her husband, and a note signed by R. Seymour jun.: 'this is the only copy remaining in the possession
of myself the only remaining member of the family.'   The
Mackenzie copy of this pamphlet realized 72*l.*"

even bewilderment : but accept the explanation, which is that this enormous price was owing to interest, not in Seymour, or his drawings—not even in the gifted author himself, but solely and exclusively to the mysterious fascination of his story. Nothing could better justify the elaborate investigation we have been making in these pages into the secret of the charm which " Pickwick " exercises on the world.

It is astonishing, indeed, to see how the almost fantastic rage for " Pickwick " memorials goes on steadily increasing; and fresh evidences of this greedy interest display themselves every day. We take up an illustrated newspaper, and on a full page is exhibited the scene of Mr. Pickwick's discovery of the " Bill Stumps " inscription—the eager antiquarian being shown on his knees, tenderly wiping the stone in front of the Cobham cottage, his friends grouped about him : only the incised characters are made to refer to a well-known patent medicine. The passion is now for the original Pickwickian illustrations, drawings, &c. Later will come the turn of the engraved illustrations, which now but rarely come into the market.

We have mentioned the astonishing price realized in the June of last year, by a few Seymour drawings. But in the month of July, a large collection of drawings by " Phiz " was submitted to competition, and brought even more astonishing prices.

"The precarious fate of such memorials," says a writer in the *Daily News*, "may be assumed from the circumstance that when the artist had etched his designs on the plates, the originals were thrown into the fire, or given away incontinently to those of his friends who had the temerity to ask for them. The illustrations to Dickens have happily escaped this ordeal, and their whereabouts may be satisfactorily ascertained. The original designs by Seymour and Phiz for the 'Pickwick Papers' are in Paris, in the possession of Mr. W. Wright, who has also secured the 'Pickwick vignette,' and several of G. Cruikshank's designs for 'Sketches by Boz.' Mr. Stuart Samuel owns, among others, part of the "Boz" series, and these may at present be studied by the curious at their ease in the galleries of the Royal Institute of Painters in Water Colours, in the Humorists' Exhibition. Several of the sketches for 'Oliver Twist,' 'Nicholas Nickleby,' 'The Old Curiosity Shop,' 'The Christmas Carol,' and others may be there seen, together with the whole of the original drawings, as transferred to his plates by the artist, for three of Dickens's novels, 'David Copperfield,' 'Dombey and Son,' and 'Bleak House.' There also is the admirable series of water-colour drawings for 'Oliver Twist,' made somewhat late in life, by G. Cruikshank for his patron, the late Mr. F. W. Cosens, who also rejoices in a unique series of illustrations in watercolours executed by Hablot Knight Browne, under similar circumstances, to illustrate nearly all Dickens's works. Another interesting souvenir is the version by C. R. Leslie, R.A., painted for his friend the author, of 'Mr. Pickwick surprised by his friends with Mrs. Bardell in his arms.' This mere sketch was sold at the Dickens' sale for 131 guineas! Mrs. Cruikshank possibly treasures up the two designs made by her husband over half a century ago—his artistic contributions to the 'Pic-Nic Papers,' and the six designs executed by Phiz for the same work, as edited by Dickens, may come into the market at any unexpected moment.

"The sum received by Seymour for the completed drawings, including the plates etched by his hand, probably did not exceed six guineas apiece. H. K. Browne, through whose facile artistic interpretation generations of Dickens's admirers must realize the novelist's universally familiar characters, it is believed, was satisfied to work for no more extravagant remuneration; the sale of his original drawings, designed to illustrate 'Martin Chuzzlewit;' and the water-colour drawings for the 'Phiz vignettes,' followed the Seymour studies on the 9th of the present month.

A few of these sketches brought prices which
might have astonished the illustrator no less than
the author. The well-known and elaborate
frontispiece, 'Tom Pinch at the Organ,' was
carried off by Mr. Lever for 35*l.*; the buyer
secured a bargain in 'Mr. Pinch and Ruth,
unconscious of a visitor,' the famous 'beef-steak
pudding' episode, which was sold for the modest
figure of 11*l.* 10*s.* 'Mr. Pecksniff on his mission' (to the abode of Mrs. Gamp) reached 15*l.*
15*s.*; the 'Pleasant little family party at Mr.
Pecksniff's' brought 14*l.* 10*s.* The design
showing the monthly nurse, Mrs. Gamp, with her
'eye on the future,' illustrating the passage—
'Would you be so good, my darling dovey of a
dear young married lady . . . . it's my card,'
fell to Mr. Wright for 15*l.* 'Mrs. Gamp makes
Tea,' 'And quite a family it is to make tea for,'
said Mrs. Gamp, went for 18*l.* 18*s.* The most
spirited struggle was evoked over the famous gin-
and-tea-drinking symposium in Sairah's bed-
chamber, between Mrs. Gamp and that 'grace-
less renegade,' Betsy Prigg; 'Mrs. Gamp pro-
poses a Toast,' brought 35*l.* 10*s.*, being secured
by Mr. Pearson, the purchaser of the preceding
lot.

"The 'Phiz' vignettes, though smaller and of
more recent execution, have the extra attraction
of being tinted in colours. 'Little Nell and her

Grandfather in the Old Curiosity Shop' went to Mr. Wright for 22*l.*; Browne's version of 'Scrooge and Marley's Ghost,' differing materially from Leech's inimitable design on the same subject, brought 15*l.*; 'The mad gentleman and Mrs. Nickleby' and 'The Nickleby Family' averaged 14*l.* apiece; 'The Pecksniff Family and Tom Pinch' fetched 13*l.* 5*s.*; and the delightful frontispiece to 'Pickwick from Italy,' one of Phiz's most successful efforts of water-colour art, was sold for the modest price of 8*l.*"

Even while I write, the old Inn in the Borough, which was described early in these pages, is being pulled down. The proprietors, Messrs. Manger, hop merchants, could not allow the crazy fabric to subsist longer, as the ground is valuable, and the necessities of their business requires more suitable accommodation. Gone, therefore, now are the galleries, whence the landlady and chamber-maids looked down into the yard, and called out to " Sam," busily engaged cleaning boots. Gone the short dark stair in the corner, up which the Pickwickians were led to the spinster aunt's room. Gone with the old Inn are the memories of the *real* personages, and their adventures, who must have figured here, for a couple of centuries. Nobody cares for them; but for the more real Pickwickians, Sam, Wardle, Jingle and the rest, who never set foot in the place.

And here, the favourite " Fanteeg " asserts
itself. The worthy hop merchants, careless as
they might seem of the traditions of the place,
were not insensible to their commercial value.
The dismantled old galleries, with their sturdy-
looking balustrades, would be welcome to your
true Pickwickian, as a souvenir, and the present
writer was offered one " in good, sound condition," for the sum of one guinea—a fair market
price under the circumstances.

XVII.

In the early part of the volume there was given a sort of rough analysis of the characters exhibited in this varied panorama. But a more detailed and exact enumeration of all the figures, "great and small," will furnish further proof of the versatile powers of the author, and the wonderful imagination that could bring together such a collection of original beings. In this list, the important, finished characters are marked in capitals, and those next in degree in italics. It will be seen that the appreciation is made, not according to the length or elaborateness, but according to the finish and workmanship; a character that fills little space being often more striking and important than one dealt with at greater length. It may be repeated that the professional workman must be lost in admiration at the few brilliant touches with which a figure is put in, and the perfect economy of the strokes, and the exact selection of what is fitting. This suggests the rules of etching, where a single line conveys the *essence*, as it were, of the object selected, divested of all details.

CHARACTERS IN " PICKWICK."

1. MR. SAMUEL PICKWICK.
2. The Secretary of the club.
3. MR. TRACY TUPMAN.
4. MR. AUGUSTUS SNODGRASS.
5. MR. NATHANIEL WINKLE.
6. The cabman.
7. "Tommy," the waterman.
8. Another cabman.
9. The hot-pie man.
10. MR. ALFRED JINGLE.
11. The Rochester coachman.
12. The mother.
13. Ponto.
14. Don Bolaro Fizzgig.
15. Donna Christina.
16. Handsome Englishman.
17. The waiter at the Bull.
18. Hon. Wilmot Snipe.
19. The Clubbers.
20. The Smithies.
21. The Bulders.
22. The brewer's wife, &c.
23. *Dr. Slammer*.
24. Mrs. Budger, the widow.
25. Boots.
26. Lieut. Tappleton.
27. *Dr. Payne*.
28. "Dismal Jemmy" (Mr. Hutley).
29. The Stroller.
30. His wife.
31. The "shoving" man (at the Review.
32. WARDLE.
33. RACHEL.
34. Emily.
35. Isabella.

36. Trundle.
37. The Fat Boy.
38. Ostler at the Bull.
39. The deputy-ostler.
40. Postboy.
41. The "red-headed man.'
42. The "tall, bony woman."
43. Emma.
44. Jane.
45. Mary.
46. Boot-cleaner.
47. Old MRS. WARDLE.
48. The clergyman.
49. His wife.
50. Hard-headed man.
51. Miller.
52. The fat man.
53. John Edmunds.
54. His wife and son.
55. Old man.
56. Rook-boys.
57. Stout gentleman.
58. Dumkins.
59. Podder.
60. Luffey.
61. Struggles.
62. Sir Thomas Blazo.
63. Quanko Samba.
64. Mr. Staple.
65. Landlord of Blue Lion.
66. Ostler.
67. Pike-keeper.
68. Ostler.
69. Post-boy.
70. SAM WELLER.
71. Chambermaid (White Hart).
72. Landlady.

73. PERKER.
74. Landlady of the Leather Bottle.
75. Owner of " Bill Stumps."
76. The madman.
77. The girl.
78. The rival.
79. MRS. BARDELL.
80. Mr. Bardell.
81. Tommy Bardell.
81. Samuel Slumkey.
82. Hon. Horatio Fizkin.
83. Hoarse man in the balcony.
84. Busy little man.
85. The mob.
86. Waiter.
87. Fizkin's agent.
88. MR. POTT.
89. MRS. POTT.
90. Jane.
91. Independent voters (pumped over).
92. Barmaid at the Town Arms.
93. Gentlemen of Committee.
94. Small boys.
95. Mayor.
96. Voices in crowd.
97. Whiffin.
98. Proposer of Fizkin.
99. The one-eyed man.
100. The dirty-faced man.
101. Red-faced man.
102. The placid man.
103. Tom Smart.
104. Firm of Bilson and Slum.
105. The bay mare.
106. Barmaid.
107. The widow landlady.
108. The tall man.
109. The Ghost.
110. MR. LEO HUNTER.
111. Solomon Lucas.
112. MRS. LEO HUNTER.
113. Count Smoltork.
114. The four "Somethingean" singers.
115. The Contortionist.
116. JOB TROTTER.
117. Sarah.
118. Servant at Westgate House.
119. Miss Tomkins.
120. The cook.
121. The teachers.
122. Miss Smithers.
123. Nathaniel Pipkin.
124. Old Lobbs.
125. Maria Lobbs.
126. Kate.
127. Henry.
128. *Goodwin.*
129. "The Lieutenant."
130. Martin, the LONG GAME-KEEPER.
131. The boy.
132. Brookes the pieman.
133. *Captain Boldwig.*
134. Hunt the gardener.
135. Wilkins.
136. Mob.
137. *Ramsey.*
138. DODSON
139. FOGG.
140. Tom Cummins.
141. Bullman.
142. *Jackson.*
143. Wicks.
144. 3rd Clerk.

220. Child and " necklace."
221. The " Prim Personage."
222. Gentleman " with pink anchors."
223. *Scorbutic youth.*
224. Large-headed young man.
225. Pale youth.
226. Noddy.
227. Gunter.
228. *Mr. Raddle.*
229. Boy with hairy cap.
230. Barmaid, Blue Boar.
231. *Antony Humm.*
232. Mudge the chandler.
233. Old lady tea-drinker.
234. Brother Tadger.
235. Foreman of Jury.
236. *Buzfuz.*
237. *Justice Stareleigh.*
238. Officer of Court.
239. Richard Upwitch.
240. *Thomas Groffin.*
241. Chemist's boy.
242. *Mr. Skimpin.*
243. Mrs. Mudberry.
244. Mrs. Budkin.
245. The Baker.
246. Booking-office clerk.
247. Jews with fifty-bladed knives.
248. Waiter.
249. Mr. DOWLER.
250. *Mrs. Dowler.*
251. Officer.
252. Moses Pickwick.
253. The " outsiders " (3).
254. *Cyrus Bantam.*
255. Gentleman of Clapham Green.
256. Mr. JOHN SMAUKER.
257. Lady Snuphanuph.
258. LORD MUTANHED.
259. Hon. Mr. Crushton.
260. *Mrs. Colonel Wugsby.*
261. Miss Bolo.
262. Miss Wugsbys (2).
263. Mr. Crawley.
264. Miss Matinter (2).
265. Mrs. Cradock.
266. Prince Bladud.
267. King Lud.
268. Daughter of an Athenian.
269. Lord Chamberlain.
270. A Reveller.
271. Long Chairman.
272. TUCKLE.
273. Harris.
274. MAN IN BLUE.
275. Man in green foil smalls.
276. Coachman.
277. *Whiffers.*
278. Old lady of the Bath-chair.
279. Young lady.
280. Bob Sawyer's boy (Bob Cripps).
281. Lamplighter.
282. Occasional charwoman.
283. Chambermaid.
284. Surly groom.
285. Scientific gentleman.
286. Pruffle.
287. The horse.
288. *Smouch.*
289. Barmaid.
290. Mr. Ayresleigh.
291. Price.
292. Crookey.
293. Namby.
294. The " Bail."

295. Clerk in spectacles.
296. *Roker.*
297. Tenants of the Fleet (3).
298. Bill.
299. " Number 20."
300. Husband and wife.
301. SMANGLE.
302. *Mivins.*
303. *Tom Martin.*
304. *Simpson.*
305. *The Parson.*
306. Pot-boy.
307. Neddy.
308. *The Chancery prisoner.*
309. The racing countryman.
310. Old man.
311. Granddaughter.
312. Characters in the Insolvent Court.
313. MR. SOLOMON PELL.
314. George, the coachman.
315. The two coachmen (brothers).
316. " The late Lord Chancellor."
317. The boy with the blue bag.
318. " Red-faced Nixon."
319. The man who died of eating crumpets.
320. His doctor.
321. *The Cobbler.*
322. The young lady peeling potatoes.
323. The boy calling for Weller.
324. Owner of " Whistling Shop."
325. Mrs. Bardell's cab-driver.
326. *Mrs. Rogers.*

327. Waiter at " The Spaniards."
328. Isaac, the bailiff.
329. Mr. Snicks.
330. Mr. Prosee.
331. The pupil.
332. *Martin.*
333. The Bagman s uncle.
334. His mother.
335. The Baillie.
336. Mail guard.
337. The young lady.
338. The son of the Marquis de Filletoville.
339. The ill-looking gentleman.
340. Irish Gentleman.
341. Mrs. Cripps.
342. Waiter.
343. Postboy.
344. Smart servant girl.
345. *Mr. Winkle, senior.*
346. Postboy.
347. Host of the Saracen's Head.
348. John the waiter.
349. Pott's reviewer.
350. *Slurk.*
351. The buxom cook.
352. Old woman with jam.
353. Old woman with camomile tea.
354. Old woman with pot of jelly.
355. Mrs. Pell.
356. *Wilkins Flasher.*
357. Simmery.
358. Boffer.
359. Daughter of Lady Tollimglower.
360. Mr. Blotton (of Aldgate).

Some three hundred and sixty characters! And the marvel is that every one is distinct and present to the memory, with their sayings and doings, without confusion or nidistinctness. This is surely one of the most astonishing feats in literature. There is nothing like it on record, as we shall find by comparing it with "Tom Jones" or "Vanity Fair."

Not less astonishing is the enumeration of the various contrasted scenes and episodes, which form the narrative, each novel and interesting in itself, to be read in detached shape, and yet blending with the whole. It will be curious to note the variety and originality of each picture.

1. The meeting of the club.
2. Attack by the cabman and rescue.
3. Adventure at the ball.
4. Winkle's duel.
5. Dismal Jemmy's story.
6. The review.
7. The drive to Manor Farm.
8. The night at Manor Farm.
9. The convict's return.
10. The rook-shooting.
11. The cricket match.
12. The supplanting of Tupman.
13. The elopement.
14. Scene at the White Hart.
15. The madman's story.
16. The presumed proposal to Mrs. Bardell.
17. Election days at Eatan swill.

T

18. The bagman's story.
19. Mrs. Pott's party.
20. West Gate boarding-school.
21. Story of the parish clerk.
22. Quarrel with Mr. Pott.
23. Another shooting party.
24. Scene with Dodson and Fogg.
25. Stories of the old Inns of Court.
26. The double-bedded room.
27. The Nupkins episode.
28. Stiggins at Dorking.
29. The wedding at Manor Farm.
30. Story of Gabriel Grub.
31. Doings at Manor Farm.
32. Interview with Serjeant Snubbin.
33. Bob Sawyer's party.
34. The " Brick Lane Branch."
35. *Bardell* v. *Pickwick*.
36. Adventures at Bath.
37. Story of Prince Bladud.
38. Dowler and Winkle.
39. The servants' " Swarry."
40. Winkle's interview with Miss Allen.
41. Incidents in the Fleet Prison.
42. Pell and the insolvent coachman.
43. Stiggins and the Wellers.
44. Arrest of Mrs. Bardell.
45. Release of Mr. Pickwick.
46. Scenes with Ben Allen's aunt.
47. Story of the bagman's uncle.
48. Mission to Mr. Winkle, sen.
49. Pott and Slurk.
50. Death of Mrs. Weller.
51. Interview with Dodson and Fogg.
52. Scene at Osborne's Hotel, Adelphi.
53. Pell proving Mrs. Weller's will.
54. Mr. Pickwick, and Sam's marriage.
55. Arabella and Mr. Winkle, sen.
56. Denouement.

This shows that there are nearly three-score episodes, all full, exuberant, dramatic, complete and mirth-moving. Further, most of these can be subdivided and are made up of smaller and shorter episodes ; as in the chronicle of the Fleet Prison life, where every page teems with incidents. Under this single heading the scenes might be thus classified : —

In the Fleet Prison.
1. Mr. Pickwick's reception. " Sitting for his portrait."
2. The night with the Zephyr and Smangle.
3. Scene of his "getting up."
4. Scene with the butcher, parson, &c.
5. Jingle and Job.
6. Voluntary arrest of Sam.
7. The Chancery prisoner.
8. The cobbler.
9. Visit of Stiggins, &c.

Dickens pursued the system of choosing natural and often " colourless " names, until " Martin Chuzzlewit " was published. " Nickleby," in which we find many episodes quite as good and fresh as anything in " Pickwick,"—witness the sketches of the country actors under Crummles' management,—offers a collection of names all " easy, natural, affecting." Nothing could be better or more appropriate to their respective characters than Kenwigs, or Lillivick ; Folair and Lenville are simply perfect, and Gride is good. On the other hand, Cheeryble is a compounded, rather artificial name, expressing the character ; Squeers

is not so probable a one; Lord Frederick Veri-
sopht's is a quibble, as is Sir Mulberry Hawk's.
Count Smorltork is intended to suggest "small
talk," yet has an original Russian sound.   But
with "Chuzzlewit" began the reign of grotesque,
compounded names, such as Pecksniff, Sweedle-
pipes, &c.

Allusion has been made to the numerous translations of "The Pickwick Papers" which have
been executed in foreign countries.   There have
been two into French.   The first, issued in the year
1838, is a rude adaptation rather than a translation,
in which the most fantastic tricks are played with
the text, most of the dialogue being left out and
the whole compressed into two small volumes.   It
is entitled "Le Club de Pickwickistes, Roman
comique, traduit *librement* de l'anglais par Mdme.
Eugenie Giboyet."   And "*librement*" translated it
certainly is; there is an avowal of the method
adopted; for the adapter not merely leaves out
whole pages of dialogue, but "improves" the
text by supplying passages entirely of her own
manufacture.   The famous passage as to the
"Pickwickian sense" is thus treated:—

"Pickwick reste ferme sur sa chaise, déclare
qu'en effet l'épithète d'épicier s'adressait à M.
Blotton; celui-ci se borne à dire qu'il rejette avec
mépris l'accusation injurieuse de l'honorable
membre (*Applaudissements prolongés*)."   The

"Pickwickian sense" is entirely omitted.   In the account of the trial, the damages claimed are put at 300,000 francs, or 12,000*l.* sterling, and we are informed that " MM. Snubbin et Finge arrivèrent, puis Dodson et Fogg et leur avocat Buzfuz, qu salua Snubbin en souriant, encore à la surprise de Pickwick.   Bientôt entra le juge Stareledgh." "Finge," it will be noted, represents our   old friend Mr. Phunkey, it being necessary to choose a word that might   sound like "singe," or monkey.   The well-known dialogue follows :—

"Je me   constitue pour le défendeur, mon second est M. Finge," ajoute Snubbin.

"Messieurs Buzfuz et Skimpin, d'une part; Snubbin et *Singe* de l'autre," dit le Président.

" Mon nom ést Finge, M. le Président."

" J'entends   parfaitement, Singe. C'est la première fois que vous prenez la parte devant nous, Monsieur—eu—eur ? "

" Finge."

" Bien."

Buzfuz then opens his case :—

"Vous avez appris, messieurs, par mon savant confrère (ils n'avaient rien appris du tout), que l'affaire qui vous est soumise est relative à la violation d'une promesse de mariage, acte sacré dans lequel toute moralité est renfermée, acte d'ou naissent, . . . je m'arrête . . . . où je n'irai— pas ? "

" La plaignant, messieurs, est veuve depuis trois ans, bien veuve. Son mari, estimable douanier, qui avait toujours joui de la confiance de ses superieurs et de la solde de l'Etat, disparut inopinément de ce monde pour aller chercher dans l'autre la paix et le repos qui manquent au douaniers."

The incident of the letters is thus represented:—

" J'ai ici deux lettres qui prouvent cette intimité passée, je ne demande qu'un moment pour en faire lecture.   Première lettre :—

" ' Ma chère Madame Bardell,—Des cotelettes à la sauce aux tomates.   Votre dévoué PICKWICK.'

" Qui oserai écrire ainsi à moins d'une grande intimité ?   Seconde lettre :—

" ' Chère Madame Bardell,—Je n'arriverai que demain par la dernière diligence du soir. Ne vous inquietez pas du chauffe-lit.'

" Qui est-ce qui parle d'un chauffe-lit sans y attacher un double sens, messieurs ? qui écrit chauffe-lit quand c'est bassinoire qu'il faut dire ? "

The translator also provides Mr. Pickwick with an entirely new story to be read in the Fleet Prison, called " *Bill le Détenu* " a rather low, farcical narrative. This seems to be carrying the art of translating " librement " beyond legitimate limits.

Every one recalls " Bob Sawyer's party " and

the disturbing claims of his landlady, Mrs. Raddle. In setting out her demands the translator found it shorter to recompose the whole scene afresh. After giving her the name of " Mistress BADDLE," he makes her ask for security for her rent. " Your watch ? " she said. " It's in pawn." " Your clothes ? " " They're all in rags." " Books ?" " Lent." Here Mr. Pickwick entered. " Forgive me, " he said, " I did not know you were engaged with ladies." " I am the landlady," said Mrs. Baddle. " How much does my friend Robert owe you." " Two guineas three shillings and six- pence,"said Mrs. Baddle. " There's your money," and Mr. Pickwick paid it down.

Presently Jack Hopkins arrived.

" What, just come from the Hospital, Jack ? " said his host. Pickwick stared at him, to see if he had the look of a patient. " Yes," was the reply, " from St. Bartholomew's, where I pass my life." " Anything new ? " " A splendid case ; a man fallen out of a four-story window, without hurting himself, and they are going to trepan him to see if his brain is all right."

" Gentlemen," said Benjamin, throwing away his cigar end, " suppose we learn a lesson of anatomy on the joint ? " " Agreed ! " All sat down. Robert brought the oysters, but one thing was wanting—they had forgotten to open them. Each did what they could. Pickwick, who had always a store of ingenious expedients, suggested *a hammer*. The beef was cold, the ham was rancid, and the cheese, from its strength, was the only article worthy of notice."

It was not until 1859 that some *amende* was made for this rough treatment, when Messrs. Hachette proposed to undertake a complete and accurate translation of our author's works, employing competent persons, under the direction of M. Lahure. The series began with the "Aventures de Monsieur Pickwick," a mistranslation of the title to start with. The author supplied an address to the French people written in his own language. He wrote :—

"I have long been desirous that a complete French translation of the books I have written should be made, and should be published in one uniform series. Hitherto less fortunate in France than in Germany, I have only been known to French readers not thoroughly acquainted with the English language, through occasional fragmentary and unauthorized translations, over which I had no control, and from which I have derived no advantage. The present translation of my writings was proposed to me by Messrs. L. Hachette and Co., and Ch. Lahure, in a manner equally spirited, liberal, and generous. It has been made with the greatest care, and its many difficulties have been combated with

unusual skill, intelligence, and perseverance."
Yet, strange to say, even the translation of this
preface was not very accurately made, as when
Dickens speaks of "the manner" in which the
scheme was proposed as being spirited, &c., the
translator makes it "qui font honneur à leur
charactère élevé, libéral et généreux;" while "its
many difficulties have been *combated*," is turned
into "*vaincus:*" alterations, no doubt, meant as
compliments to the publishers.

Dickens, however, has never been so appreciated
by the French as was his great predecessor,
Sir Walter Scott, owing to the fact that many
points of his humour turn on local dialect and
peculiarities, which it is impossible to render
in another language. Thus in this careful translation Sam Weller's oddities of pronunciation
spelling, &c., vanish altogether, as the translator
found it hopeless to supply any forms that could
represent them. Sam becomes one of the innumerable free-and-easy valets who figure so
largely, like Sganerelle, in plays and stories.
This is in part one of the many problems of
translation.

The scene of Mrs. Leo Hunter's party will
show how fairly the difficulties have been overcome. The hostess becomes Madame *Chasselion.*

Count Smorltork says :—

"Comment vous tire, Madame Chasselion ?

Monsieur Pigwig, he ? ou Bigwig—un avocat ? Je
vois, c'est ça, Monsieur Bigwig," et le comte
allait enregistrer M. Pickwick sur ses tablettes
comme un gentleman qui se chargeait de faire
les affaires des autres, et dont le nom était
dérivé de sa profession, lorsque Mme. Chasselion
l'arrêta.

"Non, M. le Comte. Pickwick."

"Ha, ha ! je vois. Pique, nom de baptême ;
Figue, nom de famille. Très fort bien. Très fort
bien. Comment portez-vous, *Figue?* "

And again, when Mr. Pickwick says gravely,—

"Le mot politique comprend en soi-même
une étude difficile et d'une immense étendue."

"Ah ! s'écria le comte en tirant ses tablettes,
"très fort bon ! Beaux paroles pour commencer
un chapitre ! Le mot politique *surprend* en soi-
même," &c. This is excellent and quite as
amusing as the original.

We turn for a moment to the "trial," and to
the sketch of the "little judge."

"Il y a quelqu'un avec vous, Maître Snubbin ? "
reprit le judge.

"M. Phunkey, milord."

"Maître Buzfuz et Maître Skimpin pour la
plaignante," en écrivant les noms sur son livre des
notes et en articulant ce qu'il écrivait. "Pour le
défendeur Maître Snubbin et M. *Tronquet*."

Buzfuz's speech is capitally rendered. "Enfin,

messieurs, que signifient ces paroles ?   La voiture est en retard " (slow coach). And then, the peroration :—

" Cependant, gentlemen, Pickwick, l'infame destructeur de cet oasis domestique, qui verdoyait dans le désert de Goswell Street, Pickwick, qui se présente devant vous aujourd'hui *avec son infernale sauce aux tomates, et son ignoble bassinoire,* Pickwick lève encore devant vous son front d'airain, et contemple avec ferocité la ruine dont il est l'auteur."

It would almost be impossible to give a full list of the numerous translations made of "Pickwick." Mr. Wright has, however, gathered all that can be procured. On his shelves are to be found translations in (1) French, (2) German, (3) Russian, (4) Spanish, (5) Italian, (6) Danish, (7) Swedish, (8) Dutch, (9) Polish, (10) Hungarian, (11) Portuguese. The Book is also said to have been translated into Flemish, and I have heard, though on not very good authority, that there is one in Japanese! Again, it may be asked, is not this an extraordinary tribute to the general impression made by the book ?

In the progress of " Pickwick," as number followed number, the young author was encouraged and stimulated by " the cheers," as it were, of clever and admiring friends, to whom, as we have seen, the proofs were read aloud, and who were privileged to make suggestions.   It was as though some popular orator were making a speech, stimulated, as he goes on, by the growing applause of his favouring hearers.   Among these none were so cordial, so practical and valuable as two gifted young men, *litterateurs* like himself, and who were then working their way to success.   These were Talfourd and Forster, the one a graceful poet and dramatist; the other a sagacious critic.   It was Talfourd who presided at the dinner which cele-brated the happy, triumphant conclusion of "Pickwick:" and it was Forster who care-fully watched the proofs in its progress, and who in the grateful words of the author, had devoted "many patient hours to the correction of the original editions:" and had furnished "counsel, sympathy and faithful friendship" to the writer. The pair showed him indeed an extraordinary and hearty sympathy, that amounted to affection, and identified themselves wholly with his work.

This admiration and support was thoroughly spontaneous, and though they and others of his friends were connected with the press, the author never condescended to invite or solicit the praise of the newspapers.   In an unpublished letter now before me, and written from Doughty Street about this time, I find him writing to Mr. George Cox: " Let me say candidly in one word, that I have never, either in my own behalf or that of my most intimate friend, made a request of any kind the most remotely connected with the noticing of a work, to any reviewer I know, directly or indirectly. I always most cautiously and carefully abstain from doing so."

This appreciation of his two friends presently found expression in sonnets, a graceful, but now old-fashioned, form of compliment. Both are pleasing specimens, and may be contrasted with each other. Talfourd's exhibits a somewhat recondite tone ; Forster's, a true, warm affection.

SONNET

To CHARLES DICKENS, ESQ.,

On reading the completed "Oliver Twist."

Not only with the author's happiest praise
Thy work should be rewarded ; it is kin
To men's, who steeling finest nerves to win
Rare blessings for mankind, explored the maze
Black with the mists of centuries, through ways
Where grief unsoftened prompts its parent sin
To make unwonted music 'mid the din
Of passions ; in the guilty spirit raise
Sweet dreams of goodness, bid the irons fall,
And hail the slave a Brother,—for within
Wan childhood's squalid haunts, whose basest needs
Make tyranny more bitter, at thy call
An infant face with patient sadness pleads,
Admitted kindred to the heart of all.

16th February, 1839.

Forster's sonnet is more familiar to the world,
indeed the last two lines have been often quoted.
It is less mystical, and more hearty in its
expression than Talfourd's :—

To CHARLES DICKENS.

Genius and its rewards are briefly told :
  A liberal nature and a niggard doom,
A difficult journey to a splendid tomb.
  New writ, nor lightly weighed, that story old
In gentle Goldsmith's life I here unfold ;
  Thro' other than lone wild or desert gloom
In its mere joy and pain, its blight and bloom
  Adventurous.   Come with me and behold
O friend with heart as gentle for distress
  As resolute with wise, true thoughts to bind
The happiest to the unhappiest of our kind,
  That there is fiercer, crowded misery,
In garret toil and London loneliness
  Than in cruel islands mid the far- off sea.

March, 1848.

XVIII.

I MUST not pass over that interesting incident in
Dickens' career, when, to the gratification of all,
he consented to introduce the writer of his books,
as well as the books he wrote, to the public. It
might be assumed that the author must be the
best interpreter of his own works: indeed, it was
held to be beyond dispute, that the tones,
emphasis, action, thus presenting the authorized
version, as it were, must be the best and most
legitimate expression. But the same difficulty
that was pointed out in the case of the would-be
illustrator, applies here. The hearer has formed
an ideal of his own ; the reader presents another.
As we have shown, a true comedy character is
general and abstract : the interpreter, unless he
be a Garrick or a Coquelin, makes it particular,
and unreal. Wagner could not interpret his
own music nearly so efficiently as his lieutenant,
Richter. In many passages of Dickens' readings,
clever as they were, it was thus felt that the interpretation was often not the correct one.

The most enlivening of all the " Readings," and
the one presented with most dramatic variety, was
the " Trial from Pickwick." It was full of contrast
and indeed introduced the leading Pickwickian
favourites, with whom all the world was familiar.
The extraordinary life and spirit infused into the
original, roused a corresponding life and spirit
in the Reader : and the perfect familiarity of the
audience with all the allusions and even sentences,
gave an irresistible *entrain* to the whole. It was
usually given on the same night with that entire,
perfect chrysolite, " The Christmas Carol," to
whose pensive and pathetic grace it affords a
happy contrast ; and which, as we have shown,
was suggested by a story in " Pickwick." In this
piece, he thoroughly identified himself with his
characters. As Mr. Kent says, who has made a
regular *étude* of the reading : " His evening
costume was a matter of no consideration ; the
flower in the button-hole, the paper-knife in his
hand, the book before him, the animated, mobile,
delightful face, that we all knew by heart—were
equally of no account whatever. Watching him,
hearkening to him, while he stood there before
the audience, on the raised platform in the
glare of the gas burners shining down on him
from behind the pendant screen above his head,
his individuality disappeared. We were as
though we saw the bald head, the spectacles,

the cloth gaiters of Mr. Pickwick. Even the lesser characters were then at last brought to the fore, and suddenly assumed to themselves a distinct importance. Reader and audience, about equally one may say, revelled in the ' Trial from Pickwick.' Every well-known person in the comic drama was looked for eagerly, and when at last Sergeant Buzfuz, as we were told, rose with more importance than he had yet exhibited, if that were possible, and said, " *Call Samuel Weller*," a round of applause invariably greeted the announcement."

The little judge with his sepulchral tones and owlish face, and the Sergeant, were perhaps the best of his sketches. Sam Weller seemed scarcely to reach the general ideal; but then, how difficult to reach that ideal! There were little strokes and touches of minor characters that showed great art; such as the nervous sincerity he put into the tones of the conscientious juryman when asking as to Mrs. Bardell's window bill: " There is no date to that document, is there ? There were other admirable little pantomimic touches, such as the Sergeant appearing to draw his gown up on his shoulders, and to set the tails of his wig free, talking behind his hand to Dodson and Fogg. The whole was pruned and compressed with much tact, and knowledge of stage effect, and the Sergeant's speech was altered all through to the first person, with excellent result. To quote Mr. Kent again :—

"Every point, however minute, told and told effectually. More effectually than if each was heard for the first time, because all were thoroughly known, and therefore appreciated. There was something comically absurd in the Sergeant's extraordinarily precise, almost mincing pronunciation, as where he said that 'never, in the whole course of his professional experience, had he approached a case with such a heavy sense of respon-see-bee-lee-ty—a respons-ee-bee-lee-ty he could never have supported," &c.

Another "reading" from "Pickwick" was the "Bob Sawyer's party," always welcomed with enjoyment. This, however, amusing as it was, had not the same dramatic power as the trial. Jack Hopkins, with his short, Jingle-like sentences, "Sister industrious girl—cried eyes out—at loss of—*neckluss :* looked high and low for—*neckluss*"—was not very striking. A stroke of genius, however, was the presentation of the Lodging House drudge, who spoke with a wheezy solemnity—her mouth formed into an O—the tones coming deep from the throat: "Please, miste' Soiyer, Mrs. Raddle seys you can't have no hot *whater !*"

The Readings were continued by this spirited, intrepid man for some ten years, entailing travel over enormous distances, under every hardship

of climate and illness : yet without the least flagging.   The last note, however, of all, and which
ended the strange, eventful history, was " Pickwick," and the trial was given with more than his
usual spirit and force, ending with " Samivel,
Samivel! vy warn't there an alleybi ? "   I recall
this last of the long · series, at St. James's
Hall, on March 15, 1870, when, I stood on the
platform, close to him, behind one of the violet
screens, and heard him utter his strangely significant farewell!   " From these garish lights, I
vanish for evermore ! "   Within a few weeks he
had indeed vanished for evermore—and his loss
impoverished the public stock of harmless
pleasure.

Early in this volume, it was pointed out, how
much uncertainty and lack of plan there was on
the part of all concerned, when the work was
started.   One thing alone seems to have been
kept in view—that Seymour, having been supplied
with a plan capable of variety and expansion,
was expected to exert all his talent, and carry
the venture through.   This is shown by the
large quantity of illustrations, in the opening
numbers, quite out of proportion to the printed
matter supplied.   Thus, in the first number, which
consisted of twenty-six pages only, we find no less
than four elaborately done etchings : so that the
purchaser of the shilling's worth would probably

buy it to amuse himself with the pictures, turning to the text for comment and explanation. The plates were all sewn together, so that this must certainly have been the intention: and it is much the same with those who purchase a number of *Punch*, and who turn to the "Cartoon."

The second number was reduced by two pages, and contained twenty-four pages, or a sheet and a half, with three illustrations. With the third, owing to the death of Seymour, the whole purpose of the venture was changed; it was no longer to be a series of illustrations, "illustrated" by the text; the author stepped into the prominent place, as indeed he was entitled to do from the merit of his work, two sheets or thirty-two pages were allotted to him, and only two illustrations were furnished. This became the official form of all his works. With these changes before him, some future Dryasdust might work out the early history of "Pickwick."

The original MS. of "Our Mutual Friend" is, we believe, in America, while those of his other novels were regularly transferred to Mr. Forster as they came out, and are now to be seen at South Kensington. Mr. Dexter possesses the interesting MS. of the "Christmas Carol," and Mr. Wright that of the "Battle of Life." It is curious to note the change that gradually took place in the author's handwriting and fashion of writing, in this

period of over thirty years, during which he was
engaged in composition ; and it is scarcely fanciful
to say, that it corresponded with the change in his
style. Mr. Forster has placed beside each other two
specimens—one written in 1837, a passage from
" Oliver Twist," which would be the same as the
writing of "Pickwick," and the last page of
" Edwin Drood." The former is clear, open,
decided, and almost mercantile, with only three
corrections in the fourteen lines; the other
crowded, hesitating—in small characters, profusely corrected, interlined, and not very legible.
Nothing is more remarkable than the manly
decision of the first specimen, and its bright,
perfect legibility.

When he came to the printing of his work, no one
was so conscientious or workmanlike as Dickens.
His proofs display little more than omission of
paragraphs and the occasional alteration of a
word. In the revisal of his followers' proofs he
was unsparing—altering, cutting, inserting, but
disturbing the arrangement of the form as little as
possible. He showed much ingenuity and cleverness in this process. " Cutting " was his grand
maxim, pruning down florid sentences and
adding little effective points of his own. We have
before us now slips of our own work, astonishingly
improved by these touchings—a labyrinth of in-
sertions, transpositions, and erasures, all in his

favourite blue ink, which he adopted when
" Copperfield " had run about half its course. The
original " copy " or MS. of nearly all his works, in
the Forster Library, is in great stout quartos. It
is curious to note how every line almost is carefully
amended or altered, and the substituted passages
written in the minutest characters. So close are
the lines and so " squeezed " the writing, that
the effect is bewildering; but his printers knew
his way perfectly. Each page holds about forty
lines of close writing, and each line some twenty
words, making about 800 words in each page.
He followed one system, and never failed in the
practice—to make the words erased illegible.
This must have cost him time and trouble ; for it
is done in thorough fashion. Instead of drawing
a line across, the sentence is laboriously effaced
by a series of minute flourishings.

We find here proof sheets of only two of his works
—" Copperfield " and " Edwin Drood." The
passages erased from the proof are interesting in
their way, and it is not difficult to find the reason
for their omission. They were mostly *de trop*, or
an amplification of some previous sentiment.
Among the most curious is the alteration of the
subject of Mr. Dick's monomania, which originally
took the shape of " the bull in the china shop."
" Do you recollect the date," he asks, " when the
bull got into the china shop and did so much

mischief ? " " I was very much surprised," says David, " by the inquiry; but remembering a song about such an occurrence, that was once popular at Salem House, and thinking he might want to quote it, replied that I believed it was St. Patrick's Day." " Yes, I know," said Mr. Dick, " in the morning ; but what year ? " This notion of " the bull and the china shop " was carried on for a number or two ; but was carefully altered into the more refined and natural idea of " King Charles the First's head." Mr. Dick, on his first introduction, was seen at the window, " putting his tongue out against the glass, and carrying it across the pane and back again : and, when his eye caught mine, squinted at me in a most terrible manner." This picture of lunacy was felt, no doubt, to be disagreeable, or too realistic, and was omitted.

As Mr. Forster has shown, the author set down at the beginning of each chapter, a few hints and catch-words for its treatment. Thus we find " First chapter funny. Then on to Emily. ' Going out with the tide.' Em'ly to go ? No. Yes, and ruined ? Next time. Miss Moucher, impossible. No Steerforth, this time. Keep him out."

There is a dialogue between Steerforth (who was originally Steerford) and Mrs. Gummidge which is worth restoring.

" Mrs. Gummidge, as usual, was taken poorly in
her spirits when we showed a disposition to be
merry ; and was, as usual, adjured by Pegotty
to cheer up. " Mr. Dan'l," said Mrs. Gummidge,
shaking her head, " I gets worse and worse ; I
had far better go into the house to-morrow
morning, afore breakfast ! " " No, no," said
Steerforth, " don't say so ; what's the matter ? "
" You don't know me, sir," said the doleful
Gummidge, " or you wouldn't ask." " The loss is
mine," said Steerforth coaxingly; " but let us
know each other better. What's the matter ? "
Mrs. Gummidge shed tears, and stated her uncomfortable condition in the usual terms ; " I'm
a lone, lorn creetur and everythink goes contrary
with me." " No, no," said Steerforth, " why, we
must be designed by heaven for each other. I'm
a lone, lorn creature myself, and everything has
gone contrary with me since my cradle. Mr.
Pegotty, will you change places and allow me to
sit next her ? " The immediate effect of this on
Mrs. Gummidge was to make her laugh. " You
lone and lorn," said Mrs Gummidge, peevishly ;
" yes, you looks like it." " As like it as you are,"
said Steerforth, taking his seat beside her.
" Indeed," said Mrs. Gummidge with another
laugh. " Ay, indeed," cried Steerforth, " let us
be lone and lorn together. Everything shall go
contrary with us both, and we'll go contrary

with all the world." It was in vain for Mrs. Gummidge to resist this logic, or to try and push him away. He sat thus all the rest of the evening, and when Mrs. Gummidge began to shake her head, repeated his proposal. The consequence was that Mrs. Gummidge was constantly laughing and pushing him."

Another speech of Steerforth's on proctors was also erased. "I confess I think it a matter of gammon and spinach, as my friend Miss Moucher would say," he returned; "a proctor's a gentlemanly sort of fellow. I don't see any objection to your being a proctor; you shall take out my marriage licence, in case I ever want one, if that is any inducement to you, and you shall separate my wife and me afterwards, and you shall prove my will if you live long enough." This is gay and spirited. The proctors were originally to be named "Aiguille and Tanquille," after which he wrote, "No; Spenlow and Jorkins." Littimer, the valet, was Lirrimer in the original.

Dickens, always eager to put down religious "cant," at first thought of introducing some severe "hits." Here is a passage which does not appear in the printed editions.

"I heard that Mr. Creakle, on account of certain religious opinions he held, was one of the Elect and Chosen—terms which certainly

none of us understood in the least then, if anybody understands them now—and that the man
with the wooden leg was another. I heard that
the man with the wooden leg had (Traddles'
father, according to Traddles, had positively
heard him) frightened women into fits by
raving about a pit he said he saw, with I don't
know how many thousands of billions and trillions
of pretty babes born for no other purpose than
to be cast into it."

He also intended to make Heep more of a
sanctimonious or praying hypocrite, as is evident
from various pious allusions struck out. Thus,
Heep says : "I passed an hour or two in the
evening sometimes with Mr. Tidd, and thought
myself in another and better world ; he is so clear,
Master Copperfield." Describing Copperfield's
youthful passion for Miss Larkins, Dickens wrote
in his proofs, "If the elder Miss Larkins would
drive a triumphal car down the High Street and
allow me to throw myself under the wheels as an
offering to her beauty, I should be proud to be
trampled under the horses' feet." And again,
" Sometimes I am persuaded she must have been
aware of it [my attachment] on account of my
agitation and the expression of my face when I
met her. Then I look in the glass, and getting
up that expression as nearly as I can," etc. The
Micawbers lived " in an unfurnished room like a

party of domesticated Arabs." A passage was
taken out of David's amusing account of his
tipsiness : " I was so far from wanting words
that I had only too many of them. I didn't know
what to do with them. I floundered among them
as if they were water in which I was splashing
about." When he was in love with Dora and
attending church, " a sermon was delivered
(about Dora, of course), beginning 'in the first
chapter of the Book of Dora you will find the
following word, *Dora*.'" In David Copperfield's
account of his mother's funeral, there was this
pathetic passage :—

" I remember being awakened in the morning
by the sharp strokes of a spade ; that I looked
out of the window and saw men working in the
churchyard underneath the tree, and went to bed
and wept. I remember that I lay there sobbing
until Pegotty came up to help me to undress myself,
and that being in her black dress the first time she
wrung her hands, a thing that turned my very
blood to see her do."

In one of the Ouvry letters, he tells a friend
that the publisher's profits during three years—
from 1836 to 1839—upon the sale of " Pickwick "
in numbers only, were 14,000*l*. It will be interesting to compare the bargain made, for " Nickleby,"
which was based upon this result :—

" First.—They give me 1500*l*. more for

' Nickleby.' Five hundred of this I have had, so there is a thousand more to pay.

"Secondly.—They pay me 50*l.* a week for the new work, out of which I pay for what assistance I require, which, upon a liberal allowance, may average 12*l.* a week, but certainly not more. They also pay all expenses of printing, advertising, and illustrations (the last being woodcuts will be very expensive), and then of all profits allow me one clear half—not deducting the expenses.

"By this arrangement, upon a sale of 20,000 copies I shall get nothing ; upon a sale of 40,000, they get half the profit upon the additional 20,000, and I add the other half to my 50*l.*—you understand ? If the work went on for two years, and were to sell 50,000 (which Bradbury and Evans think certain, but which I confess I do not, though there is a good chance of it), my profits would be between 10,000*l.* and 11,000*l.*, and theirs 5000*l.*

" I think this very good—as good as could be —and if the secret of the form and nature of the new publication is rigidly kept, as no doubt it will be, I hope it may make a tremendous stand. If so, I don't despair of making a decent thing out of some one of my works yet—and as to time if it continues to be popular, it may go on for five years as well as for two."

XIX.

In the interesting Exhibition of "English Humorist Artists," held last year, at the Institute, Piccadilly, there were to be seen specimens of illustrations from the days of Hogarth to those of Mr. R. Caldecott. Here the inspiring influence of Dickens was conspicuous, particularly in the display of the figures and scenes from his stories. These, after the brilliant efforts of Rowlandson, formed unquestionably the most attractive portion of the Exhibition. Here were to be seen the sketches for "Oliver Twist," "Copperfield," "Bleak House," "Edwin Drood," and many more. Here we could make comparison between the strength of the different illustrators. In the earlier specimens of "Phiz" and Cruikshank, there was a sort of inspiration, and a dramatic feeling, that corresponded with the author's. In Phiz's later efforts, this seemed lacking. Many were the difficulties which Dickens experienced in the selection of an illustrator for what unhappily proved to be his last work; and, after much hesitation, he selected a young artist of ability, engaged on an illustrated paper, the *Graphic*, just then started.[1]

It is with a particular interest that we pause before an original coloured, full-length of Mr. Pickwick, the work of "Phiz." This spirited drawing was clearly intended by the artist to be his "sketch model" and reference guide during the progress of the work. There we see the full, benevolent face, a little more florid, and perhaps grosser, than we would expect; but it must be recollected that, in the plates, a face done on so small a scale, is abstract and general. We could not tell, for instance, what was the exact shape or expression of the Pickwickian mouth, a simple indication or dot being all that was attempted. When we come to larger, detailed work, the general likeness which was every one's ideal, becomes too emphasized and distinct in expression. It cannot reach to the ideal of all. Thus, as we have shown, no new illustrations, however well executed, will be acceptable to all. In the corner " Phiz " has set down some notes, descriptive of the costume; as :—" *Nankeen tights, black cloth gaiters, white waistcoat, blue coat, brass buttons, square cut in the tails.*" These stage directions

---

[1] We recall a dinner-party given by our author (it was on January 30th, 1870), at which were Sir Edwin Landseer, and this young artist, now a Royal Academician, our host informing us, for the first time, that he was the illustrator he had selected for the new work.

were no doubt official, and furnished by the author himself. So earnest was the artist in his work, that we find in the top corner experiments for Mr. Pickwick's hat. There are three sketches of it, from various points of view. The figure itself seems an enlargement of Seymour's first sketch of Mr. Pickwick addressing the club *on his chair*, the right arm being raised oratorically, the left placed under his coat-tails, in which attitude there is a capital dramatic significance. It betokens that fervency and ardour which redeemed so much of that amiable person's mild absurdity.

It is curious to turn from the boldly-conceived and even elaborate " Pickwick," this masterly picture of character and manners, which supposed the knowledge and experience of a lifetime, to the portraits of the author done at the period. Few would be prepared for that bright, boyish face, full of vivacity, gracefully outlined, with the abundance of flowing hair, and with an engaging expression that was for his friends irresistible. Here was found a vigorous, practical glance, which might almost have seemed incompatible with delicacy of humour and enjoyment. Yet there is the same combination in " Pickwick," where we find an airiness of touch, and occasionally a tenderness, united with a business-like vigour. As we have so often repeated, this was

the work of a young man of only three and
twenty!

The subject of the Portraits of Dickens is
being dealt with in a sumptuous and comprehensive work, " Dickens in Pen and Pencil," now
being issued under Mr. Kitton's and Mr. Dexter's
direction.

This work has been entered upon with an extraordinary enthusiasm and industry, with the
result that about a hundred portraits and sketches
have been gathered. The contrast between these
various counterfeit presentments is surprising ;
between the early boyish exuberance, and the
later rather " grizzled " type, suggesting, according to Ary Scheffer's happy expression, some
grim Dutch Admiral of Van Tromp's day. Of the
portraits representing him at what we may call
this Pickwick era, the most notable are Lawrence's
crayon sketch done in 1837, and brilliantly
lithographed—though somewhat heavy about the
mouth ; Maclise's well-known picture ; and Count
D'Orsay's clever drawing, done in 1841.

Not the least interesting of the memorials to
be seen at the Humorists Exhibition, were the
rough pencil sketches of the author, dashed off
by Cruikshank, at convivial moments, and done
during the Pickwickian era. There is a sheet of
paper covered with attempts. There is a spirited
full-length, representing him seated, with five

heads, all of the same character—the hair droop-
ing over the eyes. There is a curious suggestion
of his son Henry's features.

The genius of Dickens during his thirty years'
course may be said to have inspired the foremost
artists of his time. Though the designing of illustrations for stories is usually found incompatible
with the labours of the professional painter—in
France it is a distinct branch—his friends were
proud and eager to associate themselves with his
work. Half a dozen of his illustrators have become
Royal Academicians; but of these Leslie and Sir
J. Gilbert only are associated with "Pickwick."

The absorbing interest of the subject has
indeed prompted all sorts and conditions of
illustration. On turning over these efforts, it is
curious to note how complete and universal is
the failure to reach the author's ideal. Shown
without preparation to a casual amateur, it
would be almost impossible to know that they
were associated with "Pickwick" at all. Neither
the faces nor the scenes themselves suggest
anything Pickwickian. Comparing the artists
engaged, we are compelled to acknowledge

[2] It may be noted here, that Leslie's monochrome oil sketch
is scarcely done justice to in the small woodcut prefixed to the
first cheap edition. It now belongs to Mr. Wright, and is
vigorously painted, though Mr. Pickwick's face has a rough or
testy expression, and the pleasant humour of the situation—
the scene with Mrs. Bardell—is scarcely brought out.

the amazing supremacy of "Phiz," and of Seymour, and we must consider it part of the unvarying good fortune of the author, that he thus secured the best talent available for his work. At the same time his own important share in the *direction* of the illustrations by way of suggestion and alteration, contributed to this result. So that in this, it may be unique, instance, the author became the inspirer and director not only of his own legitimate department, but of that of his coadjutor also. The natural result has been that the plates reflect the story, even in the most minute points. As Mr. Grego has pointed out to me, the innumerable plates which "Phiz" later furnished for Lever's works do not correspond in many points with the text, and are often founded on a misapprehension of it : for Lever was living far away at Florence or Spezia, and exercised no control over the illustrations.

Sir John Gilbert, R.A., whose richly coloured pictures, full of dash and bravura, are familiar to amateurs, was for many years much in demand as an illustrator of periodicals. Even now his bold and picturesque designs for the stories running in *the London Journal* are much sought after by the judicious collector. To "Pickwick" he furnished a series of no less than thirty-two designs, which have a pleasing correct-

ness; but which—*pace* so admirable an artist—
are highly unpickwickian. There is no trace of
humour. It is Mr. Pickwick taken *au plus grand
serieux;* or, as Elia has it, " with all the accuracy
of *ocular admeasurement.*" All the grotesque
adventures seem actual critical situations. This
lack of the ironical sense is often found in
writers. As Lamb has explained it, a " sub intention," that is, a delicate hint that you are
not to be taken seriously, is the secret of real
comedy. An illustrator of this *literal* turn
would present Mr. Pickwick in Miss Withersfield's
chamber as an actual intruder. The awkwardness of the situation becomes almost painful. But
" Phiz " seized on the precise comical point: who
shall forget the bewildered face of Mr. Pickwick,
the bed curtains drawn round it, and the unconscious spinster arranging her hair !

In addition to the skilled commentators and
" comparative explorers," there are a number of
collectors who with a generous devotion gather
everything that is associated with the " god of
their idolatry." Among the most zealous and
enthusiastic of Pickwickians, is Mr. W. Wright,
who has spared neither labour nor expense in the
pursuit. He is the possessor of all " Phiz's "
original drawings for " Pickwick," with the exception of one of the frontispieces which cannot
be traced, and has always been mysteriously

missing. According to the scale of prices that have recently " ruled," these must be of extraordinary value. Allusion has been made in the text to the difficulty, if not impossibility, of settling the priority of the different " states " of the plates, an instance of which is the etched title-page, which in some impressions displays " Tony Veller " on the sign-board, and in others " Tony Weller." This, no doubt, is a trivial point enough; but as the Bentleys and Wakefields contended fiercely over a dot or particle, so our Pickwickian controversialists find themselves hotly engaged over all that touches the exactness and due authenticity of the text and illustrations. These little controversies enliven the general drudgery of the eager bibliophilist, and often lead to important discoveries. This little " Veller " point, is, however, all but settled, as it appears to me, by a particular copy of " Pickwick " in the possession of Mr. Wright, and to which a singular interest attaches. Each number, as it came out, was presented by the author to Miss Mary Hogarth, to whom, as we have seen, he was tenderly attached, and whose death was actually the cause of the interruption of the story. In each number was written an inscription from the author, " Mary Hogarth, from hers most affectionately, Charles Dickens," which is continued until the thirteenth number, when her father's

name is substituted. The succeeding numbers
bear the initials of Miss Hogarth's friend, Miss
Walker. Thus the copy is of interest:[3] for it
seems certain that the author would have presented only the earliest copies of the numbers,
as they came from the publishers, to this friend.
Here we find "Veller," not Weller, on the
sign-board. It is curious that, in the title of
Martin Chuzzlewit, there is also a mistake of the
same kind, in the inscription or "sign," where the
"£" is placed after "100," instead of before. The
mistake was corrected, but it is evidence of the
very earliest edition.

A few weeks ago in Paris, when turning over
this interesting collection, Mr. Wright placed in
my hands a strangely interesting relic, associated
with Dickens' boyhood. This was a parchment-
bound cash-book, in which the clerks of Messrs.
Ellis and Blackmore, the firm of solicitors who

----

[3] Mr. Wright's own account is as follows:—

"Mr. George Hogarth, her father, whose name appears on a
number, gave them to her intimate friend and school companion, Miss R. F. Walker, who completed the set. The
numbers afterwards came into the possession of their son,
Edward Walker, who took them with him to India and other
places, hence the salt-water stains on some of the leaves. In
1888, Mrs. Walker commissioned Miss Langley to sell them,
and I then became the owner of this unique copy of the
'Pickwick Papers.'

"*Paris*, 1888."

employed him, entered regularly all their items of
legal expenditure. It begins in March, 1827,
when their young clerk was but fifteen, and here
he sets down in his clear, but not very steady
writing, what he paid away for swearing affidavits,
&c. From this little ledger he appears to have
received thirteen shillings and sixpence a week,
later increased to fifteen shillings—and we have
such items as these: "One week in advance,"
"4s. 11d. due to me," "Coach hire, to get will registered, 2s.," "March, 1827, to justify, 2s.," &c.

But there is something more interesting still to
be gathered from these entries. For here we find
various names of clients and of causes, which re-
curred to him, and seemed to him the most fitting
and natural for particular characters. It is
curious to think of these clinging to his memory for
over a dozen years, and of their being deliberately
chosen for their realistic effect. Thus we
find an entry, "Self to Rudge," a cause of
"Ruberough v. Corney," and "Madgwick v.
Dalley." In the cause of one Humphreys he
himself swore an affidavit. Sometimes the name
was slightly altered, as in a divorce suit of
"Barwell and Wife," and a certain "Newman
Knott," whose name recurs very often—once
with the note, "Paid N. Knott, and lent him 2s."
We have also "Breeds v. Sawyer," and the
name of "Wilkin." We find also a firm of

solicitors, Prue and Freedland, doing business at Canterbury, like Wickfield and Heep.

These and many other items, show what opportunities he enjoyed for learning the " practice " of a solicitor's office ; being often despatched, like Mr. Wicks, Mr. Jackson, and the other clerks, to swear affidavits, &c. To this we owe the extraordinary dramatic vitality of these sketches of the solicitor's life. Hence, too, it would seem that in daily life so many touches occur, which suggest and even warrant " Pickwick." [4]

The relations of " Phiz" to his author, and the important share taken by the latter in directing the illustrations, have been fully set out by Mr.

[4] Thus, in the days of the "Cock" tavern, Tennyson's tavern, I once got into conversation with a sort of decayed solicitor, who dwelt on his familiar intimacy with a Commissioner of Bankrupts, exactly as Mr. Pell did on his affectionate friendship with "the Lord Chancellor." The dialogue, as reported by the decayed solicitor, was something of this kind, but with many variations :—" Todd," said he, ' I must decide the case against you.' 'Very well, my Lord, you will decide wrongly.' ' I don't care, Todd,' he said. ' We'll see, my Lord,' said I. Well, sir, the case was reversed on appeal, when he sent for me, ' Todd,' he said, ' you were right, and I was wrong.' 'I knew you were, my Lord,' I said. 'Todd,' he said," &c.

Once our author was presenting the prizes at the Midland Institute of Birmingham, of which he was President, when a little girl came up, whose name, it was announced, was Winkle. The chairman with his usual pleasant *bonhomie*, said, "So you see, my dear—you will have to change your name."

Croad Thomson, in a handsome quarto volume. on the life and labours of Hablot Browne. Here we are shown how truly fortunate was Dickens in having so versatile a person at his command, and one so prompt in carrying out his suggestions. This artist, as is well known, was one of the most prolific and industrious of illustrators, and his plates for Lever's "rollicking" books, where he was uncontrolled, show even a greater brilliancy and dash. Here the artist was not fettered by restraints, such as preserving the likeness throughout, or of importing a particular significance to a dramatic situation. As we have seen, the drawings submitted to Dickens were returned with marginal directions, and with letters of particular instructions which the artist generally contrived to carry out.

The first plate which "Phiz" drew for "Pickwick" was the scene in the yard of the White Hart Inn, which, however, in the book, is placed after another, that of the overturn of Wardle's chaise during the pursuit of Jingle. I have before pointed out what delicacy and grace there is in this etching, which is perhaps the best of the artistic series. Mr. Thomson gives a dramatic account of its execution. Mr. Young, who is now alive, and residing in Furnival's Inn, Dickens' old place of residence, was well skilled in the important function of what is

called "biting in" etched plates, a task of nicety
and delicacy, as the effect depends on the time
the acid is allowed to work.[5]   At this time "Phiz"
was lodging in Newman Street, and, as Mr. Young
relates, one evening he came rushing in; " Look
here, old fellow," he said; " will you come to
my rooms, to help me with a plate I have to
etch?"   He had just received his commission to
work on "Pickwick."   " Mr. Young, being as
obliging a man as ever lived, readily agreeing to
go, the other bade him bring his key with him,
as they might be late.   They sat up the whole
night to accomplish the work."   I am glad to
find my opinion of the merits of this introductory
plate endorsed by so competent a judge as Mr.
Thomson, who pronounces it " an inimitable
composition, which must have made Dickens'
heart warm as he looked at it."

The elaborate nature of Dickens' promptings to
his artist will be seen from a single instance.   As
he often said, he never took the slightest liberty
with his public, but supplied the very best work
he could command.   Every one will recall the
picture of Mr. Dombey's introduction to Mrs
Skewton on the "Parade" at Leamington,

[5] Now-a-days, the artist is presumed to do this work himself,
as he can produce effects which a journeyman cannot attempt.
There are etchers also who actually print their own works,
which allows of other devices and effects being produced.

through the agency of Major Bagstock. It
would seem an ordinary incident enough; but
the author intended a deep and even mysterious
significance. Accordingly we find him writing to
his artist: " The first subject I am now going to
give is very important to the book. I should like
to see your sketch of it if possible. I should pre-
mise I want to make the Major, who is the in
carnation of selfishness and small revenge, a kind
of comic Mephistophelian power in the book."
He then goes on to describe at length the scene of
the introduction of Mr. Dombey to Mrs. Skewton
and her daughter: " Mother usually shoved about
in a Bath chair, by a page who has rather out-
grown and out-shoved his strength, and butts it
behind like a ram, while his mistress steers it
languidly by a handle in front. Nothing the
matter with her to prevent her walking, only was
once a beauty; sketched reclining in a barouche,
having outlived her beauty and the barouche. . .
The native in attendance bearing a camp stool and
the Major's great coat. *Daughter has a parasol.*
Native evidently afraid of the Major. If you like
it better, the scene may be in a street or in a green
lane. *But a great deal will come of it;* and I want
the Major *to express that*, as much as possible in
his apoplectic, Mephistophelian observation of
the scene."

Returning to the " Pickwick " plates, we find

that enormous pains were taken with one illustration, that of Gabriel Grub and the goblin. No
less than *three* drawings were made, " a unique circumstance," says Mr. Thomson, " in the Dickens'
illustrations.   The first scarcely follows the text:
the goblin's tongue is not out, his hat is not broad-
brimmed, nor are his legs crossed.   In the second
the result is better ; the hat and legs are as described, but the tongue is still not out.   In the
third, the figure is exactly as described, and St.
Alban's Church is introduced in the background,
very delicately and beautifully."   Two drawings
were made for the Warden's room, the first not
nearly so good as the present.

It is clear that many of the improvements were
suggested by the author himself while the plates
were being etched.   Thus in the " Valentine "
drawing, Mr. Weller, senior, is shown without his
hat, and his coat does not lie on the chair ; and in
Bob Sawyer's surgery a skeleton is introduced;
while in the picture of Bob on the top of the
chaise, the boy running after the chaise had a
bundle on his back, which was transferred to his
hand with more effect.

As I have said, nothing strikes us so forcibly
as we turn over these wonderful plates, as the
perfect propriety of illustration, the figures being
disposed exactly as they ought to be ; also the
extraordinarily humorous details, which are dis-

played without intrusion. They will bear study and examination, with the result of fresh discoveries each time. It may be admitted that they are a little unequal in design and execution; some have been " bitten in " a little too black, but all show the same spirit. If we were to select the best, for delicacy of execution, we should name : (1) The yard of the White Hart. (2) The scene in Nupkins' kitchen. (3) The bedroom scene in the Fleet. (4) Winkle's confession of his marriage. (5) Mary and the fat boy (where, by the way, a cook is introduced who does not figure in the text).[6]   Other plates are remarkable for the dramatic effect and grouping, such as the picturesque scene of the ghostly mail coach legend, which has quite a weird-like tone, and lingers in the memory. A few, not half a dozen, are somewhat inexpressive and conventional, but the whole series is admirable, and will bear the closest criticism. I may note here, besides the variations in the plates noted by the Dean of Lismore, a few more which Mr. Croad Thomson has pointed out. These are; in the White Hart plate, in its first shape, Wardle's smalls are dark and the dog black; in the second both are light coloured. A Wellington boot on the first step has been added.   In the

---

[6] In the battle between the Eatanswill editors, the cook, kitchen-maid, and landlord are introduced, who were not present, as " the house " had long since gone to bed.

"elopement" or overturn, the second version greatly varies, "the upraised arm of Wardle is altered; there are four horses seen; no wheel is lying in the foreground; the driver is not the same man, and the carriages and foliage are treated differently." In the sketch of the interview with Sergeant Snubbin, Dickens has written underneath: "I think the Sergeant should look younger and a great deal more sly and knowing; he should be looking at Pickwick too, smiling compassionately at his innocence. The other fellows are noble.—C. D." This is now capitally conveyed. On the plate entitled "Mr. Winkle returns under extraordinary circumstances," he writes: "Are Sam and the housemaid clearly made out? and would it not be better if he were looking on, with his arm round Mary? I rather question the accuracy of the housemaid." Which was accordingly done.

"The 'Eatanswill Election' varies greatly in the two versions, the mayor stands with his legs apart in the second plate, and in the crowd below some of the figures are in different positions. A minute variation is the boy's hat behind Pickwick; in some copies it has a cockade, thus making the figure Sam Weller's.

"In the plate of Mr. Pickwick behind the door of the young ladies' school, it is to be noted that *the bell* is only in the second version. In Mrs.

Leo Hunter's party there are many variations. In the first version there is a post in the foreground and a birdcage in the tree, and (as was before noted) a figure like Lord Brougham's. In the second, the brigand has a hat and feathers, his knees are bent, and Mr. Pickwick extends both his arms. In the visit to Dodson and Fogg's office, Sam's legs in the first plate are together; in the second, apart. In the first etching of " Pickwick in the Pound," as we before noted, there is a young ass not found in the second, and there are also more boys.

"In the double-bedded room the lady is plumper and younger in the second, and the dress thrown over the chair is bright coloured.

" In the Christmas Eve at Mr. Wardle's, the first version had a cat and dog not found either in the drawing nor in the second version. In the goblin scene there is a bone beside the skull in one plate. The " Valentine " has a newspaper on the ground in the foregrouud and in the trial scene, Perker's hat is in one and not in the other. The partition of the counsels' seats is much higher."

The connection between Dickens and his illustrator continued for over twenty years, when our author was induced to try a new hand. It must be said that by this time "Phiz" had lost his cunning, or at least his sense of

humorous inspiration; his faces, figures, and
scenes offered a rather monotonous and conventional air; he seemed to take no trouble with
the faces, and the general idea was rather indi-
cated than expressed. There was also an *extravagance* in the drawing, and what was intended to
be humorous became caricature, such as is seen
in the comic papers. It was likely, however, that
the author's stories had now become so purely
psychological as to be with difficulty represented
in black and white. Any one looking at " Phiz's "
last series will be constrained to admit that the
connection could not have been continued longer,
to the author's advantage.[7]

" Phiz " survived his friend some twelve years,
dying in 1882. He will always be associated with
the "immortal Pickwick," and have his share in
the fame of that work.[8]

[7] In one of the "versions" of the scene with the "tall
quadruped," *three* forelegs of the animal can be made out?
This was owing to an imperfect erasure of the artist's, who was
dissatisfied with one of the forelegs.

[8] In a preceding page I confessed my astonishment at the
inferior character of a set of illustrations supplied by him for
the cheaper " Household Edition " of " Pickwick." It seemed
indeed almost impossible to believe that they were his work, so
rude and coarse were the designs. I did not know that there was
a sad but sufficient reason for this failure. Mr. Thomson tells
us, "that in 1867 he had sustained a severe shock of a kind of
paralysis, and for the remaining fifteen years of his life he was
never the same man again, either as a designer or a draughts-

man.   One of the things he began after his recovery was the
Household Edition of Dickens.   In the feeble and childish
scrawls of these blocks may be seen the injury that had been
inflicted. . . . So greatly was the power of the right hand
impaired that he had to support it on the left in order to get
the glass to his mouth.''   Hence he was obliged to hold his
pencil or brush in an extraordinary and clumsy fashion.   As an
illustration of the good nature with which occasion is found to
help an old favourite, I may mention that Mr. Cozens, of
Melbury Road, gave " Phiz " a commission to prepare a coloured
series of the drawings that illustrate " Pickwick," " David
Copperfield,"   " Dombey,"   " Nicholas Nickleby,"   " Bleak
House," and " Little Dorrit ; "   which were accordingly
executed, the artist furnishing a humorous written guarantee
with a pen-and-ink sketch, representing himself sketching Mr.
Pickwick, who is standing on a raised stage.   These were, it is
believed, traced from the etchings and then lightly coloured.
It may be added that the Duchess of St. Albans is a great
amateur and collector of " Phiz's " drawings.   The rage, however,
is for those which illustrate Dickens's works, which will by-and-
by be in great demand at high prices, being so limited in
number.

XX.

WE have noted how the profane race of adapters seized on " Pickwick," to the annoyance of the author, as a special subject for the exercise of their craft. It is remarkable indeed that every one of Dickens' novels—and the list is a long one —have been thus shaped for the stage : even his slighter stories, such as the pretty Christmas books, and the stories in the extra Christmas numbers of " All the Year Round," have found their way to the stage. To the end, however, he never favoured this process, and was with difficulty induced to witness the performance. One reason may have been that the task too often fell into the hands of some rough-and-ready workman, who treated the piece in rather coarse fashion. On two occasions at most were skilled dramatists employed, as when Mr. Tom Taylor prepared a version of the " Tale of Two Cities," and Mr. Andrew Halliday treated " David Copperfield." Amusing as was this last adaptation, and admirably acted (particularly the parts of Micawber, by Rowe, and that of Pegotty by Emery) the gifted author was not wholly satisfied, and no doubt found that the delicacy of his work had evaporated in the process. In one adaptation, that of " No Thoroughfare," made by Mr. Wilkie Collins, he himself took some share, and also superintended its production on the French stage. It is impossible, we think, not to hold that Dickens' stories and characters are essentially dramatic ; but, at the same time, they require the utmost skill to fit them for the stage.

It has been often said by the critics that " Pickwick," being nothing but a series of scarcely connected and fragmentary episodes, is wholly unsuited for the stage. The great length, too, and number of characters render it, as it were, incompressible. But the answer to this objection is that, as we recall the incidents, we find a distinct story rising before us, marked by many prominent passages. In true comedy, as we have shown, character and the development of character by even trifling incidents is a legitimate source of dramatic interest ; and the exhibition of Mr. Pickwick and his friend, under their various trials—his victimization by Jingle and Mrs. Bardell—would be sufficient to form a play, and also constitute the framework, as it were, of the piece. The other episodes are more or less garnish, and unessential. But then it should be treated by dramatists of the first skill, such as MM.

THE HISTORY OF PICKWICK.

Meilhac and Halevy, who abstracted out of Goethe's tremendous and unwieldy poem the play of "Faust," which is the admiration and despair of all professional dramatists. The scenes at Rochester, the borrowing of the coat, the ball, the duel, are not a bit more farcical than the scenes in "The Rivals," with Acre's display of timidity and his duel; indeed it might be said that there is even less formal story in the "Rivals" than in "Pickwick."

"Pickwick," as we have seen, had not run half its course, having barely reached its thirtieth chapter when the attack began, and the managers of the Adelphi got their version ready with all speed.

The bill of this performance is a singular production, and must have been moral torture to the author, in spite of the nauseous compliments with which the adapters tried to propitiate him. At the same time it is difficult not to be amused at the ingenuity with which the writers made the most of, and "beat out" as it were, the meagre materials at their disposal. This mode, however, of laying out a "good bill," and piquing the readers with an anticipatory sketch of the plot, was then in high fashion, even at theatres of better standing. The bill is worthy of preservation as a "curio."

THEATRE ROYAL, ADELPHI.

☞ THE new piece of THE PEREGRINATIONS OF PICKWICK is eminently successful.—The personation of Pickwick, Jingle, and Sam Weller, is unique.—The roars of laughter are incessant—The serious interest intense—The house full.

Monday, April 10th, and during the week, will be presented an original, Serio-Comic Burletta, in three Acts, interspersed with music founded on the celebrated Papers written by "Boz," and entitled the

PEREGRINATIONS OF PICKWICK.

The Papers upon which this Drama is principally founded have obtained a celebrity wholly unexampled in that class of literature. The proprietors of the Adelphi were anxious to present it in the most favourable dramatic form to the public; a serious story (the incidents from an episode in the Papers) has therefore been interwoven with the pre-ambulations (sic) of the Pickwickians.

A great portion of the comic dialogue is extracted from the Papers by the express permission of the author, C. Dickens, Esq., better known as "Boz."

ACT I.—THE MISER FATHER.

Old Clutchley (*a wealthy speculator*),—MR. O. SMITH.
George Heyling,—MR. HEMMING.
Maria (*betrothed to Heyling*),—MRS. YATES.
Norah (*attendant on Miss Wardle*),—MRS. FITZWILLIAM.

THE CLUB.

Charing Cross—*Cab*-alistic doings—A meeting—A Journey.
Samuel Pickwick, Esq. (*Founder of the P.C., a gentleman of the inquiring sort*)—MR. YATES.
Augustus Snodgrass, Esq., M.P.C.,—MR. STIRLING.
Tracy Tupman, Esq., M.P.C.,—MR. ISMAY.
Alfred Jingle (*not*) Esq. (*a gentleman of a talkative sort*),—MR. BUCKSTONE.

THE ELOPEMENT.

Garden—A Father's denunciation—The Flight.

Air, "O' Killarney's lucid Lake" (Old Irish Melody),—MRS. FITZWILLIAM.

THE BALL AT ROCHESTER.

Ante-room at Ball—Arrival of visitors—Pickwickians pleasuring —Cutting out and cutting in—Fighting and Flirting.

A. Wardle, Esq., of Dingley Dell (*an " Old English Gentleman "*)—MR. CULLENFORD.

Dr. Slammer, M.D.,—MR. SANDERS.

Joe (*the fat boy—a peripatetic somnambulist*),—MR. DUNN.

Miss Wardle (*maiden sister of Mr. Wardle*),—MRS. Young.

Misses Wardle,—MISS A. CONWAY and MRS. FORSYTHE.

Quadrille—Another Elopement—Pursuit.

Act II.—WHITE HART INN, BOROUGH.

Arrival of Pursuers—The Interview—The Compromise.

Sam Weller (*Boots with original notions respecting things in general*),—MR. JOHN REEVE.

Mr. Perker (*an Attorney*),—MR. YOUNG.

Ostler,—MR. GIFFORD.

Chambermaid,—MISS CONWAY.

THE MARSHALSEA PRISON.

Destitution—Unforgiving Father—Generous Hibernian—Catastrophe.

Air, " The Grave where the dear one died " (Irish Melody),— MRS. FITZWILLIAM.

Sportsmen (Country and Cockney).

The Banquet—Precautions—Effects of Punch and Speech making.

ACT III.

Three years are supposed to have elapsed between the second and third Acts.

Pickwick resumes his Peregrinations in search of a new wonder.

AN APARTMENT.

An Irish Medley, by MRS. FITZWILLIAM.

Old Weller (*father of Sam, a long stage coachman*),—MR. SANDERS).

A PRISON.

Marian, the restored maniac—Repentance—Happiness.

THE FETE AT MR. WARDLE'S.

Christmas party—Good news—Denouement—Finale and dance.

Some of the touches here are worthy of Mr. Crummles' management, and the absurd statement, that with a view to present the story in the most favourable dramatic form, " an episode " from the papers " was ' interweaven ' with the perambulations " of the Club, must have made the author laugh heartily. It will be noted that a later long-established favourite, Buckstone, played Jingle; and Yates, a favourite comedian of much merit, Pickwick. The most amusing part was the character written up or rather devised for Mrs. Fitzwilliam. This lady, long after one of the main stays of the Haymarket, was Irish, and could sing Irish songs. She accordingly became Norah, Miss Wardle's Irish maid, for whom it was necessary to suspend the action while she warbled no less than two "melodies" and a " medley " ! One, as we see, was entitled "The *grave* where the dear one *died !* " There can be little doubt that this suggested, however remotely, passages in the Crummles' episode.

Encouraged by this attempt, another theatre, the new Strand, now took the book in hand, calling in the aid of Moncrieff, whose adaptation of the refined "Tom and Jerry" had drawn all London. That a compliment was intended to the authur by thus employing so eminent a "haud," will be seen from an introduction—where, we are told, the piece was

"Arranged from the celebrated PICKWICK PAPERS, of the inimitable Boz."

NEW STRAND THEATRE.

(Near Somerset House.)

ON Monday, July 10th, 1837, and during the week will be presented for the first time, with new and extensive scenery dresses, and decorations, &c., &c., an entirely new Peregrinating Piece of incidents, characters and manners, interspersed with Vaudevilles, called

SAM WELLER,

OR THE

PICKWICKIANS,

founded on Boz's Posthumous Papers of the PICKWICK CLUB, by the author of "Tom and Jerry." The scenery by Mr. Dearlove and assistants ; the music arranged by Mr. Collins, the dresses and decorations by Mr. Nallion, &c. The piece produced under the sole direction of MR. W. J. HAMMOND.

☞ If the author should be considered to have overlooked, or not to have perceived, any part he should have taken, he can only plead in excuse that he has been obliged to perform his work in the *dark !* which he trusts will procure him pardon. Late experience has enabled him to bring Mr. Pickwick's affairs to a conclusion rather sooner than his gifted biographer has done, if not so satisfactorily, at all events quite legally.

This precious piece, which out-heroded its predecessor, was the work of a dramatic " hack," who had adapted, altered and disfigured a vast number of works, and whose chief qualifications was the having fitted for the stage Pierce Egan's degrading chronicle of " Tom and Jerry, or Life in London." In these congenial hands the Pickwickians became a set of jovial, rollicking fellows, " *pre*-ambulating " the country in search of adventures. Indeed, with much effrontery, the admirers of Mr. Egan's story claimed that it had supplied the model for Pickwick, and pointed to his description of the King's Bench which became the Fleet in the novel, and to an archery meeting, instead of the shooting party.[1]

This, however, ran but a few nights. Nothing daunted, however, the spoilers proceeded with their work; and presently brought out, " Sam Weller's Tour ; or, the Pickwickians in France,"

[1] The author of "Charles Dickens: the Story of his Life," has noted as a curious coincidence that, in " The Finish " (a sequel to " Life in London ") one of the characters, " the Fat Knight," is first met by " Corinthian Tom " at the village of Pickwick. It would almost seem, indeed, that this name was associated with him from his birth almost. The last coaching stage on the Bath Road, where Moses Pickwick's coaches changed horses, was "Pickwick," where was " Pickwick Lodge," Mr. Dickenson's residence. It is stated that, in the Register at Portsmouth, under the date of May 8th, 1814, is found the baptism of one Francis Pickwick, with immediately after it Francis Dickens, followed by the name of Shakespeare.

when the whole was taken over to Paris, where there were scenes in the Palais Royal, &c., all set out in the bills in the usual half-jocular and would-be appetizing style. It wound up with a spectacular pageant and procession, representing the coronation. A specimen or two from this production will be found to more than justify the author's indignation at the treatment of his work. When the club is first setting out, Mr. Pickwick thus addresses his friends :—

" Now then, *brother Pickwickians*, now then to commence our memorable peregrinations.

Chorus—OMNES. *Air, " Vive le Roi."*
Pickwick's on, o'er hill and dale,
We'll from all knowledge draw ;
Far and near, spread the tale,
Boys, hurrah ! boys, hurrah !
Hearts that fame like ours inspires,
Critic frowns ne'er shall awe,
Till our Club's last name expires,
Boys, hurrah ! boys, hurrah !

Exit OMNES, L.

But the *dénouement*, which takes place in the Fleet Prison, is more extraordinary :—

Enter SAM *and* JINGLE, L.

SAM. Hurrah, hurrah, hurrah ! Pack up your things, sir !

PICK. Sam—Sam—compose yourself—I have provided beds, a pair of bellows, and——

SAM. Beds ! bellows ! burn the beds and blow the bellows. Hurrah! hurrah !

PICK. Sam, you're mad! My friends here wish to walk with me awhile—get my stick.

SAM. Stick—you must cut your stick, and prepare to take a very long walk. Hurrah! hurrah!

PICK. Sam! I have no hesitation in saying, I can't walk without my stick?

SAM. Beg pardon—my heart's too full to speak —Mr. Jingle here is the very best scoundrel as ever vas, and the long and short of it is, you're a free man agin—Mother Bardell is married—the rascally lawyers are in Newgate—all a conspiracy —Jingle here proved it—he's Mother Bardell's husband; here's your discharge (*gives paper*).

PICK. Amazement!

SAM. And vhat's more—three hundred pounds to compromise the felony—and all this clever scoundrel Jingle's doings!

JINGLE. Friend Pickwick—can't say much— feelings won't let me—fact simply this—account —your debtor ow'd you much—yes much—this, per contract—let us strike balance; if in my favour give me your note of hand (*takes hand*).

PICK. This repays all, still all is not repaid; take this three hundred pounds—'tis fairly yours —it will release you—live honest, and live happy!

JINGLE. Study new character—play new part—

eh!—give up the villains—bad line of business—
unprofitable, very! I will, I will, bless you, old
fellow! eternal blessings, repentance, gratitude!
(*repressing his feelings*) Damme, I want the word
—good-bye—heaven bless you all!

Exit, L.

An American actor was then playing at the
theatre, and entrancing the town with a song, the
burden of which was, "Turn about, and wheel
about, and jump Jim Crow." It was felt that this
might in some fashion be utilized for "Pickwick,"
and we find Sam Weller accordingly fitted with
a song, called "Rooks and Daws," which must
have been agony to the author.

Song.—SAM. *Air,* "*Jim Crow.*"
Rooks and daws must look out when
  Rook shooting cockneys go,
For those who shoot at pigeons
  Very often kills a crow.
Hop about and skip about
  And jump jist so,
Keep for rooks a sharp look out—
  Nor kill the crow!

Nor was this all. The perseverance of the
marauders was extraordinary. As soon as
"Nicholas Nickleby" appeared, it was also
seized upon, cut up, and distorted generally, under
the title of "Nicholas Nickleby and poor Smike;
or the victim of the Yorkshire school!"

The author's high-strung nature was deeply

wounded by this series of deliberate outrages, which he was powerless to hinder. Towards the end of "Nickleby," we find Nicholas at Mr. Crummles' supper, breaking out into excited protest against the shameful doings of so-called dramatists, and addressed to an astonished "literary gentleman" who was of the party. This protest was somewhat inartistic and out of place at such a scene; but the author could not resist the opportunity of gibbeting the person who had done him such injury. Mr. Moncrieff must have felt uncomfortable as he read this description of himself and his work. "There was a literary gentleman present who had dramatized in his time two hundred and forty-seven novels, as fast as they had come out—some of them faster than they had come out—and *was* a literary gentleman in consequence.—"What, dramatize a book," said the literary gentleman, "*that's* fame—for its author." "Oh, indeed," said Nicholas. "That's fame, sir," said the literary gentleman. "So Richard Turpin, Tom King, and Jerry Abershaw, have handed down to fame the names of those on whom they have committed their most impudent robberies." Then speaking of Shakespere, he who embodied traditions and stories in the magic circle of his genius, he went on, "You drag within the magic circle of your dulness *subjects not at all adapted to the purposes of the*

stage, and debase as he exalted. You take the
uncompleted books of living authors fresh from their
hands, wet from the press, cut, hack, and carve
them to the powers and capabilities of your actors
and the capability of your theatres."

This very genuine and excited outburst must
have mystified many an ordinary reader, who could
not understand why the tranquil Nicholas should
feel so acutely on the subject.

He was even more enraged by the shameful
burlesques upon his work, the "Pickwick
Abroad," in America, &c. His annoyance and
anger at this treatment by these pirates is shown
by the fantastic address which he inserted in
Bentley's Magazine :—

PROCLAMATION.

𝔚𝔥𝔢𝔯𝔢𝔞𝔰 we are the only true and lawful " Boz : "

And 𝔚𝔥𝔢𝔯𝔢𝔞𝔰 it hath been reported to us, who are commencing a new work to be called the

LIFE AND ADVENTURES OF NICHOLAS NICKLEBY,

that some dishonest dullards, resident in the by-streets and
cellars of this town, impose upon the unwary and credulous
by producing cheap and wretched imitations of our delectable
works. And 𝔚𝔥𝔢𝔯𝔢𝔞𝔰 we derive but small comfort under this
injury, from the knowledge that the dishonest dullards aforesaid cannot by reason of their mental smallness follow near
our heels, but are constrained to creep along by dirty and little
frequented ways, at a most respectful distance behind.

And 𝔚𝔥𝔢𝔯𝔢𝔞𝔰, in like manner, as some other vermin are
not worth the killing for the sake of their carcases, so these

kennel pirates are not worth the powder and shot of the law, inasmuch as whatever damages they may commit, they are in no condition to pay.

𝕿𝖍𝖎𝖘 𝖎𝖘 𝖙𝖔 𝖌𝖎𝖛𝖊 𝖓𝖔𝖙𝖎𝖈𝖊 :—

Firstly to Pirates :

That we have at length devised a mode of execution for them, so summary and terrible, that if any gang or gangs thereof presume to hoist but one shred of the colours of the good ship "Nickleby," &c.; and he threatens them with the gibbet accordingly.

This is just as bitter as the attack on the dramatic pirates in "Nicholas Nickleby" itself.

XXI.

ALL which suggests how curious it is to find this humorous work, ever engendering other humours, and *bizarre* situations as it were, by sheer contagion. Sometimes the result took the shape of something truly absurd, as where sham or spurious humours would connect themselves with it, to which we owe the imitation Pickwicks, and these vulgar dramatic versions. But whatever it touched there is certain to follow some grotesque exhibition. As we have seen, there was something comic in the reception of the book by the pundits and sober persons of the day, who pronounced it "low," and were shocked at the obstreperous hilarity it caused. We cannot resist describing a certain convivial meeting which took place as the work was coming out in numbers, and which is typical of much more that was going on in the same spirit. Messrs. Longman, the eminent publishers, gave a dinner to their friends at which were assembled Sydney Smith, Mr. Hayward, Thomas Moore, Mr. Merivale, Canon Tate, Mr. McCulloch and Dr. Lardner, known as "Dionysius the tyrant." Now here was a fairly

representative gathering, including the chief
wit of the day, the vivacious "Tommy Moore,"
who had a pliant wit of his own, a good *raconteur*
who knew how "to cut a story down to the bone"—
with various critics, and men of vigorous mind.
Moore tells us how the conversation turned "on
Boz, *the new comic writer*," that is, on the new
"funny" young fellow who was writing those
trifling "things" which made people laugh.
Strange to say, Sydney Smith "cried him down,"
and this too "without having given him a fair
trial," that is, having as it were skimmed his
pages and noted a good thing or two.   It actually
appeared that the party, with the exception of
Mr. Hayward and Moore, took the same view.
Moore confesses (in his diary) that he was sorry
for this, and declares that he thought it proof of
good taste in the "masses" that they appreciated "Pickwick," "there being," he says "some as
nice humour and fun in the 'Papers' as in any
work I have seen in our day."   Mr. Hayward
supported him and asked him to dinner.   This
criticism of Moore is characteristic and diverting.   "Nice humour" is good; as though he
should say, "very fair, very fair indeed, a very
promising young man;" and the phrase somehow
recalls the compliment of the Bath Footman to
Sam when he told him that "without any
flattery at all, he seemed to have the makings

of a very nice fellow about him." The Fudge Family is almost forgotten, but the " nice humour" of Boz is still heartily relished.

As we have pointed out, Dickens seems to have had the art of investing old inns—generally mouldy places enough—with dramatic associations. All the Pickwickian Inns we know thoroughly;—have put up at, dined, slept, wandered through their passages, and leave them with regret. They live in our memories, and have each distinct associations. In " Pickwick " they are the welcome background of some of the pleasantest scenes. Our author seemed to think with Dr. Johnson, that " a tavern chair was the throne of human felicity." It recalls the oft-quoted lines of Shenstone on the still inviting old " Red Lion " at Henley :

> " Whoe'er has travelled life's dull round,
> Where'er his wanderings may have been,
> Will sigh to think he still has found
> His warmest welcome at an Inn."

How many inns will the reader suppose, are introduced in Pickwick ? Each has a physiognomy of its own, as distinct as the man with his "four cats in the wheelbarrow—four distinct cats —I give you my honour, sir." They are twenty-two in number !

1. The Golden Cross, Charing Cross.
2. The Bull, Rochester.
3. The Bull, Whitechapel.

z

4. The Blue Lion, Muggleton.
5. The White Hart, Boro'.[1]

---

[1] It was a surprise, and perhaps a shock, to find it seriously put forward that the old, lately demolished White Hart Inn, of the Borough, whose memory is so dear to all Pickwickians,— was not the one intended by " Boz," when he introduced his travellers to Sam! This may seem a trivial matter : but we cannot thus lightly be divorced from one of the most cherished associations of Pickwick. It is comforting to have to say that there is no foundation for this rather rash assumption. Thus shaken, our faith in the rest of the " Boz " topography might fairly totter. Mr. J. Ashby Sterry, who has written many agreeable papers on Dickens's " London," lately stated :—

" I had especial opportunities for comparing the George and the White Hart years ago, and in acquiring information from those who were intimately acquainted with them in the days of Pickwick ; and I have no hesitation in saying there is not the slightest doubt that it was at the George, not the White Hart, where Alfred Jingle and Miss Rachael were discovered by the irate Squire Wardle. These changes, as your correspondent remarks, were frequently made by Dickens. If I mistake not, in his last work, 'Edwin Drood,' the Bull at Rochester is described under the sign of the Blue Boar."

Another writer, Mr. Gordon Stephenson, adds that " it is more than probable that Dickens simply borrowed the name of the White Hart—a sign which struck his fancy— and transferred it to another inn, the George, a little higher up. If Mr. Fitzgerald will visit the George, he will see " curious tiers of open galleries, and an open yard," similar to those which existed at the White Hart ; and *the spot where Sam Weller used to clean the boots* will be gravely pointed out to him. He will also, upon inquiry, ascertain the fact that coaches did not run from the White Hart, but from the George. Dickens either intentionally or by accident frequently made these changes." " If you like to go upstairs," adds Mr. Sterry, " you can see the very room where Mr. Jingle consented to forego all claims to the lady's hand for the consideration of one hundred and twenty pounds. Cannot you

6. The Old Leather Bottle, Cobham.
7. The George and Vulture, Lombard Street.
8. Town Arms, Eatanswill.
9. The Peacock, Eatanswill.
10. The Angel, Bury.
11. The White Hart, Bath.
12. The Bush, Bristol.
13. The Great White Horse, Ipswich.
14. The Spaniards, Hampstead.
15. The Fox under the Hill, Adelphi.
16. The Magpie and Stump, London.
17. The Markis o' Granby, Dorking.
18. The Bell, Berkeley Heath.
19. The Hop-Pole, Tewksbery.
20. The old Royal Hotel, Birmingham.
21. The Saracen's Head, Towcester.
22. Osborne's Hotel, Adelphi.

The marvel is, that these old hostelries, each and all, awaken the most agreeable associations, being the scenes of diverting adventures, which could not have occurred anywhere else with propriety.

fancy too the landlady shouting instructions from the galleries?" A rather fanciful picture that adds nothing to the argument. As to the coaches plying from the George, it may be said that Boz states distinctly that the coaches had, at the period of his story, ceased using this inn, which was given over to the waggons : and, within late years we have often seen waggons lying up in order in the yard of the White Hart. In fact little turns on the point, as we are told that both Jingle and the Wardle party arrived in chaises.

It seems inscrutable why Dickens should have wished to call his inn by the name of the White Hart, and yet really furnish the description of an inn only a few doors off. Dickens, we are told by Mr. Sterry, " changed the sign in order that the place should not be too closely identified." But why should notoriety be attached to the White Hart, from which the

Many of them still remain.   But what cannot be
said of the sympathetic genius of the humorist,
who has contrived to make each distinct, and to
live in the memory without confusion!

It has been shown how the current of daily
life is perpetually furnishing some illustration of
the truth and accuracy of our " Pickwick."   As
these occur, the original passage, or apophthegm of
the story suggests itself, and, as it were, furnishes
an interpretation.   Not a day passes without its
Pickwickian allusion.   Thus, the counsel in the
Cronin case make this flourish : " Not content

George was to be shielded? In the case of the George and
Vulture, the Golden Cross, the score of inns above enu-
merated, he had no scruple in naming them *tout bonnement*.
The only argument given for the gratuitous assertion is the
instance of the Marquis of Granby, which was shifted from
either Chatham or Esher to Dorking. But the author had
good reasons for this, connected with his own family; there
was beside a gain of pictorial effect. It is seriously urged that
" he did the same thing in 'Edwin Drood,' where the Bull is
described under the sign of the Blue Boar." But as Cloister-
ham was a fictitious title, its inns had to follow suit. It is a
different thing to transfer a real sign to another real inn.

The whole is in fact an assumption founded, not on any
discrepancy in the author, but on " Phiz's " picture which
appears to represent the yard of the George. But the
White Hart passed through many phases of dilapidation before
its dissolution. Its galleries were filled up, portions torn
away. Even twenty years ago, it was in a state of decay.
The George is in a sound state, like the Bell at Holborn. But,
we may repeat it, Dickens states that the incidents occurred
at the White Hart, and in his time the White Hart stood there.
It is not worth while going beyond this.

with having beat out his life, *not content with
having laid him to rest in a sewer*," when it was
noted that this suggested Sergeant Buzfuz's description of Mr. Bardell " peacefully gliding from
this world," having been knocked on the head
with a quart pot, in a cellar. The spirit of both
passages is the same. On the same day a half-
witted being is brought up in the police court,
and pleads that he was only looking up to the
sky. For what? " *For Samuel Weller.*" " Do
you mean the person we all know? " asked the
magistrate. " Yes," said the man. Sergeant
Robinson, in his recently published " Reminis-
cences," describes a judge behaving exactly like
Mr. Justice Stareleigh. " Well, witness, your
name is John Tomkins." Witness : "No, my lord,
Joe Taylor." Judge : " Ah, I see—you are a
sailor, and you live in the New Cut." Witness :
" No, my lord."

But few Pickwickian illustrations or " apoph-
thegms " have been so serviceable as that of the
" Pickwickian sense " which has been found valuable in explaining away an offensive expression.
I have stated that this passage was intended to
ridicule some such explanation given by Mr.
Joseph Hume. I have since discovered, in "The
Squib Annual," 1837, some satirical verses, which
prove that Dickens had this incident in his
mind.

THE CODE OF HONOUR.

From Sir R——— P——— to Jo——— H———e, Esq.

I wish to be inform'd aright,
  Touching the speech you made last night,
  You are reported by the press,
(Indeed, myself I heard you say so,
  But surely I can do no less,
If you deny its truth, you may so,—)
  To have asserted I had broken,
So oft my pledges to the people,
  That all the speeches I had spoken,
Proffer'd good faith which I must keep ill,
  Or else, for so your comment ran,
  I could not be an honest man;
That, not to make the inference greater,
  Which to establish I were loth,
You thought me either rogue or traitor,
  And said, perhaps, I might be both;
Nay, if I understood your rule,
  With no exception in't to save,
You thought that I must be a fool,
  And hinted I must be a knave.
The speech you made, say, was it made so?
Or what you said, pray, was it said so?
And tell me, (which is most of all),
Were your words meant as personal?

No. II.

From Jo——— H———e, Esq., to Sir R——— P———l, Bart.

SIR,

  But, if such charges I let fall,
  Why should you think me so personal?
  As sure as groats are boil'd for gruel,
  Warm words, I know, will cause a duel;
  Then without scruple, I confess,
  Sir Robert, I meant nothing less;

And let me tender this admission,
  Since candour is so much in vogue,
I meant that, as a politician,
  I thought you knave, and fool, and rogue.
May I be burnt like Bishop Bonner,
If once I meant to touch your honour.
Far from me, therefore, to infer
Aught 'gainst your private character.

No. III.

From Sir R—— P——l to J—— H——e, Esq.

I just tuck in my twopenny,
To tell you in two words, that I,
Receive with due consideration,
Your satisfactory explanation,
Nought can be more precise, or better,
Than what you write me in your letter.

This shows the largeness of Dickens's humour, which dealt with the deep-seated failings that belong to every generation. This happy jest, trifling as it is, has obtained, therefore, a prominent popularity and application.

I have given illustrations of the extraordinary influence exercised by " Pickwick " on " the form and pressure of the time." Were there space, it would be interesting to show how, of all modern books of fiction, it has insensibly worked good, in furnishing scenes of unaffected good-nature and benevolence, with types of true and honest dispositions, so natural and familiar as to convey the idea that they are common and universal. This sort of revelation has the greater effect, as the characters are of the Bourgeois type.   It may be said, without exaggeration, that the ardent reader of "Pickwick" will have learned much from its pages which he would have had no other opportunity of knowing, while even the cynical will have their harsh views of life and character softened.   This view, it is likely enough, will seem fanciful; but the mere fact that between two and three hundred characters of this pleasant type have been introduced into the community whose sayings and doings are familiar to all, must have had an extraordinary influence.

Even as I write the magic circle of Pickwick's popularity continues spreading, and foreign countries, like our own, seem to find equal relish for the humours of the book.   Lately a traveller in Stockholm noted to his astonishment that the play announced for the night at the Svenska Theatre was "Mr. Pickwick."   "I went to see it," says the writer, in *Vanity Fair.*   "The curtain had already risen.   Upon the stage stood three men; and in one of these, arrayed in a blue coat with brass buttons, drab tights and gaiters, with a bald head and spectacles, I recognized the hero, even before they addressed him as Meester Peekveek.   As to the others, I was more doubtful; one wore a green coat and drab small clothes, the other had long hair and a poetical-looking suit of black; but soon I heard them called Meester Veenkle and Meester Snodgrâs.

"Later on, a middle-aged female, referred to as Meesis Bardale, came in and fainted in the arms of Meester Peekveek, who was consequently pitched into by a youth known as Tommee, the latter being in turn violently assaulted by Meester Veenkle. Finally, there entered a weird and wild creature, with spasmodic movements and fragmentary utterances. They called him Yingl. The scene of Act II. was laid in the inn 'i Eatonsvill.' A public election was apparently in progress; Meester Pote delivered a brief harangue, and a fussy little man in quaint black costume, Meester Pairker, dodged about everywhere. Then I made the acquaintance of Meester Vardle, Mees Râshale, Mees Arabella, Mees Amelee, and a fat boy called Yoey. An excited crowd passed and repassed the door with military drummings. Yingl was foiled in an endeavour to elope with Mees Râshale. Meester Veenkle and Mr. Snodgrâs carried on shockingly with the other two young ladies; Sahmmee kissed the servant girl Marie; the election of somebody was announced, and Meester Peekveek was set upon by very free and independent electors, who were eventually cleared out in fine style by the uncoated Meester Vayler and his son.

"The fourth act was the best. The famous trial was conducted in a Gothic chamber that savoured more of the Church than the Law Court. The seat of judgment was in the middle of the stage by the footlights; in front of it, to the right and left, were two small pews, in which a couple of red-robed gentlemen took their places, whereupon a black-robed usher removed from a tall hat-stand two grey wigs and solemnly placed them upon their respective heads. Yards behind, in a long pew at the back, sat three more red-robed persons—junior counsel, probably—but they took no part whatever in the proceedings. In a low gallery on the left sat the foreman of the jury; behind him stood two of his brethren, one clad in a flaming scarlet waistcoat; the other nine jurymen, perhaps, were round the corner. On either side sat the Plaintiff and the defendant, with their professional advisers; two ushers sat in the middle of the Court; the red-robed judge came to and occupied the Bench, with his back to the audience, and the trial began. Advokat Boozfooz rose in his pew on the right and delivered an oration; in which I am sure he said something about chops and tomato sauce, after which Advokat Snoobeen delivered an oration from his pew on the left. Then, in turn, the plaintiff, Meesis Cloopeens, Meesis Sahndares, Meester Veenkle, and Sahm, were brought alongside the pew of Advokat Boozfooz, who confidentially put a few questions to those individuals. There was no cross-examination at all. When done with, the witnesses shook hands with plaintiff or defendant, as the case might be. The latter's friends, especially Meester Vayler, interrupted from the dress-circle. The Judge never summed up; but the foreman of the jury immediately pronounced a verdict with damages, and the curtain fell on Meester Peekveek expressing extreme indignation." [1]

[1] When Sam was reproaching Mr. Winkle for his elopement from Bath, he used this remarkable phrase, "all sorts o' *fanteegs*," which has excited an extraordinary amount of speculation and discussion. Even the lexicographer, Dr. Murray, the learned editor of the new monumental dictionary, has furnished me with a theory, and Professor Skeat, of Cambridge, has discussed it in his "Notes on English Etymology." "*Fanteague*, a worry, or bustle, also, ill-humour; Halliwell. To be 'in a *fanteague*' or 'in a *fanteeg*,' i.e. to be in a state of excitement, is a familiar expression. The word is in Pickwick, chapter xxxviii., where *fanteegs* means 'worries,' or 'troubles.' It is clearly from F. *fanatique*, adj., 'mad, frantick, in a frenzie, out of his little wits;' Cotgrave. Hence it is allied to *Fanatic*." Sam of course, had no idea of these profound meanings. But here the art of the author is shown. Persons of Sam's class, and of the same intelligence, are fond of coining or distorting some word or phrase which they have picked up, and which has struck them as expressive. In the writer's family was an old servant who had travelled, and who had picked up a stock of strange terms, such as "*rocoma-wollia*," for a state of confusion, "rook'em-rack'em," for disorder. He would account for a person's death on the ground that "he had *no stanniner*."

XXII.

THE true Pickwickian humour is found in a large portion of "Nickleby," "Oliver Twist," "Humphrey's Clock;" later this gave place to another form, which the author seemed to prefer. Occasionally we find the same subject treated under both systems; and thus is offered an interesting and convenient mode of comparison; as between Stiggins and Chadband. We are lost in admiration at the skill with which the author's intention is carried out, and the rich variety of touches of humour with which the Pickwickian figure is presented, or rather presents itself, for all is action and movement: whereas Chadband displays himself in forms of words and phrases to which the author points attention by comments of his own. When Stiggins paid his visit after Mrs. Weller's death, he describes himself as " a vessel," as does also Chadband, on one of his visits.

"Oh, my young friend" said Mr. Stiggins, breaking the silence in a low voice, "here's a sorrowful affliction." Sam nodded very slightly. "For the man of wrath too!" added Mr. Stiggins; "it makes a vessel's heart bleed." Mr.

Weller was heard by his son to murmur something about making a vessel's nose bleed; but Mr. Stiggins heard him not. "Do you know, young man," whispered Mr. Stiggins, drawing his chair closer to Sam, "whether she has left Emmanuel anything?" "Who's he?" inquired Sam. Here is the reserve of true humour. Mr. Weller's remark of "making a vessel's nose bleed" is murmured to himself; were it heard by Stiggins, the situation would be "coarsened" and rough. Stiggins' queries are put, as is natural, in a low tone, so as not to be heard by Mr. Weller. Indeed the attitude of Sam—between the two—is not only exquisitely humorous, but dramatic. We then turn to Chadband. "From Mr. Chadband's being much given to describe himself, both verbally and in writing, as a vessel, he is occasionally *mistaken by strangers for a gentleman connected with navigation:* but he is, as he expresses it, 'in the ministry.' . . . Mrs. Snagsby has but recently taken a passage upward by the vessel, Chadband, and her attention was attracted to that bark, A 1, &c." Supper being got ready for him, he was, we are told, "rather a consuming vessel, the persecutors say, a gorging vessel." This elaboration of the "vessel" idea is more ingenious than humorous; and we prefer the first airy method, which just touches it and then lets it go.

We recall Sam's well-told story of the sausage-maker, who disappeared, and who, it was found, had allowed himself to be drawn into his own machine to be converted into sausages. The discovery, it will be recollected, was made by a customer. In an old Irish song-book is to be found an account of much the same kind of inci dent, but which the author of Pickwick could never have seen, and which begins :—

> " At the sign of the Bell
> In the town of Clonmel
> Paddy Hegarty kept a shebeen."

He is roused up by his friends in the middle of the night, and required to prepare them a supper. There were no victuals in the house, and in his despair he bethought him of his trousers.

> " He cut them in sthripes
> By way they was sthripes
> And he boiled them, his ould leather breecks."

The guests found this food extraordinarily tough, and protested that it was

> " Quare sort of mutton,
> When Andy M'Quirk
> With the point of his fork
> He picked out an ivory button.

In proof of the extraordinary vitality of " Pickwick " it may be repeated that hardly a day passes without some allusion or discussion, or quotation, connected with the story and its characters. It would seem that we cannot do with-out it. Now a valse is published, entitled " The

Pickwick Valse ; " or now, a patent medicine proprietor offers a cartoon, showing Mr. Pickwick
discovering his medicines, as he did the " Bill
Stumps " inscription ; or a gigantic cartoon shows
a carpet cleaned by machinery, representing
Sam and the pretty housemaid holding up the
carpet. Now a caricaturist exhibits Mr. Glad-
stone on the ice, like Mr. Winkle. Even as I
write, there is a curious little controversy going
on, on the subject of Sam's dialect, and his
constant substitution of the letter " v " for " w "
and of " w " for " v." It is insisted by some
that this was an ingenious invention of the
author's. Others contend that the substitution of
the " v " for " w," was a common Cockney form
of the time, but that the turning of " veal ' into
" weal " was unknown. Lately, a dog named
" Sam Weller " was brought into court at
Wokingham, on the charge of being found
without a muzzle. This sagacious animal—
who must surely be descended from Mr. Jingle's
Ponto—is stated to have actually presented
himself on a Monday morning to the astonished
magistrate—without his master, to meet the
charge, and took his seat solemnly. His mistress stated in evidence, that when the baby was
lying ill of the influenza, the animal was accustomed to listen to the doctor's report, and carefully avoided intruding himself ; but when he

heard the doctor state that the child was "out of danger," he resumed his daily visits to the cot. Lately, a case came before the courts, in which a husband resisting payment of his wife's debts, declared loudly in court, that he would be found "*as stubborn as Pickwick*" in the matter. Nay, so deeply ingrained is the Pickwickian tradition, that an allusion to the name "Samuel" seems to challenge recognition. At a late meeting of the Alsopp's Brewery Company, when some very critical interests were being discussed, a gentleman named Harrison interrupted :

Secretary. "What is your Christian name ?"

Mr. Harrison. "Samuel."

A Voice. "Who gave you that name ?"

Secretary. "Did you say Samuel?" (Great laughter.)

A Voice. "*Spell it with a wee!*" (Roars of laughter.)

Only this morning, a leading journal, alluding to Stanley's account of his travels, remarks that the natives of Africa appear to have as rooted an objection to a note-taker among them "as had Mr. Pickwick's cabman."

Much of this "actuality" is no doubt owing to the vivid living sources from which the author drew his inspiration. He was not attracted by merely superficial transitory manifestations, but pierced deeply to what was purely essential. I lately came upon a curious illustration of this. It has always seemed a puzzle why the author attached so much importance to the "Stroller's Tale," a rather melodramatic story, yet of which he wrote with a sort of pride and satisfaction; he was so dissatisfied with the illustration furnished, that he had it redrawn. On making some investigation into the curious history of Grimaldi the clown, I found that this wretched stroller was almost a literal reproduction of Grimaldi's dissipated son, who, four years before, had closed his miserable career under most tragic circumstances. The incidents, it will be found, are almost the same in both cases; both being engaged ' at a theatre on the other side of the water," and performing there on the night previous to the seizure ; there is the same frantic attempt to act during the delirium, with the restraint and surrounding squalor. The story seems to have made a deep impression on Dickens, though he does appear to have had the life of the father in hand at the time.

It has been mentioned that in families bearing the name of Weller, it is often the practice to christen a son " Samuel." The most mysterious incident, however, in this connection is the question how one of the most eminent of Shake-

A a

spearian commentators and scholars came to be
called " *Samuel Weller Singer*."

As was mentioned in the earlier pages of this
work, one of the family of Pickwick appears to
have found the bearing of this honourable name
so inconvenient, owing to its grotesque associations, that in the year 1880, the usual proclamation appeared in the *Times* announcing that
he had abandoned it for ever, and would henceforth bear the name of Sainsbery. Yet this
simple act instantly attracted public attention,
as though it were a serious step taken by a
member of Mr. Samuel Pickwick's family ! One
journal even made it a matter of reproach to the
gentleman, as though he were *ashamed* of belonging to the house of his eminent relative.
He was reminded that it was an ancient and
honourable name, founded on the heraldic motto,
" Piquez Vite."   This might have been suggested
by Count Smorltork himself.[1]

[1] Mr. Forster, humouring this pleasant illusion, has preserved
among his papers an actual letter of old Eleazer Pickwick's,
dated Jan. 5th, 1802, and which runs :—

" DEAR SIR,—I beg to acknowledge the receipt of your favour,
including a bill for seventy-five pounds, seven shilling and sixpence, which I have acknowledged as directed on the back of
the bill ; and permit me to acknowledge myself much obliged
by your kind attention to the business.

" I am, sir,
" Your most obliged,
" ELEAZER PICKWICK."

L'ENVOI.

WE have now come to the close of our "Peram-bulations," and I think it will be admitted that there is no story of modern times that could have furnished such an amount of varied "exe-gesis," extending in so many directions. Nor have, as I think, the Perambulations been unentertaining; and it will be some satisfaction if they lead to a renewed study of this truly humorous work. In conclusion we may join heartily in "Father Prout's" hymn composed when Pickwick was appearing :—

"A RHYME! a rhyme! from a distant clime,—from the gulph
    of the Genoese :
O'er the rugged scalps of the Julian Alps, dear Boz! I send
    you these,
To light the *Wick* your candlestick holds up, or, should you
    list,
To usher in the yarn you spin concerning Oliver Twist.

"Immense applause you've gained, oh, Boz! through conti-
    nental Europe ;
You'll make Pickwick œcumenick ;[1] of fame you have a sure
    hope :
For here your books are found, gadzooks ! in greater *luxe* than
    any
That have issued yet, hotpress'd or wet, from the types of
    GALIGNANI.

---

[1] εἴδωλον τῆς γῆς οἰκουμένης·

'But neither when you sport your pen, oh, potent mirth-
compeller!

Winning our hearts 'in monthly parts,' can Pickwick or Sam
Weller

Cause us to weep with pathos deep, or shake with laugh spas-
modical,

As when you drain your copious vein for Bentley's periodical.

" Write on, young sage! still o'er the page pour forth the flood
of fancy;

Wax still more droll, wave o'er the soul Wit's wand of necro-
mancy.

Behold! e'en now around your brow th' immortal laurel
thickens;

Yea, SWIFT or STERNE might gladly learn a thing or two from
DICKENS.

" A rhyme! a rhyme! from a distant clime,—a song from the
sunny south!

A goodly theme, so Boz but deem the measure not uncouth.

Would for thy sake, that 'PROUT' could make his bow in
fashion finer,

'*Partant*' (from thee) 'pour la Syrie,' for Greece and Asia
Minor.

" GENOA, 14*th December*, 1837.'

APPENDIX.

~~~~~~~~

BIBLIOGRAPHY OF "PICKWICK."

I shall now proceed to deal with a subject which will be
interesting to the select, but important class of Pickwickians,
who spare neither their time nor their money in securing the
choicest editions, best impressions of the etchings, &c. I shall
go through the numbers, noting all the "points" which make a
true first edition valuable, and then furnish a regular Biblio-
graphical Table—perhaps the fullest and most complete yet
offered.

The first number of "Pickwick" offers the well-known,
pale green wrapper, the author's familiar, serial "livery" which
he retained for over forty years. Lever adopted pink, and
Thackeray yellow, as their distinguishing colours. We have
noted that the emblems and sketches all portended a regular
sporting novel. At the top was a Cockney sportsman in
gaiters, firing at a robin; at the sides were trophies —fishing-rods,
landing-nets and a fowling-piece; while below, Mr. Pickwick is
shown asleep in a punt, his head drooped upon his breast, a
bottle and glass beside him, with Putney bridge and church in
the background. It is remarkable that Mr. Pickwick through
the whole story did not display the slightest acquaintance
with sporting, though he relished going out with shooting
parties. He is described as having written a paper on the
ponds of Hampstead and on "tittlebats." "With illustrations by Seymour," of which there were four. These four,
however, did not bear the artist's name : but in the
second number we find "Seymour del" under each of the
three stitched in at the beginning. There was no description
under the plates, but merely a reference to the number of the
page where the subject of the illustration was to be found. On
the back was a displayed advertisement of a new venture of
the publishers. "This day is published, &c., The Library of

Fiction," of which the first article is the " Tuggs' at Ramsgate, by Boz," while a couple of pages of the publishers' other advertisements are sewn in. No II. contained three etchings by Seymour, and only 24 pages of type—the first had twenty-six—and the following Address was inserted in a leaf :—

" Before this number reaches the hands of our readers, they will have become acquainted with the melancholy death of Mr. Seymour, under circumstances of a very distressing nature. Some time must elapse before the void which the deceased gentleman has left in his profession can be filled up ;—the blank his death has occasioned in the Society which his amiable nature won, and his talents adorned, we can hardly hope to see supplied. We do not allude to this distressing event in the vain hope of adding, by any eulogium of ours, to the respect in which the late Mr. Seymour's memory is held by all who ever knew him. Some apology is due to our readers for the appearance of the present number with only three plates. When we state that they came from Mr. Seymour's last efforts, and that on one of them, in particular (the embellishment to the Stroller's Tale) he was engaged up to a late hour of the night preceding his death, we feel confident that the excuse will be deemed a sufficient one.

" Arrangements are in progress which will enable us to present the ensuing numbers of the Pickwick Papers on an improved plan, which we trust will give entire satisfaction to our numerous readers.

" *April 27th,* 1836."

Number III. announced " With illustrations by R. W. Buss," and contained 32 pages. There was also a leaf inserted, an " Address from the Publishers," but written by Dickens :—

" We announced in our last that the ensuing numbers of the Pickwick Papers would appear in an improved form, and we now beg to call the attention of our readers to the fulfilment of our promise.

"Acting upon a suggestion made to them from various influential quarters, the Publishers have determined to increase the quantity of letterpress in every monthly part, and to diminish the number of plates. It will be seen that the present number contains eight additional pages of closely printed matter, and two engravings in steel from designs by Mr. Buss—a gentleman already well known to the public as a very humorous and talented artist.

"This alteration in the plan of the work entails upon the Publishers considerable expense, which nothing but a large circulation would justify them in incurring. They are happy to have it in their power to state that the rapid sale of the two first numbers, and the daily increasing demand for this Periodical, enables them to acknowledge the patronage of the public, in the way which they hope will be deemed most acceptable.

" *May* 30*th*, 1836."

Postscript from the Editor.

" Always anxious to amuse our readers by every means in our power, we beg to present them with the following *verbatim* copy of a letter which was addressed and sent by an anonymous correspondent to the Editor of the Pickwick Papers, a fortnight since. Our correspondent's notions of punctuation are peculiar to himself, and we have not ventured to interfere with them.

" ' Sir,—In times when the great and the good are largely associating for the amelioration of the animal kingdom, it seems remarkable . that any writer should . counteract their . intentions . by . such careless paragraphs as . the one . I enclose.

" ' if it is carelessness *only* . it may be corrected if it is . bad taste . I am afraid it . will be more difficult . but perhaps you could . in another paper point out . to the obtuse . like myself, the wit or humour, of depicting . the noblest of animals faint, weary, and over driven,

" When the Knees quiver and the Pulses beat."
Subjected . to a . Brute ; only to be . tolerated because he *at* . *least* is *ignorant*, of the Creature and his Creator . to whom he is responsible, and whose " admirable frolic and fun " consists in giving . his brutal history of his horse . in bad English ! ! " '

" Then follows an extract from a newspaper containing the cabman's description of his ' Horse from p. 6 of our first number.' This is evidently a very pleasant person—a fellow of infinite fancy. We shall be happy to receive other communications from the same person—and on the same terms."

In a leaflet of two pages we find an announcement of the author's " Sunday under Three Heads, to be published in a few days ; " the illustrations of which were by Hablot Browne, who was presently to be chosen the artist of Pickwick. There was also some " favourable notices " of the story, taken from such obscure chronicles as the *Lincoln Gazette*, the *Tyne Mercury*, and the *News*. The second of these journals wrote, " Heaven help the man who gets hold of this book in the midst of business, for if it do not cause him to neglect it, he can have no taste for the ludicrous."

Pickwick described as " now publishing," is, we are told, " to be completed in *about* twenty monthly numbers, each monthly part to be embellished with two illustrations by R. W. Buss." [1]

Mr. Buss, as we have seen, was dismissed after a single trial. The "about" is significant, but the young author made up his mind, towards the middle of the work, not to exceed twenty numbers. Yet half a dozen more would have been welcomed, for there is no sign of flagging towards the close. No. IV. simply bore the announcement " with illustrations ; " it was felt, no doubt, after the two miscarriages, that they had but a precarious hold of any artist. In this number, Hablot Browne, or "Phiz," made his *debût* with two singularly delicate etchings, full of grace and promise. A critical eye will note in a few of the earliest attempts a certain constraint and even stiffness, and there is a single plate which, in its first shape, is inferior in drawing to the rest. This is the scene of Mr. Pickwick being surprised with Mrs. Bardell in his arms.

"Phiz del" is found under every plate save one, viz., the scene in the Fleet Prison where Mr. Pickwick is shown in bed. The meeting with Jingle in the Fleet is signed "Phiz" only. Sometimes this name is in capitals, but more often in running hand. These trivialities are of interest only to the " *bibliophile enragé.*"

So successful was the work that we now find a well-filled "Pickwick Advertiser" with notices from the publishers, Macrone and Tilt. Rowland and his Macassar oil had figured in the preceding number. In some early issues we find "Nemo" signed to the artist's first two plates. In No. V. "Phiz" is signed to the second plate. In No. IX. we have this characteristic announcement :—

" New Burlington Street,
" *November* 28*th.*
" Edited by 'Boz.'

" On the first of May, to be continued monthly, price 2*s.* 6*d.*, with a portrait and other embellishments.

Mr. Bentley

will publish the first number of

The Wit's Miscellany

Edited by ' Boz.'

[1] Each is signed, " Drawn and etched by R. W. Buss," which is scarcely accurate, as the artist employed another to etch them.

With contributions by the most distinguished personages of the day."

The venture never appeared under this title, for it was at once changed. It was the occasion, however, of a pleasant *mot* —attributed to James Smith, we believe. " I was thinking," said the Publisher, " of changing the title to simply ' Bentley's.' " " Would not that be going to the other extreme ? " said the cynic. The worthy Bentley, to whom it did not apply, himself would have smiled at this jest. Other magazines were presently launched in its wake, which also engendered wit :

> " Says Ainsworth to C——
>   A plan in my pate is
> To give my romance
>   As a supplement gratis.
> Says C—— to Ainsworth,
>   'Twill do very nicely,
> For that will be giving
>   Its value precisely."

In No. X., December, 1836, we read this ADDRESS :—

" Ten months have now elapsed since the appearance of the first number of the PICKWICK PAPERS. At the close of the year and the conclusion of half his task, the author may perhaps, without any unwarranted intrusion on the notice of the public, venture to say a few words for himself.

" He has long been desirous to embrace the first opportunity of announcing that it is his intention to adhere to his original pledge of confining this work to twenty numbers. He has every temptation to exceed the limits he first assigned to himself—the brilliant success, an enormous and increasing sale, the kindest notice, and the most extensive popularity can hold out. They are, one and all, sad temptations to an author, but he has determined to resist them ; firstly, because he wished to keep the strictest faith with his readers; and secondly, because he is most anxious that when the POST-HUMOUS PAPERS OF THE PICKWICK CLUB form a complete work, the book may not have to contend against the heavy disadvantage of being prolonged beyond his original plan.

" For ten months longer, then, if the author be permitted to retain his health and spirits, the PICKWICK PAPERS will be issued in this present form, and will then be completed. By what fresh adventures they may be succeeded is no matter for present consideration. The author merely hints, but he has strong reason to believe that a great variety of other documents still lie hidden in the repository from which these were taken, and they may one day see the light.

"With this short speech, Mr. Pickwick's stage-manager makes his most grateful bow, adding, on behalf of himself and publishers, what the late eminent Mr. John Richardson of Horsemonger Lane, Southwark, and the Yellow Caravan with the Brass Knocker, always said on behalf of himself and company at the close of every performance :—

"'Ladies and Gentlemen,—For these marks of your favour we beg to return you our sincere thanks; and allow us to inform you that we shall keep perpetually going on, beginning again, regularly until the end of the fair.'

"*December*, 1836. (No. X.) "

In No. XII. the system of omitting all reference to the page where the subject of the illustrations is to be found—an odd omission—was continued to the end of the book. Here another lavish advertiser—Mechi and his "Magic Strop "—begins his contributions.

In No. XIV. there is an announcement at the top of the "Pickwick Advertiser "—" 20,000 of the advertising sheet will be printed, and stitched in each number."

In No. XV. there is a Notice to Correspondents :—" We receive every month an immense number of communications purporting to be 'Suggestions' for the Pickwick Papers. We have no doubt that they are forwarded with the kindest intentions ; but, as it is wholly out of our power to make use of any such hints, and as we really have no time to peruse anonymous letters, we hope the writers will henceforth spare themselves a great deal of unnecessary useless trouble."—And an ADDRESS dated June 30, 1837:—

"The author is desirous to take the opportunity afforded him by his resumption of this work, to state once again what he thought has been stated sufficiently emphatically before, namely, that its publication was interrupted by a severe domestic affliction of no ordinary kind ; that this was the sole cause of the non-appearance of the present number in the usual course ; and that henceforth it will continue to be published with its accustomed regularity.

"However superfluous this second notice may appear to many, it is rendered necessary by various idle speculations and absurdities which have been industriously propagated during the past month ; which have reached the author's ears from many quarters, and have pained him exceedingly.

"By one set of intimate acquaintances, expressly well impressed, he has been killed outright ; by another driven mad ; by a third imprisoned for debt ; by a fourth sent per steamer to the United States ; by a fifth rendered incapable of any mental exertion for evermore—by all, in short, represented as doing anything but seeking in a few weeks' release, the restoration of that cheerfulness and peace of which a sad bereavement had temporarily bereaved him."

There is also inserted among the advertisements a finely-engraved steel plate, as a specimen of an illustrated work on Scotland, edited by Dr. Beattie.

In No. XVII. " The Pickwick Advertiser" informs us that, " The impression of the advertising sheet is limited to 20,000, but the circulation of the work being 26,000, that number of bills is required." That is, of bills that were to be stitched in ; but it is not very clear why as many copies of the Advertiser could not be printed as there were of the number. There was this important announcement :—

" August 26th, 1837.

"NEW WORK BY 'BOZ.'

" Messrs. Chapman and Hall have the pleasure of announcing that they have completed arrangements with Mr. Charles Dickens for the production of an entirely new work, to be published monthly, at the same price as the PICKWICK PAPERS. The first number will appear on the 31st March, 1838.

" They also announce an edition of ' Sketches by Boz,' having purchased the whole copyright, for the purpose of enabling the subscribers to the Pickwick Papers to obtain the whole in one book of the same series, and at the same price, propose to publish it in twenty numbers."

There was stitched in a regular pamphlet descriptive of Lockhart's " Life of Sir W. Scott," with all the praises, &c., a curious advertising picture, dealing with " Spinal Support," exactly of the pattern issued now.

In No. XVIII., October 2, 1837, we are told that the circulation was now 29,000. And there is this important announcement :—

" No. XVIII. *September* 29th, 1837.

" COMPLETION OF THE PICKWICK PAPERS.

"The subscribers to this work and the trade are respectfully informed that Nos. XIX. and XX. (with titles, contents, &c.) will be published together on 1st of November ; and that the complete volume, neatly bound in cloth, price one guinea, will be ready for delivery by the 14th of that month, and for which country producers are requested to send early orders to their respective agents."

This is followed by a notice of the new work which was to be published monthly at the same price, and in the same form, as the Pickwick Papers, with illustrations by Phiz, and to appear on 31st March, 1836.

The last two numbers were issued together, and with it the title-page, frontispiece, preface, dedication, errata, and directions to the binder. The full semi-burlesque title ran : "The Post-humous Papers of the Pickwick Club. Being a faithful record of the perambulations, perils, travels, adventures, and sporting transactions of the Corresponding Members. Edited by 'Boz.' With illustrations by Seymour." An announcement changed in the third number to " R. W. Buss," and in the fourth to " with illustrations " simply. It should be noted that this expanded title, " The Perambulations," &c., is found only on the wrapper, and is, as it were, the *temporary* title ; but collectors have now the fashion of retaining their copies in this form, the highest shape of the " uncut," and hold that the covers and advertise-ments even legitimately belong to the book.[2]

On the official title-page, however, we find this flourish, " Perambulations, &c.," discarded, and it stands, "The Post-humous Papers of the Pickwick Club, edited by Charles Dickens." Though this title was issued for those who had subscribed for, and taken in numbers from the beginning, it states that it contains " forty-three illustrations by R. Seymour, and Phiz," which is not accurate, as they would have had two plates by Buss.[3] This seems to convey that, in the re-issued work, the two plates had been withdrawn, and Phiz's substi-tuted. And, as we have seen, Phiz also re-drew Seymour's, so that the whole issue became the work of his etching needle. The Bibliophilist will look carefully at the bundle of

---

[2] This appears to be the view also of the authorities at the British Museum, who bind up the serials, such as magazines, exactly as they come out. No doubt, from one point of view, this theory is correct enough : and it may be held that a copy in numbers is a distinct and special form of the work. Thus " Boz's " addresses in " Pickwick " are official utterances, and contribute something to the history of the work. For the reader who concerns himself with the story only, these additions would be a mere intrusion and a disfigurement.

[3] Seven were by Seymour, two by Buss, and thirty-four by Phiz.

numbers offered him for sale ; and in most cases will find "with illustrations" in all, which are therefore re-issues. The genuine first number should have "With illustrations *by Seymour*."

The prefatory matter, dedication, &c., filled 14 pages ; the body of the work, 609 pages.[4] It is curious to note what changes have been made in the introductory matter. As we have mentioned, the dedication to Talfourd has been omitted ; which seems to have been effected by a gradual process. Thus, in the edition of 1847, we find it compressed into three or four personal lines. "To Mr. Serjeant Talfourd, with much regard, &c." I find in Mr. Forster's papers the directions to the printers to make this substitution—in the author's own hand. We get to the Library Edition of 1858, where the dedication disappears altogether, as it did from all later editions. For the preface and the various curious changes that were made in it the reader is referred back to the early portion of this work.

By January or February, 1838, "Pickwick" was issued complete in one volume, as we gather from an announcement of the publishers :—

"One volume 8vo, bound in cloth, 1*l*. 1*s*. ; half morocco, 1*l*. 4*s*. 6*d*. ; morocco, gilt leaves, 1*l*. 6*s*. The Posthumous Papers of the Pickwick Club, by 'Boz.' With forty-three illustrations by 'Phiz.' 28th Feb., 1838."

The capricious vitality is such that we can scarcely follow it. The legitimate title-page, issued with the numbers, announces that it is by "Charles Dickens," yet here we go back to "Boz," which name he retained in three more of his works.

Just ten years after the completion of "Pickwick," its genial author conceived the idea of what was then a novel and daring venture, viz. that of issuing it and his other works in the cheapest form, and in weekly numbers at three halfpence each, and also in monthly parts. For this shape of publication he always had a fancy. The tradition is preserved at the office of the enormous rush on the first day of publication. Barriers had to be put up to restrain the crowds who pressed to purchase the first "cheap" number. The form of weekly numbers, at three halfpence, was, I am informed, discontinued

---

[4] There were fifty lines in each page in the earlier portion, later reduced to forty-nine. On a rough calculation, the work will be found to contain the matter of over four volumes of the ordinary novel.

after the completion of "Pickwick." That the author felt he
was taking a very serious step is shown by the grave and
responsible tone he assumed in a manifesto which he issued on
the occasion.[5]

" ADDRESS.

"On the 31st March, 1836, the publication of 'The Posthumous Papers of the Pickwick Club' was begun, in what was
then a very unusual form, at less than one-third of the price in
the whole of an ordinary novel,[6] in Shilling Monthly parts.
On Saturday, the 27th of March, 1847, the proposed re-issue,
unprecedented, it is believed, in the history of cheap literature,
will be commenced.

"It is not for an author to describe his own books. If they
cannot speak for themselves, he is likely to do little service by
speaking for them. It is enough to observe of these that eleven
years have strengthened in their writer's mind every purpose
and sympathy he has endeavoured to express in them; and
that their reproduction in a shape which shall render them
easily accessible as a possession by all classes of society, as at
least consistent with the spirit in which they have been
written, and is the fulfilment of a desire long entertained.

"It had been intended that this CHEAP EDITION, now announced, should not be undertaken until the books were much
older, or the author was dead. But the favour with which they
have been received, and the extent to which they have circulated, and continue to circulate at four times the proposed
price, justify the belief that the living author may enjoy the
pride and honour of this widest diffusion, and may couple it
with increased personal emolument.

"A new preface to each tale will be published on its conclusion
in weekly parts. A frontispiece to each tale, engraved on wood,
from a design by some eminent artist, will also be given at the
same time. The whole text will be carefully revised and
corrected throughout by the author."

It was further announced that it would be completed in about
thirty-two numbers. Pickwick was to cost four shillings, and

---

[5] This characteristic address is little known, and the only
copy I have seen is found inserted in one of the numbers of
Vanity Fair.

[6] It would thus seem the cost of "an ordinary novel" was
then over 3*l.*

to be followed by Nickleby, and its fellows, down to Martin Chuzzlewit.[7]

The frontispiece of the new Pickwick was the well-known sketch by Leslie, of Mr. Pickwick surprised with Mrs. Bardell in his arms.

Among the advertisements stitched up with the serial, " The Library of Fiction," is found a curious programme, or proclamation, which throws some further light on the author's earlier plans for the treatment of his story. Mr. Pickwick, it will be seen, was intended to be a burlesque personage, and to exhibit himself in grotesque situations :—

" Now publishing,
to be completed in about twenty monthly numbers,
Price one shilling each,
No. 1 of the
Posthumous Papers
of
THE PICKWICK CLUB,
containing a faithful record of the
Perambulations, perils, travels, adventures,
and
sporting transactions
of the corresponding members,
with biographical notices by the secretary.
Edited by " Boz,"
and each monthly part
embellished with four illustrations
by Seymour.

'THE PICKWICK CLUB, so renowned in the annals of Huggin Lane, and so closely entwined with the thousand interesting associations connected with Lothbury and Cateaton Street, was founded in the year one thousand eight hundred and twenty-two, by Mr. Samuel Pickwick—the great traveller, whose fondness for the useful arts prompted his celebrated journey to Birmingham in the depth of winter; and whose taste for the beauties of nature even led him to penetrate to the very borders of Wales in the height of the summer.

" This remarkable man would appear to have infused a con-

---

[7] The revision of the text, however, thus promised, was not attempted, for we find most of the oversights retained ; such as Mr. Magnus being described as having " blue spectacles," which a few pages further on become " green glasses."

siderable portion of his restless and inquiring spirit into the
breasts of other members of the Club, and to have awaked in
their minds the same insatiable thirst for travel which so
eminently characterized his own. The whole surface of
Middlesex, a part of Surrey, a portion of Essex, and several
square miles of Kent were in their turns examined and
reported on. In a rapid steamer they smoothly navigated the
placid Thames ; and in an open boat they fearlessly crossed the
turbid Medway. High-roads and by-roads, towns and villages,
public conveyances and their passengers, first-rate inns and
roadside public houses, races, fairs, regattas, elections, meetings,
market days—all the scenes that can possibly occur to enliven
a country place, and at which different traits of character may
be observed and recognized, were alike visited and beheld by
the ardent Pickwick and his enthusiastic followers.

"The Pickwick travels, the Pickwick diary, the Pickwick
correspondence, in short the whole of the Pickwick Papers,
were carefully preserved, and duly registered by the secretary,
from time to time, in the voluminous transactions of the Pickwick Club. These transactions have been purchased from the
Patriotic Society at an immense expense, and placed in the
hands of " Boz," the author of sketches illustrative of every-
day life, every-day people—a gentleman whom the publishers
consider highly qualified for the task of arranging these
important documents, and placing them before the public in an
attractive form. He is at present immersed in his arduous
labours, the first-fruits of which appeared on the 31st of March.
Seymour has devoted himself, heart and graver, to the task of
illustrating the beauties of Pickwick. It was reserved to
Gibbon to paint, in colours that will never fade, the Decline
and Fall of the Roman Empire ; to Hume to chronicle the strife
and turmoil of the two proud houses that divided England
against herself—to Napier to pen in burning words the history
of the war in the Peninsula ; the deeds and actions of the
gifted Pickwick yet remain for 'Boz' and SEYMOUR to hand
down to posterity," etc.

It will be seen from this how large and broad was the
original plan laid out. We were to have letters, diaries, adventures in boats and steamers, and roadside public houses ; we
were to be taken to Wales; and there was the " celebrated
journey to Birmingham." The *locale* of the club would appear
to have been somewhere in Lothbury—and was likely enough
to have held its meetings at the George and Vulture. It is
stated to have been founded five years before the opening of
the story : though, in the later plan, it would seem to have been

only recently formed ; as it will be recollected, the " uniform "
and button had been just adopted.

I will now lay before the *Bibliophile* Reader all the various
editions, illustrations, and other matter, that have been engendered by this wonderful book.

The Posthumous Papers of the Pickwick Club,[8] with forty-three
  illustrations by Phiz. PP. xiv. 609. Chapman and Hall.
  London, 1837. 8vo.
Ditto. With illustrations after Phiz. Van Diemen's Land.
  Launceston, 1838. 8vo.
Ditto, in Baudry's "Collection of British Authors." Paris,
  1841. 16mo.
Ditto. London, 1847. 8vo.
Ditto. With illustrations, London, 1867. 8vo.
Ditto. The Charles Dickens Edition, with eight illustrations.
  1867.
Ditto. New York. Fifty-two illustrations by Nast. 1873.
  8vo.
Library Edition of the Works. 22 vols. 1858.
Library Edition, with the original illustrations. 30 vols. 1861,
  1873, 1874.
The Household Edition. With illustrations. 1873.
Popular Library Edition. 16mo. 1880.
Cabinet ditto. 1885.
Posthumous Papers of the Pickwick Club, and thirty-three
  additional plates by Onwhyn, Phiz, and others. Published
  by E. Grattan, 1837.
The Posthumous Papers of the Pickwick Club. Cassell's Red
  Library, 1885.
Another Edition, illustrated by A B. Frost. 1881.
Dick's Edition. London, 1883.
Tales from Pickwick (Routledge's Pocket Library). 1888. 8vo.
Pickwick Papers. With notes and illustrations. Edited by
  C. Dickens the younger. Jubilee Edition, 1886.
Ditto. Chapman and Hall, and Routledge. Price one shilling.
Ditto. G. Routledge. Price sixpence. 1887.
Ditto. Warne. Price sixpence.

---

[8] This title, in part, had been anticipated a few years before :—
Posthumous Papers, Facetious and Fanciful, by a Person
  lately about Town. Cr. 8vo, half calf, 3s. 1831.
Includes the Humorous Man, or what the Ladies call " Nice
  Men," Tunstile Hall, the Eccentric Poet, a Chapter on Pigs,
  etc., etc.

Ditto. Goodhall's edition. Price one penny (half a million copies printed).

Ditto. In shorthand, in the Phonographic Library. 1887.

A Pickwick Klub. Pest, 1862.

Klub Pickwicka. 1869.

Pickwick Klubbens Efterlemnade Papper. Stockholm, 1861.

Uplně vydání Spisu Dickensovych (S. illustracemi od F. Barnarda.). Prekládá Prof. J. Váná. V. Praze, 1883. 4to.

Geillustreerde complete Werken. (By Mensing.) Barnard's illustrations. Published at Arnheim, 1887.

Boz's Sammtliche Werke (von Dr. C. Kolb). 1860-76.

Udtog af. Pikvik Klubbens efterladte Papirer. Kjbenhavn, 1881.

Samuel Pickwick en zijne Reisgenooten. Schiedam, 1868.

Le Club des Pickwickistes, Roman Comique. Mdme. Niboyer. Paris, 1838.

Aventures de Monsieur Pickwick. P. Grolier. Paris, 1859.

Die Pickwickier, &c. 1837.

The Pictorial Edition. 1889.

Geillustreerde complete Werken (translated by C. Mensing and others). Nijmegen, 1887.

Dickens Gesammelte Werke, in 20 vols. Leipzig, 1852.

Contes de Dickens, traduits par R. de Cerisj. 12mo. Paris, 1888.

Fantasifas. Historia de un Clown, Los Duendes, &c. (Mostly selections from the Pickwick Papers.) Valencia, 1888.

In Kent with C. Dickens. By Frost. 1880.

Dickens Memento, with Introduction by F. Philimore, and Hints to Dickens' Collectors. by J. Dexter. 1884.

C. Dickens, the Story of his Life. 1870.

Life by John Forster. 1872.

The Pickwick Treasury. 1845.

Quarterly Review, v. 59, p. 484.

Westminster Review, v. 27, p. 194.

Portrait of Mr. Pickwick. G. A. Sala. Belgravia, v. 12, p. 165.

Dickens, by Pen and Pencil. F. Kitton. 1890.

Bentley's Miscellany.

Edinburgh Review, v. 68.

London Quarterly Review, v. 59.

Blackwood, v. 52.

N. American Review, v. 56.

About England with Dickens. A. Rimmer. 1883.

Bibliography of the writings of C. Dickens. James Cook, Paisley. 1879.

Ditto. J. Anderson. [9]
Bibliography of Dickens. R. Herne Shepherd. 1880.
The Dickens Dictionary, a Key to the characters and incidents. G. A. Pierce. 1872.
On the Origin of Sam Weller, and the real cause of the success of the Posthumous Papers of the Pickwick Club. By a lover of Charles Dickens. 1883.
A Pickwickian Pilgrimage. J. R. Hassard. 1881.
Scenes from the Pickwick Papers, designed by A. Dulcken. 1861.
Bardell v. Pickwick, versified. T. H. Gem. 1881.
Six Illustrations to the Pickwick Club. 1854.
The Pickwickians, or the Peregrinations of Sam Weller. Arranged from Moncrieff's adaptation, by T. H. Lacy. 1850.
Sam Weller, or the Pickwickians. W. T. Moncrieff. 1837.
C. Dickens and Rochester. R. Langton. 1880.
Twenty Scenes from the Works of Dickens, designed and etched by C. Coveney. Sydney, 1883, 4to.
"Wellerisms" from Pickwick and Master Humphrey's Clock, selected by C. F. Rideal, and edited by C. Kent. 1886.
Bardell and Pickwick—as condensed by the author for his readings. Boston, 1868.
The Ivy Green. By Henry Russell. 1840.
Mr. Bob Sawyer's Party, as condensed by the author for his readings. Boston, 1868.
Dickens' London. T. E. Pemberton. 1876.
Dickens and the Stage. T. E. Pemberton. 1888.
A series of character sketches for Dickens. F. Barnard. Folio. 1879-85.
Dickensiana.—A Bibliography of the literature relating to C.D. F. G. Kitton, 1886.
"The London Singer's Magazine, a collection of all the most celebrated and popular songs as sung at the London Theatres, with fine character portrait of Mr. Ransford, and about 64 most humorous engravings by Cruikshank, T. Jones, Findlay, &c. 2 vols. in 1, 8vo. Duncombe, N.D.
"At page 147 of vol. 2 is—An original comic song written by 'Boz,' and sung at the London Concerts, entitled—'The Tetotal Excursion,' undoubtedly an early production of C. Dickens. The volumes also con-

[9] I have received much assistance from this admirable collection, and the author has further allowed me to make use of his MS. additions.

tain—'Smike's song to Nicholas Nickleby,' 'The Fat Boy' (with engraving), 'The Loving Ballad of Lord Bateman' (with an engraving), 'Sam Weller's Adventures, a song of the Pickwickians,' as sung at Pickwick Club, Long Acre (with an engraving). From the internal evidence the date of the volumes is circa 1839."

"Another copy of the 2 vols. in 1, with numerous engravings by Cruikshank, &c., coloured frontispieces, 8vo, original pictorial boards, uncut (slightly imperfect) £1 1s. Duncomb, N.D.

"Including 'The Old Man and the Child,' a favourite ballad written by Boz, 'The Ivy Green,' by Boz, 'Sam Weller's Adventures,' &c. This appears to be a different issue from the preceding. Both the songs and the illustrations differ."

The Pickwick Comic Almanack for 1838, containing Sam Weller's Diary of Fun and Pastime, and 12 comic engravings by R. Cruikshank, post 8vo, wrappers, sewn. Marshall.

An evening with Pickwick. C. Parker. 1889.

The Weller Family. A Comedy. F. Emson. 1878.

Pen Photographs. Kate Field. 1868.

Der Humorist. Zotlingen, Switzerland.

Two English Humorists (Lamb and Dickens). Percy Fitzgerald. 1863.

L'Inimitable Boz. De Heussey. 1889.

Mézières, Histoire critique. Tom III., "Le Club Pickwick." 1841.

The Pickwick Club. A Burletta, by E. Stirling. 1837

Peregrinations of Pickwick. W. Leman Rede. 1837

Pickwick Songster. 1837.

Mr. Pickwick's collection of Songs. 1837.

Sam Weller's Pickwick Jest Book. 1837.

Beauties of Pickwick. 1838.

The Penny Pickwick (issued in numbers), 1838.

Pickwick Abroad; or, The Tour in France. G. W. Reynolds. With forty-one plates. 1839.

Pickwick in America.

Posthumous Papers of the Cadger Club.

The Posthumous Papers of the Wonderful Discovery Club, formerly of Camden Town. Established by Sir Peter Patson. With eleven illustrations designed by Squib, and engraved by Point. 1838.

The Posthumous Notes of the Pickwickian Club. Edited by Bos. 132 engravings, 1839.

Twenty Scenes from the Works of Charles Dickens. Sydney. 1883.

Twenty-four Illustrations to Pickwick, by Frederick Pailthorpe.

Illustrations to Pickwick. Antoney.

Ditto, Appleyards.

Sam Weller's Scrap Sheet.

Dickens Aquarelles. Twelve illustrations by " Stylus." New York.

Illustrations by " Kyd."

Racy Sketches of Expeditions from the Pickwick Club. 1838.

Illustrations by Sir John Gilbert.

Grattan's series of etched illustrations.

32 plates by Sam Weller. Onwyn. 1837.

Chapters with revived Pickwick Characters, ' Mr. Weller's Watch,' &c., in ' Master Humphrey's Clock.' (First Edition.)

Philosophy of Charles Dickens. Hon. Albert Canning. 1880.

It may be added here, that it is somewhat difficult to discriminate exactly the editions of the " collected works "—as the issues of the same edition underwent alteration—the illustrations being added in some cases, and new titles supplied. Some took several years to issue.

It was natural that a work of such claims should be celebrated in all the glories of typography. Some years ago it was determined to do honour to Dickens by bringing out a really sumptuous edition of his writings. Here was the programme :—

" The Publishers of the works of Charles Dickens, who have from the first to last been associated with the writings of this great Humorist, have made arrangements for the publication of an

EDITION DE LUXE,

COMPLETE IN THIRTY VOLUMES, IMPERIAL 8VO.

" There exist at this moment several editions of the works of Charles Dickens, but not one that sufficiently represents his place in the library as the foremost English writer of fiction of his time, the vigorous reformer of social abuses, and the household friend of readers of every rank and nation. The present edition is intended to offer the appropriate tribute to his genius which has been too long delayed. The Letterpress is printed, from the Edition last Revised by the Author, by Messrs. R. CLAY, SONS, and TAYLOR, on paper of the finest quality, made for the purpose by Messrs. SPALDING and HODGE. The Work will be illustrated by upwards of Seven Hundred Engravings, on Steel, Copper, and Wood, comprising the whole of the Original Illustrations drawn by CRUIKSHANK, SEYMOUR, 'PHIZ' (Hablot K. Browne), CATTERMOLE, TENNIEL, DOYLE, D. MACLISE, R.A., Sir EDWARD LANDSEER, R.A,, F. WALKER, MARCUS STONE, JOHN LEECH, CLARKSON STANFIELD, R.A., and FRANK STONE, as well as a selection from those by L. FILDES, A.R.A., C. GREEN, F. BARNARD, and other Artists in the later Editions. The wrappers in which the works originally appeared in Monthly Numbers will also be reproduced. All the Illustrations will be printed on *Real China Paper ;* the Woodcuts and Vignettes being mounted with the Letterpress, and the Steel and Copper Plates being mounted on *Plate Paper* expressly made for the work. A complete work will be issued every month, commencing with THE PICKWICK PAPERS, in two volumes. The Edition for sale will be strictly limited to ONE THOUSAND COPIES: and as each sheet is printed the type will be broken up. As seven Hundred Copies *have already been subscribed,* the price has been raised. The present terms of subscription may be learned from all Booksellers."

This is an astonishing monument. The volumes are of massive size—thirty in number—and, when fittingly bound, would gladden the heart of any Bibliophilist. This was later followed by another handsome tribute known as the "Victoria Edition," in which the original drawings—not the etchings— were reproduced. It was thus described :—

" Pickwick Papers, illustrated with Facsimiles of 50 Drawings made for the engravings by Seymour, Buss, Phiz, and Leech ; also facsimiles of the blue cover and a page of Dickens' manuscript ; copies of the original prospectus, &c. Two octavo volumes on hand-made paper.

" The two substantial volumes which Messrs. Chapman and Hall, the original publishers of the work, issue this week are not a facsimile reprint either of the old monthly parts in their famous green wrappers, or of the first completed edition which was given to the world just fifty years ago. . . . The original illustrations by Seymour and Phiz—even the drawings done by Buss in the intermediate time between the sudden and tragic end of the first-named artist and the regular engagement of Mr. Hablot Browne—are here reproduced, not from the original etchings, but, what is better still, from the artists' drawings. Even cancelled 'alternative' drawings and suppressed plates, which have hitherto not been seen by the public eye, are included, and all these have been reproduced with marvellous delicacy and fidelity by photogravure, or the process of photographic engraving upon copper-plates."

We have already made allusion to the edition prepared by " Boz's " son, " Charles Dickens the younger," in which the book was " worked on " like a classic, illustrated with notes and commentaries, explanatory of local and obscure allusions, obsolete manners and customs ; and also set off by pictures of the old inns, towns and other objects of interest. Unluckily the effect was marred by introducing the notes at the end of each, and thus interrupting, if not violating the continuity of the narrative. It is difficult, therefore, to read it with comfort or with the old security.

Finally, we have the " Crown " edition, now being issued ; a convenient, brightly printed volume ; with all the original illustrations, which are really essential for the proper understanding of the text.

LONDON
PRINTED BY GILBERT AND RIVINGTON, LIMITED
ST. JOHN'S HOUSE, CLERKENWELL ROAD.

13653986R00213

Printed in Great Britain
by Amazon.co.uk, Ltd.,
Marston Gate.